MAKING A LIVING

MAKING A LIFE

MAKING A LIVING
MAKING A LIFE

Essays *&* Speeches

by

Daniel Rose

Published by Half Moon Press, Essex, New York.

Printed in the United States by Cenveo Publisher Services, Philadelphia, PA

Library of Congress Control Number: 2014949727

ISBN: 987-0-692-27972-4

Cover painting by Herbert Katzman

To my father, Samuel B. Rose,

who taught me how to think;

to Alfred Baruth, my Horace Mann teacher

who taught me how to read;

to Vincent Scully, the Yale professor

who taught me how to see;

and to my wife, Joanna,

who taught me how to write.

CONTENTS

PREFACE

As one who has tried to "share the actions and passions of his times" and to comment on them publicly when asked, I confess to having enjoyed the exercise over the years of observing, reading, pondering and speaking out.

These speeches have been assembled here in the hope that they may stimulate the reader's own reflections.

The recurring themes – education, economics, social problems, religion, history, philanthropy and real estate development – have been my concerns for over half a century.

As André Gide noted, "Everything that should be said has been said, but since they weren't listening, it must be said again."

Underlying everything I write and say is the belief that "doing good" and "doing well" are not inconsistent and that the surest path to satisfaction and fulfillment involves dedication to causes greater than oneself.

Daniel Rose

MAKING A LIVING, MAKING A LIFE

The ancient Greeks loved words, and one of their best was "oxymoron," a contradiction in terms, such as a hot ice cube or a tiny giant.

At times, it seems that my subject today, "business ethics," qualifies perfectly as an oxymoron. This year's headline stories about the atmosphere of corruption that prevailed at General Dynamics, the nation's third largest defense contractor, recall the bribery stories at Lockheed in the 1970's, the General Electric scandals of the decade before, and so on.

In the broader society, municipal corruption seems so widespread; shabby influence-peddling even at the level of the white House staff; insider trading accepted matter-of-factly on Wall Street; the casual indifference with which our country's largest and most respected banks laundered huge amounts of what was obviously criminal cash – all of these (and the other scandals that will undoubtedly be revealed in next week's or next month's headlines) pose fearful problems for those leaving university and entering the business world.

The public today seems to believe that throughout the business world sharp practice is admired, duplicity and deliberate misrepresentation are the norm, and the only crime involved in outright fraud is getting caught. The average businessman is seen as echoing Mark Twain's view that while he believed in honesty, he didn't "make a fetish of it."

Worst of all is a widely-held perception that such a low standard is expected of you, and that you cannot succeed in business without it. Perhaps even your family and friends are nervously wondering if, for business success, you must make some Faust-like pact with Mephistopheles.

Relax; your souls are safe.

That is, they are safe if you want them to be. For that is what history tells us.

Morality and worldly success are not now and never have been, necessarily incompatible. Just as every society contains some people with larceny in their hearts, so every society known to man has had people who conducted themselves honorably and who led satisfying and fulfilling lives in the process.

Sir Thomas More, a moral giant and author of *Utopia*, was the most successful private lawyer of his day. Cicero, the moral voice of republican Rome, was also the most successful (and perhaps the richest) lawyer of his time. Michel de Montaigne, the great essayist, a man who could be called "wisdom personified," was also a successful vineyard owner and wine merchant, the mayor of Bordeaux, and an effective diplomat. And of Benjamin Franklin, it could be said that while "Richard" may have been "poor," Ben himself was not.

Ours is clearly what R. H. Tawney called "The Acquisitive Society," run to a great degree by the profit motive, resulting in what has been called a "money culture" or a "business civilization."

So be it. If we do not have the moral atmosphere of a medieval monastery or of King Arthur's Round Table, they did not have antibiotic medicines, symphonic recordings or fresh raspberries in December - all the result of someone's desire to make a dollar.

Some people mistakenly believe that economic transactions are "zero sum games," in which a gain for one must mean a loss for another. They gag over the bewildering paradox that blatant private self-interest can work for the public benefit, and that unlovely people with unlovely motives can actually advance the goals of society; but that's the way the world works now.

Someday it may be otherwise; and in the imaginative essay entitled "Economic Prospects for Our Grandchildren," John Maynard

Keynes forecasts a society of such prodigious abundance that misers, workaholics and ambitious "Type A" personalities will be put in mental hospitals.

In the meantime, the workaholic is a hero, and society's challenge is to channel his energies, talents and resources productively while making sure that the Devil does not take the hindmost.

We in the real estate world can take satisfaction in being in the "productive" rather than the "predatory" part of the business economy, creating wealth rather than merely transferring it. Junk bonds, leveraged buy-outs, mergers and acquisitions – none of those adds to the true wealth of the society, but building housing, offices, hotels and so forth really does.

Another point about real estate development we tend to gloss over is that it is a lot of fun. For all I know, commodity speculators, insurance actuaries, perhaps even undertakers, enjoy their work and look forward to getting to the job, or the morgue, each morning. I know developers do.

Even the richest and most successful men in our field tend to work almost indefinitely; to such exuberant types, profit is a way of "keeping score" in a game they play for sheer delight.

"Understated good taste" and "becoming modesty" may be in short supply in our field, but there is certainly no lack of energy, imagination or willingness to take risks; and a typical developer pursues his goals with the intensity of a salmon swimming upstream to spawn.

A business civilization ours is, indeed; and your professors hope that Adam Smith's "invisible hand" will guide you into unwitting pursuit of the public good while you make large sums of money (some of which, they probably hope you will contribute to the M.I.T. Alumni Fund). But in the process of making that money, you do not have to forego the normal standards of civilized people.

In the business world, as in life generally, there are temptations, pressures, morally "gray" areas. In many fields, what is technically "legal" may not be truly ethical. The used car dealer who, with a straight face, swears that the car was driven "only by a little old lady to and from church," is following accepted practice, as is the renting agent who uses "luxury" to describe any housing unit with electricity and running water. The international oil man dealing with Middle Eastern potentates convinces himself that there is indeed a difference between a "bribe" and a "shakedown," just as the publisher who bemoans the use of narcotics happily prints all the cigarette advertising he can get; and in virtually all fields, political contributions will pose a very real problem to anyone dealing with government so long as politicians have to finance expensive television campaigns by gifts from constituents.

But one always has choices, exercises judgments, makes personal decisions.

Speaking as one rational person to other rational people, I maintain that not only is it possible to function effectively in the business world today as a moral individual, but that such conduct will lead to a more satisfying and fulfilling career.

On an occasion like this it is appropriate to spell out the real-world ground rules by which civilized people have always functioned, and to shout from the rooftops that: a) morality is a personal matter for each individual to wrestle with, and that you are morally responsible for your own actions; b) that morality is demonstrated not by what you believe or say, but by what you do; and c) that morality is not a question of theoretical dilemmas; it consists of attitudes, habits, and outlooks developed over a lifetime through the influence of parents, teachers and religious leaders, attitudes that are reflected in everything one values, one respects and one does.

It would be naïve to close one's eyes to the moral climate in which we live. At the highest levels of government, industry and the professions, the examples we can recite are heartbreaking. "Abscam" only confirmed what many already felt about elected officials. Leading accounting firms are seen as mere bookkeepers for amoral clients. Leading lawyers are regarded as little more than "hired guns" able to confuse or "guide" juries and to tie in knots less-skilled public prosecutors.

4

Even those trusting souls with faith in our court system are sorely troubled by well-publicized recent jury verdicts—one, for example, letting go scot-free a former automobile manufacturer despite motion pictures clearly showing his cocaine sales. That decision calls to mind the story of the sanctimonious attorney who cabled news of a successful verdict to his mobster client with the message, "Justice has triumphed;" the client cabled back, "Appeal at once."

How, in such society, does a rational person justify moral conduct?

The answer, I believe, is to try to understand that society and one's own place in it.

At the moment, our society is driven by a mad desire for success with such success measured almost exclusively in dollar terms. All other values seem to be subordinate, and our present moral climate is a result. Physicists describe the relationship of oxygen to a fire as "necessary but not sufficient." You cannot have a fire without oxygen, but oxygen alone is not enough. For success in the business world today a certain degree of economic achievement is also "necessary but not sufficient."" In such a case, the dollar becomes one – but surely not the only – measure of success.

That is what the wisest men have always said. Self-respect; pride in a job well done; the satisfaction of productive contribution; the legitimate esteem of those you respect – those values and others like them play a part in the moral landscape of those we most admire and should wish to emulate. To such people, integrity, loyalty, responsibility, sincerity and what modern philosophers call "authenticity" are not meaningless or hypocritical terms. They are watchwords to live by, especially for people who want to be able to look at themselves in the mirror each morning with a clear conscience.

The goal, then, is clear; the problem is how to achieve it.
Back in the days when a title of nobility presumably meant that one followed a noble code, two interesting concepts were taught the young: "noblesse oblige" and "obedience to the unenforceable." The first meant that since you had greater advantages, more was expected

5

of you; the second, that there were some things in life that were "done" and others that were "not done." In such a context, "rights" implied "duties," "privileges" implied "responsibilities."

By and large, these concepts are still reasonable guides today, although we might add the wisdom of the Lord's Prayer, which says, not "Let me be good," but rather, "Lead me not into temptation."

In more specific terms, as the basis for a practical code for here and now, let me propose a modern decalogue for the real estate field today.

THINK "PROFESSION" RATHER THAN "TRADE"

A trade is an activity carried on to make money, period. A profession has overtones of a formal body of knowledge, standards, a code of ethics, and a sense of responsibility to the general public and to one's professional colleagues, as well as to one's own pocketbook. The Roman writer, Tertullian, could have been referring to the world of real estate when he wrote that, "Any calling is noble if nobly pursued."

MASTER YOUR FIELD

Easier said than done, of course. Solid professional skills, appropriate knowledge, and relevant experience should be your goals as you seek to acquire true expertise. Remember Nicolo Machiavelli's single religious insight that, in the short run at least, the armed Biblical prophets triumphed, whereas the unarmed prophets failed. In a similar vein, an old Russian saying has it that, "A fine character is of no help in a chess game." Have a fine character and learn to play chess well, too!

CHOOSE YOUR BATTLEGROUND CAREFULLY

Where the deck is stacked against you or where your opponents are playing with marked cards, do not try to compete. If what William Safire calls "corruppies" are ready to use bribery or outright chicanery, for example, making agreements they try to renegotiate as soon as the contract is signed, you should realize that there are some games in which you do not choose to play, since you know at the outset that you cannot win.

If everything you do can be written up without embarrassment on the front page of The New York Times, you may lose some opportunities, but you will have peace of mind and are apt to gain other opportunities as well.

There are clients or partners who understand that your refusal to steal for them is the best guarantee that you will not steal from them, either.

THINK "RELATIONSHIPS' RATHER THAN "DEALS"

Try to have each transaction you complete be your recommendation for the next. Continuity builds reputation, and reputation, for better or worse, becomes part of what you bring to the table. Presumably, in another go-around, even the Trojans would not have accepted the gift of, say, a large Wooden Cow.

Our field has its share of P.T. Barnums and hokum experts, but there are also role models who built careers doing their best to "give fair value." They are trusted because they have proved that they are trustworthy.

BE ACCURATE AND COMPLETE IN AGREEMENTS

Thieves will try to wriggle out even of ironclad agreements, and honorable people will abide by handshakes. But everyone loses when painful, but legitimate differences arise through sloppy or incomplete documentation of original understandings. Robert Frost observed that, "Good fences make good neighbors"; a commercial equivalent might be, "Well-drawn agreements help make good relationships."

DO NOT TRY TO WIN THE "BATTLE OF THE HEADLINES"

To a degree that would surprise the public, the business press largely reflects flackery and blatant public relations puffery. Ben Sonnenberg, the PR master, once defined his role for his clients as "putting very large pedestals under very little men." A somewhat different point of view was that of Cato in ancient Rome who, in rejecting a proposed statue of himself in the Forum, said that he would rather people asked why there was not a statue of him than why there was.

It is a fact of life that the American public refuses to differentiate among "fame," "notoriety" and "celebrity." Albert Einstein, for example, is famous; Al Capone is notorious; and Zsa Zsa Gabor is celebrated.

It is an interesting sign of our times that the Watergate crew are delighted at their present "name recognition," that the so-called "Mayflower Madam" claims that American Express wants her to do a promotional ad and that the deliberate, illegal demolition of a building at midnight in Times Square has proved absolutely no social or professional handicap for those involved.

For some reason that is not entirely clear, the real estate development field seems to attract many flamboyant megalomaniacs. There's nothing really wrong with that, I suppose—just a question of taste— but newcomers to the field should not feel that wide "name recognition" is a mandatory part of development life.

To be "well-known" and perhaps feared seems to be the aim of many prominent people of our time. Others seek respect. But for some, "honor," a term that sounds quaint to 20th century ears, can still be a living concept to be pursued. To live so that you reflect well on yourself, your family, your schools and your career field is not an unrealistic goal.

PUT MONEY IN PROPER PERSPECTIVE

At this stage in your lives, determining your personal goals and values is an important challenge. Wise people try to think them through carefully, and only a fool would put costs and benefits in purely monetary terms. It might be a worthwhile exercise for each of us to define for himself the word "greed."

It was here in Cambridge that Oliver Wendell Holmes observed that, "The reward for the successful general is not a bigger tent but a more challenging command."

Whether you pursue a career in the private sector or the public, whether on your own or in a large organization, conduct yourself well and good things are likely to follow.

Don't be stampeded

Peer pressure; the plea that "it's for the company"; the promise that "no one will ever know"; the excuse, as expressed by one prominent real estate man on the front page of The New York Times, that "The world is a jungle, and you gotta get them first"— be prepared to hear all of these excuses again and again through the years. You will be tempted by them. Yeats was thinking of real-life situations when he wrote that," The best lack all conviction and the worst are full of passionate intensity," and that can apply to your colleagues, too. There are times in life when one must just say "No."

Include a "Pro Bono Publico" Component in Your Life.

Whether through charitable work as a volunteer, teaching or writing in your career field, mastering some outside activity as a hobby, or working politically for some cause you believe in, devoting time and effort to some activity other than your own pocketbook will add a dimension to your life and give it a resonance that the wisest individuals have always sought.

Robber baron types who gave shiny new dimes to street urchins sought the appearance of public spiritedness; those who strove for the reality were fuller human beings who led more admirable and satisfying lives.

In perhaps the saddest lines in all American literature, Robert Frost wrote of a man who lived with "nothing to look back on with pride, nothing to look forward to with hope." Thoughtful people try to live otherwise.

Well, I have rambled on; but before I get to my last bit of advice, let me point out that it could have been worse.

At a Yale commencement once, a minister gave a lengthy moral sermon, taking for his theme Y for "youth," A for "age," L for "life" and E for "eternity." When he finally finished, someone said "Thank heaven we're not at the Massachusetts Institute of Technology!"

For my tenth and final point, let me note that in a play written over 300 years ago, a long-winded, pretentious and somewhat foolish figure gave tedious advice to his son; yet ever since, thoughtful people have taken Polonius' last comment to heart: "This above all, to thine own self be true, and it shall follow as the night the day, thou canst not then be false to any man."

Graduates, it has been M.I.T.'s responsibility to teach you to make a living; now it is your responsibility to make a life.

Center for Real Estate Development
Massachusetts Institute of Technology
1986 Commencement Address

THE COMPLETE LIFE

The topics for today's discussion -- ethics in business and in our personal lives – imply a third important question, the relationship between business and personal life: I will try to deal with all three topics by giving my personal credo.

A conference participant yesterday referred in passing to "eudaimonia", a classical Greek word I love for its varied meanings. One definition is "the prosperous life", another is "the happy life", a third is "the good life". But the fourth definition is the most thought-provoking of all: "the complete life".

My own view of all those states -- so separate and distinct in English -- presupposes a balance of five factors:

a) My *personal* life -- which to me means my family;
b) My *professional* life -- which to me means Rose Associates;
c) My *public* life -- which involves politics, civic organizations and professional groups;
d) My *philanthropic* life -- which involves those charitable causes, such as the Harlem Educational Activities Fund, to which I give my time, my thought and my money; and,
e) My *inner* life -- which means my intellectual and spiritual concerns, those inner voices one hears when no one else is listening.

These five lives intersect and interact; each is important in itself and is not to be sacrificed for the others; each at times takes precedence over the others. Successfully balancing the demands of all five lives is my continuing challenge.

Another concept the ancient Greeks had was that of "leisure", which to them did not mean doing nothing, but rather, having the opportunity to do something of one's own choosing.

I think of myself as "a gentleman of leisure" whose engine is constantly running at full speed, whose time is over-committed and over-programmed, who occasionally grouses, but would have it no other way.

In each role in life I try to "do the right thing", and on occasion like to recall the old expression of "obedience to the unenforceable". Except for the competition among them for my time, my five concerns have been no cause of conflict.

In my business life I like to think of "relationships" rather than "deals" and assume that my performance in one transaction will be a recommendation for the next.

The standing position of our firm is that all of our employees conduct themselves so that they may perhaps be annoyed, but not ashamed, to find their activities on the front page of The New York Times.

We all were proud of the comment made about our firm by a long-time institutional partner to the effect that if Rose Associates made a mistake, there was a 50/50 chance it was in your favor.

In the rough-and-tumble real estate field, are there costs of such conduct? Yes. Are there benefits? Certainly. Do the benefits outweigh the costs? I think so; but in any case I find it a more satisfying way to live and would not change.

Am I aware that other people do not always have the luxury of making such choices? Absolutely; and I count among my most important blessings the fact that I do.

The classical Greeks (to refer to them one last time) defined "tragedy" as the conflict between two rights; and I realize that if my children were starving I would probably try to steal food for them. The choice would be tragic, but I would think that on balance, it was the right choice.

We each must live with the rest of the world; but with ourselves, too. And we must try to reach multiple goals.

Our company developed and for many years owned and managed 280 Park Avenue, the home office of the Bankers Trust Company. The year it opened we received an award for it as the best New York office building of the year. I remember sending a photocopy of the certificate to my father who was on vacation. His reply, which delighted us all, was that he was pleased to note that the ink on the award was as black as the ink on our corporate books. We had hit a home run.

Even with multiple goals, there are priorities, however; and a thinker named Abraham Maslow came up with a famous "hierarchy of values" to help understand and sort out those priorities.

At the bottom of Maslow's pyramid was the satisfaction of one's material needs; next up came one's social needs, which, as I recall, included impressing one's mother-in-law and earning more than one's next-door neighbor.

Then came your psychological needs, which started with your sense of self- respect and the esteem of the world at large, followed by the ability to earn the respect and admiration of those whom you yourself respected and admired.

At the very top of the pyramid -- after your material satisfaction had passed the point of diminishing returns, after you felt good about yourself and after you had received whatever accolades you felt you needed -- the goal was "to become all you were capable of being". On reflection, we all realize that working toward that goal can start long before we achieve the others.

The Talmud is a vast compendium of Hebrew theology, philosophy, poetry, folklore and a fair share of ancient legal jargon and hairsplitting; but here and there are stories and parables that are real gems.

One of my favorites concerns an old rabbi named Zusha, who dozed off while listening to the droning recitations of his devout students. He suddenly sat bolt upright, his face reflecting terror, tears flowing down his cheeks.

"Rabbi, what happened?" the students asked; and Zusha said sadly, "I just dreamt that I had died and was standing before God, face to face."

"Zusha", he thundered, "Why were you not Moses?"

"God", I replied, "You did not give me Moses' talents and I did not have Moses' opportunities."

"Then", said God, "Why were you not Zusha?" And I had no reply."

Each of us would do well to reflect on what accounting we could render when, like Zusha, we consider our own talents and opportunities.

Tucson, Arizona
February 9-11, 2001

GOOD CITIES VS. GREAT CITIES

A conference on "The Role of the Arts in Urban Redevelopment" suggests any number of topics for a keynote address; but one obvious theme is that of the "Hawaiian Missionary." The families of the 19th Century missionaries who went out to proselytize the Hawaiians ended up owning the islands. It was said of them that, "They went to do good, and they did very well indeed!" "Doing good while doing well" could also apply to those buildings that contribute to the delight of the public and the "bottom line" of the developer.

Ever since John von Neumann, the father of Game Theory, pointed out that, while some people think of life as a "zero sum game" in which any benefit is at someone else's expense, we have come to realize that in practice, it can be a "positive sum game" in which everyone wins!

Our national experience in urban development is a prime example, especially over the past two decades during which an increasingly sophisticated public has shown itself not only willing, but eager to pay a premium for beauty and amenity, for buildings that represent not just construction, but architecture, that do not merely occupy space, but fill it exuberantly, dramatically, and for the benefit of all of us!

Worthwhile buildings are sought, and worthwhile urban context as well, leading to cities that aspire not merely to be good, but to be great.

And we are coming to understand the difference.

Great cities are not only "showcases" for culture, but incubators of it; they make provision for the talented, energetic, ambitious young in every field who supply the adrenalin in our civic system.

A great city of the 20th century would have a crowded, bustling, contagious sense of energy, excitement and human interaction— instead of strangling congestion, choking traffic, swarming sidewalks, blocked sunlight and cut-off views. It would contain buildings that function well for their occupants and owners, but also relate well to the streets they face, the neighboring buildings and to the city as a whole.

A great city presents a coherent and civilized environment, a blending of old and new, a distinctive sense of character and of place. A great city permits a street life of human scale, with opportunities for chance meetings of friends and colleagues, for agreeable experiences on the way to or from one's place of work, at mealtime, or at odd moments during the day. It would have vistas, where a surprise sight of a park or square, a public monument or a grand building brings a sense of delight that might be uncommented upon but that brightens the day.

A great city vibrates with vitality that comes from variety—variety of ages, occupations, activities, and conditions of life, in many cases with different people doing different things at different times of day or night.

A great city represents a certain symbiosis and synergism, with permanent residents, transients and visitors reinforcing one another, with neither blue collar worker, "yuppie," entrepreneurial tycoon, government worker nor professional manager dominating or constricting the life of the city, but with all contributing to its quality of life.

A great city boasts public buildings that express community rather than power, buildings that don't shout "Hey, look at me!" but that are appropriate for a particular time, place and function.

A great city exudes a zest for life and serene self-confidence.

It knows what to do and how to do it.

We are increasingly coming to understand the wisdom of appropriate public encouragement of, and involvement in, desirable private development efforts which might not take place without public intervention.

16

In such a climate, relations between the private sector and the public sector could become cooperative rather than adversarial, as they are so often today. The public sector might have to become more aware of what the private sector defines as "the discipline of the marketplace" or the "time-value of money"; the private developer might have to become more conscious of what economists and planners call "externalities," or the impact of our actions on third parties. It could mean that public figures would be encouraged to consider development problems not only from the standpoint of short-term politics, but of long-term economics as well. It may mean that aesthetes would consider the social impact of their designs; that social engineers would be forced to face hard economic problems flowing from their decisions; that planners would have to ask themselves, "Who bears the risks and the pains of failure?"; that architects would focus on the comfort, safety, and efficiency of the occupants of their buildings; and that all of us might relate more directly to the success of the project.

The vehicle for such activities will increasingly be a de facto partnership among municipal government agencies, the private developer, the private institutional lender and other entities such as cultural institutions.

We will need to create means by which risks and rewards are shared, by which each partner has a vested interest in the success of a project, and by which the benefits that flow from it are appropriately apportioned.

For example, the provision of expensive structured parking and major infrastructure costs must be seen as joint problems requiring joint solutions.

Such tools as tax-exempt bond financing (to the extent the federal government will continue to permit it), or subordination of real estate taxes to mortgage financing charges, practices such as partial application of tax loss sales proceeds to development capital (once again, at the pleasure of Washington)—must be rethought and used imaginatively.

Each historical era has its characteristic problem resolved by a characteristic solution. In the years ahead, working out the ground rules for successful accommodations among public sector, private sector, financial institution and cultural institution partners deserves our best thinking.

Why? Because the game is clearly worth the candle!

It is not necessary to dwell on the benefits to the private developer, because developers as a sub-species have finely-developed economic antennae and, like ants at a picnic, will intuitively zero in on a good thing.

Developers do not require exhortation to perceive the economic advantage of bonuses for plazas, atria, etc. from a physical point of view, or the higher rents they can charge for a prestigious building as opposed to a mundane one.

Government functionaries and the general public, on the other hand, often do not fully understand the dynamics of urban life, the complex factors that make some cities wax and others wane, that make some cities bubble with vitality and others bore to tears their own citizens and the occasional visitor.

Some factors that affect the "tone" of a city are obvious, such as an exciting array of shopping opportunities, restaurants, hotels and recreational facilities and, of prime importance, major cultural institutions, art galleries, theater districts and the like.

Other factors are often not apparent, however:— a sound economic underpinning; buildings and public places that are "user-friendly"; areas in the city that surprise and delight and perhaps even astonish; "walkable" areas that invite rather than repel the pedestrian; cheap and available housing for bright and ambitious youngsters from elsewhere who come to seek their fortunes; varied neighborhoods with differing characters; the pace and tension of a 24 hour-a-day cosmopolitan center and a vital cultural life.

Sometime before he became President in 1960, John F. Kennedy was heard to comment that Washington, D.C. was a major national capital strategically located between our North and South. "And look what we have," he is reported to have said, "an intellectual backwater with southern efficiency and northern charm!"

Today, when Washington, D.C. is discussed as reaching world-class standing in the ranking of cities, references are made to blockbuster art exhibitions like "The Treasure Houses of Britain" by-passing New York to come directly to the National Gallery's new East Wing, or to leading international ballet companies, orchestras or plays going directly to the Kennedy Center without stopping further north.

When residents of Houston or Atlanta wish to indicate the eminence of their respective home bases, they point to their new art centers, just as Australians from Sydney speak proudly of their world-famous opera house or Edinburghers refer to their Festival.

Conversely, Brasilia or Canberra, although capital cities of major nations, attract the attention only of those who have to go there. In a recent Sunday N.Y. Times, a full page discussion of "What To Do In Brasilia," implied that foreign visitors fly to that massively planned, immensely expensive capital of South America's largest country early in the morning and leave by nightfall, but that (in the words of the Times), "24 hours or even 48 hours is preferable to avoid a mad rush."

Can anyone imagine that being said of Paris or London, New York or Rome?

The implied questions are fair ones. What would Brasilia need to achieve "world-class" status; and what would, New York have to lose to suffer a drop in its standing?

A gradual but perceptible change of status between San Francisco and Los Angeles may be instructive.

The mood of San Francisco is seen as increasingly "anti-business." In the words of The New York Times, "business and civic leaders are beginning to question whether the city will continue as the center of business it has been since the Gold Rush more than 100 years ago… the Los Angeles area has been growing rapidly as a center of business and finance, sometimes at the expense of San Francisco. . .relations between business people and San Francisco City Hall have reached a low point."

The cultural balance also seems to be shifting. Observers are beginning to think of San Francisco like Kyoto or Florence—a gracious and charming place out of the main stream of life.

My own conclusion is that the business leaders who lead and support our major cultural institutions are municipal assets and should be treated as such.

We have learned a lot about what makes cities tick, but one lesson that we tend to forget is that no city ever became great or stayed great without a solid economic base.

We have been talking of great cities, but it might be worthwhile to close with a thought-provoking image of an ideal city for the 20th Century.

This ideal city might have a relaxed and civilized meeting place like Venice's Piazza San Marco; a bohemian intellectual center like Paris' Left Bank; parks like Boston's Public Garden or New York's Central Park, with London's Hyde Park Speakers' Corner and the book stalls on the Seine near Notre Dame.

It might have the business dynamism of Wall Street; the elegance of the Place de la Concorde; the sparkling waterfront life of Sydney Harbor; the imagination of Boston's City Hall, the street activity around the Pompidou Center; the sophisticated complexity of Rockefeller Center; the relaxed graciousness of San Francisco's Telegraph Hill; the majesty of Beijing's Forbidden City, and the nobility of the Acropolis.

Good cities we have; the ideal city eludes us, although a vision of it should guide us. Great cities are within our grasp if we will them and are willing to pay the necessary costs.

And in such process the Arts will lead the way.

Institute for Urban Design Conference
Museum of Modern Art, New York City
April 3, 1986

CHAZAK, CHAZAK

A four-year stint at the helm of the National Jewish Welfare Board provides the opportunity for a rare perspective on changing Jewish life in America; and the view from such a vantage point shows an American Jewish community of far stronger vital signs than conventional wisdom would have believed possible.

Those looking backward often see American Jews as still uneasy aliens on the fringe of the national culture; uprooted, displaced persons who do not quite belong. In the words of one observer as recently as 1960, they were "psychologically still in exile, marginal people with an undiminished sense of strangeness."

The current reality is quite different, for the American Jewish community has clearly achieved a level of material well-being, prestige, acceptance and influence unparalleled in Jewish history, with virtually all the worthwhile doors of our society open to it. Our plays, poems and novels do not yet reflect this, but the facts are beyond dispute.

In America today Jews constitute roughly 2½ % of the population, yet they consistently win some ten times that percentage of the country's Nobel Prizes, Pulitzer Prizes, National Book Awards, etc. It is estimated that over one-fifth of the members of the American Bar Association are Jewish; and Jews buy an estimated one-fifth of all hardcover books other than dictionaries, cookbooks, Bibles and "how-to-do-it" manuals. This past fall, after Anwar Sadat's visit to Jerusalem, when Pravda (certainly no sympathetic observer) tried to explain to its Russian readership the impact of U.S. Jews on American national policy, it pointed out that one-fifth of American millionaires are believed to be Jewish, and that Jews are well known to vote, to write for publications and to contribute to political candidates of all parties far out of proportion to their numbers in the population.

If a generation ago, anyone had ventured to guess that in 1978 the Mayor of New York and his immediate predecessor would be active and practicing Jews, as were the immediate past Secretary of State, the past U.S. Attorney General, and a past Ambassador to the United Nations, he would have been dismissed as a visionary crackpot. If, further, he had predicted that the President of DuPont would be named Irving Shapiro, his listeners would have assumed they were being set up for an elaborate joke. If he added that the current Secretary of the Treasury, the Secretary of Defense, the recently replaced Chairman of the Federal Reserve Board, and the newly created energy czar had all at least been born Jewish, his listeners would politely have excused themselves and gone elsewhere.

It is hard for many of us to realize how substantially and how quickly conditions have changed. Although it was actually in 1947, it seems only yesterday that I entered Yale and agreed to serve as U.J.A. solicitor for my 1,110 freshman classmates; neither I nor anyone else was surprised when the admission office promptly sent over a list of 111 Jewish freshmen who constituted, to the button, the prescribed 10% permitted by the informal quota system. Today there is almost no Ivy League college with less than one-fifth of its roster composed of Jewish students, and some reportedly approach one-half.

By virtually every accepted index of social health, the American Jew emerges with flying colors—whether in per capita receipt of Ph.D.'s (high) or of penitentiary incarcerations for crimes of violence (low); whether of per capita charitable contributions and communal participation (high) or incidence of alcoholism or paternal desertion of the family (low), the picture is clear and sometimes poignantly so. When the Census Bureau reports that the approximately 350,000 Jewish poor in New York City receive far below their proportionate share of federal aid, investigation shows that poverty aid formulas cause funds to flow to specific districts on the basis of such factors as

22

incidence of juvenile delinquency. Since, in New York, two–thirds of Jewish poor are over 65, and the remaining one-third are Hasidic families with virtually no juvenile delinquents, the numbers tell a dramatic story: the American Jew has created for himself a sub-culture whose carefully documented, statistically delineated characteristics are impressive when set against those of any comparable group.

Not to recognize this reality is to be blind to the obvious; not to ask why is to do an injustice to the socio-cultural tradition of which it is a reflection.

Yet this end result was not obvious nor even apparent when, at the turn of the century, English author and historian H. G. Wells looked at the bedraggled Jews pouring into America from eastern Europe. He said it was a tragic error to let them enter because they would "never be more than a semi-literate urban peasantry." His fear seemed borne out by the charge of New York's police chief, Theodore Bingham, in 1908 that, although Jews constituted one-fourth of the city's population, they accounted for one-half of the crime.

Few non-Jewish voices were raised in their defense, and for the most part those were muted; but one prescient observer had loudly and clearly stated his conviction that the Jew in America would not only succeed, but would succeed gloriously. Hutchins Hapgood: a young Midwesterner writing about four specific characteristics that set the immigrant Jew apart and would insure his successful adaptation to American life. In his now famous series, The Spirit of the Ghetto, in *The Atlantic Monthly*, he said they had 1) a fierce self-confidence and determination to succeed; 2) an all-abiding conviction of the importance of education; 3) remarkably strong family ties and a commitment to mutual aid, and 4) a sense of community support that made the family feel it was not isolated.

Hapgood was correct about the future of the Jews; I believe he would have been intrigued to see that the characteristics he noted were merely the symptoms or manifestations of a cultural pattern that would stand in good stead not only those immigrants but their descendants far into the future.

Though the debate about what Judaism is may go on forever, what is clear is that those who form that sub-culture and adhere to its standards have a statistically demonstrably better chance today of leading richer, fuller, more meaningful lives, lives with greater probabilities of self-fulfillment and self-realization; better chances of leading lives of grace and dignity, meaning and purpose.

Two conclusions follow: first, that this group is indeed different, and different not in trivial aspects, but in something profound and fundamental; second, that the crucial and significant factors which cause the difference should be analyzed, understood, and, where possible, perpetuated.

This message is an important and, I believe, a new one. Past generations of Jews affirmed their relation to Judaism because a theological covenant on Mt. Sinai designated them a Chosen People. Today, not only the devout but the questioning, the agnostic, and the theologically indifferent can affirm traditional Jewish values, can inculcate them in their children, and can move to perpetuate them in their communities, for life-enhancement today, as well as tomorrow.

The questions of whether Judaism has survived beyond its time and whether Jewish group existence is an anachronism have answered themselves. The life of the Jew in America is better because of his Judaism.

Neither the individual Jew nor the American Jewish community exists in a vacuum; it is important to note the mutually supportive relationship between vibrant, vital American Jewish sub-culture and the general American society, for the two are not only compatible, but each benefits from and reinforces the other.

Magical, unbelievable America—the 'goldene medina' of the immigrant, the one nation in modern history where the majority consists of minorities; where, in practice as in law, it is safe to be unpopular; where equality of opportunity has always been a national goal—that America has been good to the Jew and the Jew has been good to America.

The American creed celebrates "life, liberty, and the pursuit of happiness;" but the obtaining of happiness is the responsibility of each individual or voluntary grouping of individuals. If the strong and continuing affirmation of traditional Jewish values helps draw the American Jew toward what Abraham Joshua Heschel called "the authentic life, authentically lived," then everyone benefits.

American society's strengths today are economic, social and political; they are not spiritual, and more's the pity. T.S. Eliot speaks of "the decent godless people; their only monument the asphalt road and a thousand lost golf balls." That is a harsh way of putting it, but we must live with the realization that aspects of life which give resonance to existence are more than the material or sensual celebrated today by American mass media. Perhaps the American Jewish sub-culture can remedy the deficiencies, at least for its adherents, and perhaps it can do so indefinitely.

Outlining feasible scenarios for a successful American Jewish sub-culture of the future should be an important part of our agenda, in the hope that worthwhile self-fulfilling prophecies may be created. In any case, we must be clear in our goals: the structuring of a self-sustaining, self-perpetuating American Jewish community dedicated to maintaining those aspects of Jewish culture and tradition which are 'life-enhancing' for its members.

Such a Jewish community would not conflict with the finest American traditions, but would strengthen them in precisely the spirit reflected in George Washington's memorable letter to the Jewish community of Newport. Its members would be assimilated, not acculturated; they could look, dress and speak like everyone else, but would maintain a traditional Jewish outlook about the goals of life, the nature of home and family, the role of education, the significance to the donor of charity and compassion, and all other components of the traditional Jewish value system.

What specific characteristics such a Jewish community would possess are open to debate. Traditional Zionist theory, for example, has as yet no ideological framework for a long-term, vibrant, self- sustaining Diaspora and David Ben Gurion's thesis was that none was possible.

My own belief is that such a Diaspora is already emerging, but that, for realistic hopes of continuity, a number of mutually reinforcing factors must be present.

For example, a sustained knowledge and use of the Hebrew language is imperative. For ritual purposes and as a worldwide psychological bond, its role in strengthening Jewish identification will be increasingly critical. In this regard, it is interesting to recall that the one large Jewish community in history which quietly evaporated was Alexandria, where the use of Hebrew was permitted to languish and disappear.

Continuing relationships with fellow Jews abroad, especially in Israel, are essential for a number of reasons, not the least of which is the beneficial impact on both giver and receiver of the fruits of communal solidarity. The social and educational effect of UJA, Israel bond and local Federation drives is at least as important as the economic transfer payment involved. And the effect on the morale and self-image of U. S. Jews of the role they have played in the life of world Jewry in these last decades is incalculable.

The importance of vital religious and Jewish educational institutions is self-evident, and the increasing sophistication of the American Jewish community should be matched in time by the increasing sophistication of those institutions. Although the role of religious ritual in the life of the American Jew can be judged by the level of Friday night synagogue attendance, the synagogue has other important roles: it often serves as a surrogate for the extended family; as a vehicle for education and the transmission of values, and as a center for Jewish rites of passage (birth, death, marriage and that much maligned Jewish experience, the bat or bar mitzvah.) In time these affairs will become more restrained and more tasteful, but I hope we retain indefinitely the ritual act of affirmation when the individual stands before family, friends and congregation and says loudly and clearly, "I am a Jew."

The Jewish school is a separate and complex subject, but for now, let it be said that the caliber of the school and the caliber and professional status of the educator must be raised dramatically. The day of the old-fashioned melamed has passed.

26

The final important factor in Jewish continuity will be the constant revitalization and renewal of a vibrant, appropriate Jewish communal social service network, a sine qua non, "that without which" such a community could not survive.

Jewish communal services have been and are outstanding, but must strive to be even better, even more responsive to emerging needs.

What Jung called key racial memories must be kept fresh and alive: the sense of historical continuity; the values and ideals of the 'extended family' carried out to one's neighbors and the community beyond; and the sense of being 'chosen'—not in terms of privilege, but of obligation. Jews should feel not that they are better, but that they should be.

The "lives of quiet desperation" led by so many today, full of joyless pleasures and meaningless strivings, may reflect the materialistic tenor of our time, but as Jews we should hope for more. When Clemenceau commented a generation ago that the modern world was going "from barbarism to decadence with nothing in between," he intended the comment as a warning rather than a prediction. Each of us, as individuals or members of a group, can make it true or false for ourselves.

Strengthening and perpetuating the American Jewish community in our own way may be the best means we have to affirm our choice, and our efforts will benefit our own generation as well as those to come.

The story is told of the traveler in Biblical times watching three men struggle down a mountain with one of the great cedars of Lebanon. When asked what they were doing, the first man replied that he was trying to move the tree; the second said he was transporting building material; but the third said quietly that he was building the temple for King Solomon.

"Building the temple" may be an appropriate metaphor for some of the ostensibly mundane work discussed at this convocation of the National Jewish Welfare Board, where the nuts and bolts of communal work are analyzed and discussed, where lessons are learned, experiences exchanged, friendships made, and the work of the field advanced. JWB is an organization aiding thousands of volunteer and professional workers who spend some $100 million a year on behalf of the one million members of America's Jewish community centers, Y camps and affiliated groups; it is an organization through which the Jewish chaplaincy services military personnel and their families, an organization which sponsors the Jewish Book Council, the Jewish Media Service, and other activities,

If the American Jewish community survives and flourishes (and I am convinced it will), in no small part it will be because of the efforts of large numbers of dedicated individuals doing day-to-day communal work and in the process "building the Temple."

As I complete my heartwarming and immensely satisfying four years as President of JWB, I find myself grateful for the experience of working with the remarkable men and women of this organization, proud of what we have accomplished together, and mindful of all that remains to be done.

To Bob Adler and the other incoming officers, I extend my warmest good wishes and pledge of support, and as my term ends, I echo the words repeated at the end of the Torah:

Chazak, chazak, venischazak – Be strong, be strong, and let us strengthen one another.

JWB Biennial Convention
Montreal, Canada
April 8, 1978

DENIAL IN AMERICAN LIFE

Thirty-five percent of registered U.S. Democrats believe George W. Bush knew in advance of the 9/11 World Trade Center attack, according to Rasmussen polls; and between 31% and 46% of registered Republicans believe Barack Obama is a Muslim, according to other polls. Neither group seems troubled by the lack of supporting facts.

Most of us casually dismiss holders of those views as oddities, and we are equally casual about our public's growing inability to engage in rational exchanges of opposing views on a number of important questions.

"Denial"—the refusal to accept the reality of unpleasant facts— has become a common feature of American life. We hear what we want to hear, and the ancient concept "audi alteram partem"—"hearing the other side"—has been forgotten. The absence of reasoned discourse and thoughtful examination of opposing positions is itself a subject meriting discussion, since the price we will pay without it will be painful.

On some subjects, our denial is self-evident; on others, it is curious; on others still, it is self-destructive.

The state of the American economy, for example, is a clear instance of *"self-evident denial."* One half of our Congress refuses to entertain any thought of revenue increase (called taxes), the other half refuses to consider substantial decreases in expenditures (called entitlements); yet both realize that our current and projected deficits indicate impending catastrophe.

To be specific, the 40-year average of our debt-to-GNP ratio has been 37%; today it is twice that and rising. Interest charges on that debt have historically averaged 5.7% per annum but today our interest rates are at an artificial low of 2.5%. Unchecked, those interest payments must in time rise and strangle our economy.

Without a major immediate restructuring of our *short term, intermediate term* and *long term* economic thinking, all our economists acknowledge the likely prospect of a severe crisis whose timing, depth and length defy prediction. The example of Greece is very much on everyone's mind.

At a moment when militant extremists in Congress control their respective political parties, virtually no discussions of compromise are taking place in Washington, while the nation at large watches in stunned fascination like a mesmerized frog about to be eaten by an approaching snake.

The International Monetary Fund's annual report discusses the prospect of a profound shock to global financial markets if the U.S, protector of the world's reserve currency, defaults on its debt payments. Moody's Investor Service foresees the possible downgrading of U.S. debt to Double A from its present Triple A rating, with other ratings (such as Fannie Mae and Freddie Mac) dropping accordingly, with unpredictable consequences.

Meanwhile, "back at the ranch," that prominent economic savant Michele Bachmann dismisses such talk as "scare tactics." Her team tells her that if our debt ceiling of $14.3 trillion is not raised by August 2nd, our government can easily pay its monthly interest charges of $18 billion by "greatly scaling back other functions." What that will do, both to domestic peace and to international confidence in our bonds, is not mentioned.

So much for the short term. For the long term, the IMF forecasts U.S. economic growth at below 3% per annum through 2016, and Laura Tyson, former Chair of Bill Clinton's Council of Economic Advisors, says the U.S. might not see employment reach pre-recession levels until 2023.

"SELF-EVIDENT DENIAL" seems the appropriate term for the American public's relative serenity concerning our economy. With the world's highest medical costs, its largest military, an aging population, taxes that are among the world's lowest and relentlessly growing deficits, we refuse to look ahead. The level of national debate is embarrassing—"irritable mental gestures that seek to resemble ideas" (Lionel Trilling's phrase) have displaced thoughtful presentations of facts and their consequences; Tea Party leader Grover Norquist's characterization of bipartisanship as "date rape" is one example among many. Debaters on both sides seem oblivious of where—absent compromise—their respective positions are leading us.

"CURIOUS DENIAL," on the other hand, is demonstrated by the total lack of discussion in the American Jewish community of the long term ramifications of a two-state vs. one-state solution for the Israelis and Palestinians.

American Jews are generally considered a rather astute group; and they care deeply about the well-being of Israel. However, the blank check they are encouraging for Israel's leaders (who are driven by domestic politics of which most Americans are unaware) may in time make a viable Palestinian state impossible.

No rational person dismisses the complexity of the problems involved: the profound mutual distrust and the fears it engenders, the ancient grievances, the troubling 'facts on the ground'; and no one thinks successful resolution will be either easy or quick. But few American Jewish voices are heard asking whether time is working for or against the Israelis.

The ramifications of the failure to create two stable adjoining states receives almost zero discussion among your Jewish neighbors or friends. The 1.3 million Arabs living in Israel today seem willing now to accept second-class status. At some point in the 21st century, however, with one man/one vote and an Arab majority in "one state," life will look different. Failure to contemplate the demographics of a one-state solution with a Muslim majority is one case of "curious denial" by those who should know better, and the dismaying possibility of a "failed state" like Somalia or Yemen on Israel's borders is another. "Curious" today, "tragic" tomorrow.

"SELF-DESTRUCTIVE DENIAL" is the saddest of the cases because, as with a self-inflicted wound, seeking someone else to blame just exacerbates the problem. The evolving situation of blacks in America today is a case in point. The remarkable contrast in all aspects of life between those American blacks who are successfully entering the American mainstream and those who remain trapped in a mindset of anger, nihilism and alienation is profound.

The traditional black American narrative of disenfranchised, victimized, marginalized people angrily pounding on closed doors, demanding admission, is becoming less and less relevant. In our increasingly pluralistic and ever-evolving society, the time has arrived for a new black American narrative, one that looks forward with hope and determination rather than backward with despair, and one that acknowledges the growing diversity—in mindset and in socio-economic conditions—among blacks in America. Those with education and with stable families, with the skills, aspirations and determination to invest in their own 'human capital,' are rising in all areas of our society.

The situation of many blacks in the inner city, however, where prominent demagogues send a counter-productive message of defeat to nihilistic, semi-literate young people trapped in a dead end counter culture, is a fact of life that should be faced.

Despite heart-breaking rates of school dropouts, unmarried teenage births, prison incarcerations and HIV-AIDS infections, painfully few voices are heard encouraging inner city youth to stay in school, to acquire the education required for upward mobility, or to change the anti-social mindset that in the 21st century will prevent young people from competing successfully in an increasingly automated, globalized and competitive world.

Is denial of the importance of education today self-destructive? Yes. Necessary, no. Society loses, but the greatest losers are inner city young people themselves. Education is the true civil rights issue of our day. It is the great equalizer, the only 'magic bullet' we know to bring submerged groups into the economic and social mainstream; and we must shout that from the rooftops.

Americans are in denial about many other problems—our short term reliance on fossil fuels, for example, and our long term ecological challenges. If Japan has a nuclear crisis and Germany forswears all atomic energy while France embraces it wholeheartedly, we should at least discuss the question.

What can be done to raise the level of public debate today? First, no subjects should be 'off the table' for examination, research and discussion. Second, we must rethink how we consider these subjects. Two approaches would help—remembering the Moynihan Dictum and forgetting ad hominem reasoning.

Daniel Patrick Moynihan's statement that, "Everyone is entitled to his own opinion, but not his own facts," should be pounded into every undergraduate. Objective and dispassionate examination of all relevant facts, especially those of 'the other guy,' would be an important first step for all of us to take.

A second step would be to recall the concept that "facts are not responsible for those who believe them." Just because I find Noam Chomsky's anti-American diatribes repellent doesn't mean that every word out of his mouth must be mistaken; and just because I admire Albert Schweitzer, doesn't mean that I must agree with everything he says.

Dispassionate consideration of the factors involved in the major questions facing us should concern us all. It may no longer be a luxury, but a necessity for us to recognize and combat what Richard Hofstadter called The Paranoid Style in American Politics and for us to return to civilized discourse. Our well-being and survival may depend on it.

Yale Class of 1951
60th Reunion
June 3, 2011

TIMES THAT TRY MEN'S SOULS

The failure of America's political leaders across the spectrum to explain to the public the serious long term, intermediate and short term challenges we face has caused unnecessary pain, turmoil and widespread loss of public confidence in government. Their failure to deal effectively with those challenges has put our national well-being in jeopardy. Widespread protests from left and right may lack a coherent agenda, but the public knows that something is wrong and they demand the truth.

Liberals refuse to acknowledge that we must live within our means; conservatives refuse to acknowledge the economic and social imbalances that threaten to strangle our society. Both confuse symptoms with causes and the cyclical with the structural; both use the current turmoil to further their ideological goals. As a result, both give the impression of being long on cleverness and short on integrity. Neither faces the long term ramifications of an economy shifting from industrial production to services and information, or the emergence of a single global market for goods, labor and capital, or growing intergenerational economic tensions. Neither encourages the deferred gratification and future-mindedness that underlie all successful societies.

America's declining rate of social mobility, our diminishing ability to influence the world beyond our borders, the relative shabbiness of our national physical facilities, the deteriorating quality of life—none is pre-ordained, none is inevitable. All are the result of bad governmental decisions and a public demanding much, but willing to pay for little—'self-inflicted wounds' that can be reversed.

When we deal effectively with the problems of education, infrastructure, foreign trade, industrial policy and social mobility, we will regain the forward momentum we had before this lost decade, and our government will regain the public trust it has lost.

Subtle changes in the American psyche, influenced by European thinking, have caused our public to focus on today vs. tomorrow, on rights vs. obligations, on entitlements vs. their financing. All spell trouble, as does the Left's demand for equality of result rather than equality of opportunity or the Right's belief in 'everyone for himself and the Devil take the hindmost.'

Our common goals—a fair and just society, with opportunities for advancement for talent and effort, with a balance between public and private amenities, with the rewards and obligations of citizenship rationally apportioned— are achievable over time; but current realities are discouraging, and public expectations are unrealistic.

Aristotle might cite the 'efficient cause' of our current predicament as our dysfunctional mechanics of government— electoral gerrymandering, arm-twisting political lobbyists, the legalized bribery we call 'campaign contributions.' The 'formal cause' he might cite as the preposterous cost of political campaigning. Until we address these causes, we are unlikely to get the kind of responsible legislative bodies—and responsible legislation—our Founding Fathers envisioned.

The coming American "new normal," a society stratified along educational lines, with growing numbers of the under-educated having no economically-productive role, is rapidly becoming a fact of life. The wage premium of intellectual over manual labor continues to surge, even as recent college graduates find jobs scarce. How we increase the size of our national economic pie and how we divide it appropriately are challenges we must face; the sooner the better.

We have seen middle class wages stagnate so that workers can no longer afford the goods and services whose purchase the economy requires to keep growing. The top one per cent of our public receives one quarter of our national income, the top five per cent receive 37%;

and 95% of the public must limit their expenditures. The last time we had similar numbers was in 1928.

The national macro-numbers today are frightening. With a GDP of $15 trillion, U.S. public debt to others is now $10 trillion and intergovernmental debt is over $4.5 trillion, with the total growing at the rate of $1.5 trillion a year. The present value of our existing unfunded domestic entitlements is huge; common estimates put them at $66 trillion: $35 trillion for Medicaid, $23 trillion for Medicare and $8 trillion for Social Security. Of 51 million private homes with mortgages, 15 million are worth less than their debt. Three million homes were foreclosed last year; another six million are in arrears. Our national unemployment rate is over 9%, and millions of workers have given up looking for work. The unemployment benefits of some four million may expire this year. Student loans total over a trillion dollars, and the rising default numbers are ominous. Opinion polls show a public anxious and pessimistic, pleading for government's pragmatic compromise on vital issues.

We must consider—calmly and rationally—where our economy is and where it is heading. We can no longer afford the luxury of allowing political polemic to drive reasoned argument from the stage nor permit political candidates to see no further than the next election.

Just as our political parties cooperated in the national interest during the crises of WWI and WWII, they must cooperate in the current economic crisis. 'Loyal opposition' is one thing; 'rule or ruin' political maneuvering is another, and the climate in polarized Washington today is rightly called 'obsessive obstructionism.'

In light of the international embarrassment of Standard and Poor's credit downgrade, history will deal harshly with our Congressional leaders, and those like Grover Norquist, leader of the "No Tax Increase—of any kind, at any time, for any reason" movement and his efforts to demand No Tax pledges from all Republican candidates (with the threat of running further-to-the- right primary opponents against them).

The Left must face the ramifications of an aging and longer- living population, of a public education system falling seriously behind global standards, of government employee benefits out of sync with those of the rest of society.

Grover Norquist may wish government reduced to "the size where I can drag it into the bathroom and drown it in the bathtub (sic)," but most of us do not. We want government services and we must pay for them by taxation. Edmund Burke, the father of modern conservatism, put it succinctly—"To tax and to please is not given to men." Europe has found that Value Added Taxes, although regressive, are the least objectionable way to raise revenue. If we cannot face other forms of taxation, we, too, must consider them. (A 5% VAT would raise some $500 billion in annual revenue.) One way or another, cutting expenditures and increasing revenues lie ahead of us.

Few observers would disagree that free market economies are more productive than rigidly controlled ones—leading to what Winston Churchill called "the unequal sharing of blessings vs. the equal sharing of miseries." Few would disagree that to achieve optimum productivity and socio-economic stability, free market economies require some degree of government regulation. What that degree should be is the question.

John Maynard Keynes' 'interventionist' followers and Frederick von Hayek's 'hands off' supporters will always battle, but neither Keynes nor Hayek approved of swollen government, and both agreed that over-indebtedness leads to financial nightmares. Short term 'stimulus,' (preferably on desirable repairs to our deteriorating and inadequate infrastructure) to provide immediate employment, and longer term 'austerity' (with renewed savings and investment for continuous growth) reflect the best thinking of both. The two trillion dollars respected engineers tell us we must spend on infrastructure— for repairs, upgrades and expansions— will provide short term jobs and long term economic and social benefits. Had we created an infrastructure bank (with an accelerated review process) three years ago, the results would already be apparent. Short term fears of deflation, long term fears of inflation and recurring fears of stagflation must be dealt with realistically and prudently.

A healthy economy requires a sensible balance between consumption and saving/investment. In America today consumption is tilted in favor of private consumer goods and against public goods such as airports, parks, highways, mass transit, etc. We mistakenly consider expenditure on education and scientific research as personal consumption rather than as national investment for the future. We are heavily over-invested in housing, which is not productive of future wealth.

Other countries do not share our fetish of home ownership nor our conventional wisdom that house prices must rise more than inflation.

Our financial services industry, whose function should be to oil the wheels of society and to channel savings into productive enterprise, has become a world of its own, skimming a disproportionate share of the national income. In 2008, for example, the country's top 25 hedge fund managers personally received $25 billion among them, largely through the legal scam of low tax "carried interest"; corporate CEOs receive huge bonuses even as their companies post major losses. Rewards for risks on the upside have not been balanced by penalties for bad guesses on the downside. No wonder our best and brightest are seduced by financial paper-shuffling rather than careers in the productive world. Eventually, even the investment world will realize that a smaller share of a growing economy is better for them than a larger share of a stagnant one.

National wealth cannot be distributed (or redistributed) until it is produced; we must focus as much on wealth production as on its division. Albert Einstein noted that, "In the real world, there are neither rewards nor punishments—only consequences." We must act so that the consequences of our actions take us where we want to go.

Our economic problems are remediable— but not in the immediate future. America is a resilient society and we will muddle through, but we must modify our expectations for the
short run and again think long run. As Adam Smith wrote, "There

is a lot of ruin in a country," and we have great strengths. To regain our national momentum—to refute those who speak of "American decline"—we must act vigorously and wisely. Three specific areas cry out for governmental attention: infrastructure, foreign trade and industrial policy. Our public intellectuals are remiss in not demanding that we address them.

Finally, and most importantly, we must address the long term challenge of providing productive employment for all those ready, able and willing to work. Today, one quarter of our young people drop out of high school before graduation, and we have no economic role for them. Those with college degrees do somewhat better, but not really well. Graduate degrees or specialized skills are increasingly required for success in this information-fueled, high-tech world. Our workers are in competition with those of the rest of the world who are becoming better educated and vocationally-trained than U.S. workers. We either raise our educational and skill levels in STEM fields (Science, Technology, Engineering, Mathematics) or suffer accordingly. Increasing poverty, downward mobility and social turmoil are not impossible.

That is a worst case. A best case could occur if our disadvantaged poor—whether whites in the rural South or minorities in the inner cities— develop the attributes demanded by a high tech, globalized, competitive world. Future-mindedness, self-discipline, the capacity for sustained hard work and a passion for education are the underpinnings of the self-confidence and high aspirations that lead to economic productivity and personal fulfillment.

Skin color, religion and ethnicity are fading rapidly as major factors in American life. Social culture (as reflected in attitudes, values and mindset) is paramount today, regardless of the fulminations of demagogues. Entrepreneurship, for example (which we need to encourage), requires a mindset of risk-taking, thinking outside the box, the ability to rebound from failure with vigor and the tenacity to hold fast to a creative vision, all of which are cultural, not ethnic. Jesse Jackson's 'perpetual victim' view of life should give way to W.E.B. DuBois' call for the minority Talented Tenth to lead the way to the promised land.

Continuing economic growth is the answer to our employment problem, but such growth requires a revival of what Keynes called our "animal spirits," confidence in prospects for the future. That confidence must be based on real world factors, and only political and legislative leadership can create those factors: improved education and vocational training, improved infrastructure, more astute foreign trade policy, a rethought national industrial policy and a more balanced national distribution of income and wealth.

Lowering the cost of political campaigning (by some form of public financing, or free access to TV) and tightening—not loosening—the regulation of political contributions (thereby lessening the influence of lobbyists), are important first steps, along with an end to political gerrymandering. Undue influence—whether of 'fat cats' or of labor leaders—must be lessened. Political term limits and specific steps to increase transparency and accountability to voters should follow. In the meantime, we need more politicians like Teddy Roosevelt, of whom the bosses complained, "We bought him but he didn't stay bought!"

"Let no good crisis go to waste" is a useful thought; but we must be sure that Schumpeter's "creative destruction" is indeed creative. It will be worth our present pain and sacrifice if a healthier, more responsive political and legislative system results from it.

This past decade has been a difficult one for us, but we can snap back. "American exceptionalism," in which I believe, has traditionally been based on underlying premises of "can do" pragmatism, fair-mindedness, generosity and optimism. We must not forget that.

Sheer demographics and economic projections indicate that with a global population of 7 billion people, America's position in the world must in time change relatively. In absolute terms, great days can still lie ahead for our country.

The following points would speed our recovery:
• Budget deficits should be recognized as short term expedients

to "tide us over" cyclical downturns, and our debts must be paid down significantly as soon as budget surpluses from a growing economy permit.

- Health care costs must be financed by actuarially-sound measures that are transparent and understood by all. In 2010 the U.S. spent 17.6% of its GDP on healthcare vs. an average of 9% for European countries, yet their life expectancies are higher than ours. We need better value for our health dollars. "Defined benefits" as a concept should yield to some form of a "defined contribution" approach because we can no longer afford the former today, much less when the WWII baby boomers retire.

- Our system of taxation must be considered afresh, to promote investment and to raise future revenue. Eliminating many deductions and credits (e.g. from eliminating $150 billion a year to stimulate race horse breeding, whale hunting, etc., to re-thinking deductibility of interest on home mortgages) in favor of lower marginal tax rates will provide a simpler and more efficient system. The byzantine U.S. Tax Code, thousands of pages written in technical jargon beyond the ken of a typical small businessman without expensive lawyers and accountants, is a national embarrassment without parallel in the developed world.

- Lower taxes on U.S. corporations' foreign earnings would encourage them to repatriate the cash (tax revenues for us, domestic investment money for them). Tax havens (such as the Cayman Islands or the Faroes), that serve no role other than tax evasion and money- laundering, should be subject to public scrutiny and international regulation.

- Legislation which protects the banking system by distinguishing "depository" (savings/lending) banks from riskier "investment" banks (that trade for their own account) should be reinstituted, as advocated by the wise Paul Volcker. The capital requirements of all banks (large and small, savings or investment) should be examined carefully. Protection of savers and investors and encouragement of lending are the goals. Private entities "too big to fail" are too big.

- Unfunded, unaffordable pension programs of federal, state and municipal employees should be re-examined and discussed publicly. Logic calls for them to be brought into line with those in the private sector, regardless of the short term political battles that will cause.

- Legal tort reform, regulatory reform and entitlement reform should be reviewed periodically for costs and benefits, goals and actual effects. There should be full and frank discussions before an informed public on these sensitive issues. Frivolous law suits should be discouraged by using the British practice of having losers pay court costs and legal fees.

- Foreign trade should be encouraged, not discouraged, with the informed cooperation of business, labor and government, all concerned with the national interest. A clearly-enunciated national trade policy is long overdue. We must again become a successful trading nation, with high-wage, high-productivity jobs located in the United States profitably providing goods and services for the growing middle classes of the BRICs (Brazil, Russia, India, China). Trade policy should be all-encompassing; for example, tariffs on industrial production "inputs" should be eliminated so that U.S. producers are more competitive in the global economy.

- Charges of growth-strangling costs of counter-productive federal regulations (especially on small business) must be investigated and, where justified, modified. Sarbanes-Oxley and Dodd-Frank legislation should be treated as 'living documents' whose consequences and unintended consequences are reviewed periodically. Necessary environmental controls (which some business groups fight even in good times) must be differentiated from excessive controls (which ideologues support regardless of cost vs. benefits).

- Our housing problem must be faced realistically. Americans have lost $7 trillion in home equity, and necessary "de-leveraging" will be slow and painful. It requires orderly debt restructuring, debt reduction and conversion of debt into equity, until normal market forces again bring equilibrium. Permitting fore closed home owners to remain in residence as tenants, with modest rents and an option to repurchase, will prevent vandalism to the house and homelessness for the occupant. (The mortgagee will receive some income and some "shared appreciation" on the property's eventual sale but would face some write down in the short run.) Enabling non-profit groups to own—and to rent out— foreclosed single family homes is another approach; private investors can be encouraged to buy and rent out distressed single family houses. With housing production less than family formation, markets will stabilize in time, but in the meantime, first-time home buyers should be helped to absorb the current surplus of available houses; and existing home owners should be able to avail themselves of current low interest rates.

Those fortunate countries without a 'sub prime' problem either required a significant down payment on home mortgages and borrower incomes sufficient to pay debt service or did not let mortgage originators bundle and sell loans.

- Visas and 'green cards' for post-graduate students, high tech practitioners and others who help our economy should be expedited, not only for their benefit but for ours. A remarkably high percentage of our innovative practices have come from immigrants or their children who have started 40% of our Fortune 500 corporations.

- "Prevailing wage" laws have had a distorting impact on employment. General Motors, for example, has been able to hire thousands of workers recently when unions agreed to permit some "below-prevailing wages."

- Legitimate charitable contributions should be encouraged, not discouraged. The suggestion that they be taxed is the most counter-productive idea recently proposed, since a thriving philanthropic sector is now more important than ever. $300 billion in annual contributions employing 9% of the U.S. work force should not be diminished.

- The multi-trillion dollar long term reductions in government expenditures being proposed are necessary, but some proposed cuts (such as Pell scholarship grants) are ill-advised, and our public universities must be maintained.
- The successful industrial policies of Germany, whose high-wage manufacturing sector is flourishing, should be an example for America. The manufacturing economic 'multiplier effect' is much greater than that of the service sector.

Other questions to be pondered:

- Why should "second home" owners receive interest deductions on their mortgages?
- What inheritance should heirs receive free of all taxes, and what should graduated taxes be on larger estates?
- Should seniors, regardless of their ability to pay, receive medications free?
- Should Social Security be "means tested?"
- How should Internet purchases and services be taxed?
- Is it psychologically sound for one half the public to pay no federal income taxes at all?
- Why should tax rates on short term capital gains (less than one year) not be raised, while those on longer term (over a year) not be lowered? And how about a zero tax rate on newly-issued securities which fund growth?
- How should 'short selling' be regulated, taxed and reported, and what are appropriate regulations and taxation for the $600 trillion derivative market? (Yes, the $600 trillion figure is "notional," with much double- counting, but what a number!)
- Given our conflicting desires for energy independence and for a green world, how should oil and gas companies be taxed? Would not higher taxes at the gas pump curtail consumption

45

as well as provide revenues?

- America's great days may lie ahead, but "the mode by which the inevitable comes to pass is called effort," said Oliver Wendell Holmes.

It remains to be seen if the American public will make the effort.

Bard College
Hannah Arendt Center
October 28, 2011

QUO VADIS REDUX

At this first national conference of the Yale Alumni Real Estate Association, it seems appropriate to address two important questions: First, looking at the real estate field in perspective, we should ask where we have been, where we are and where we are going. Second, as individuals seeing ourselves in perspective, we should ask where we have been, where we are, and where we should be going.

To deal effectively with the first question, we must realize that real estate economics has micro and macro aspects. Local challenges of site acquisition, building design and construction, leasing, management and so forth are obviously crucial, and they are the fundamentals of our day-to-day activities. But the macro problems of real estate cycles and the financial conditions that determine a project's success are influenced by national and global factors not readily apparent.

Local market conditions and global capital flows must both be understood; and, in 2008, the macro economic question is more challenging.

No one has an unclouded crystal ball, and it is sobering to realize that, for example, the U.S. credit crunch of 2007 took virtually all economists by surprise. In 2006, the term "subprime mortgage" was unknown to the general public, and most economists (except for a few such as Yale's Professor Robert J. Shiller) seemed unconcerned with housing finance practices.

Today, the current volatility of the stock market, with its three-digit surges and crashes, shows how nervous investors are; the fluctuating interbank lending rate shows how wary banks are of lending even to one another; and the conflicting signals we receive are bewildering.

On the same day that the Blackstone Group announced it had raised a fresh $10.9 billion fund to invest in real estate opportunities ahead, JPMorgan Chase analysts predicted the U.S. commercial real estate market could decline by as much as 20% over the next five years. And at the moment when most observers anticipate a softening of the Manhattan office market because of an expected loss of 20,000 to 30,000 financial services jobs, the General Motors Building is rumored to be close to a sale at $2.9 billion that would give its purchaser a negative cash flow.

On Friday, March 14, I heard President Bush tell the Economic Club of New York how strong and resilient the American economy was and how government should not over-react to current problems. As he spoke, Bear Stearns informed the government it was contemplating Chapter 11 protection, and Messrs. Bernanke and Paulson spent the weekend pulling rabbits out of their financial hats.

The President's relaxed reaction, then and since, recalls the comic version of Kipling's poem If—"If you can keep your head when all about you are losing theirs and blaming it on you, perhaps they know something you don't."

This week, Federal Reserve Chairman Bernanke told Congress that he expects the economy to grow in the second half of 2008 and to be solid in 2009. Yet this same week's Michigan Consumer Confidence Survey showed public confidence (historically the best predictor of recession) had declined to its lowest level in 16 years; the Conference Board's index of leading indicators fell for the fifth consecutive month; and forecasts indicate that residential construction this year will fall below one million starts for the first time since 1991. Traditional economic forecasting signals—such as job loss/creation, home foreclosures, credit card delinquencies, bankruptcies—are negative.

Optimists, who want to believe in good times, but who contemplate grim fundamentals, feel like the fellow in the Tom Lehrer song who was "as nervous as a devout Christian Scientist with appendicitis."

At this moment of financial turmoil it is useful to remember some basic economic "facts of life":

a) leverage works in both directions, with smiles on the way up and tears on the way down, and our financial institutions and vehicles are wildly over-leveraged in these difficult times;

b) a "liquidity crisis" can easily be solved by the Federal Reserve (as lender of last resort) but a "solvency crisis" is a different problem entirely—monetary policy cannot make bad investments turn good;

c) supply and demand are complex factors, with "demand" referring to those ready, able and willing to buy, and "supply" often varying with price. A public worried about falling home values, rising interest costs and possible unemployment may be reluctant to spend;

d) with national and international inflation rates clearly rising, we note that Jimmy Carter did not copyright the term "stagflation" in the 1970's, so it will be available for use next year should conditions warrant it. It is difficult to understand why our economists continue to use the term "core inflation," which does not include energy or food prices, since Joe Six-pack is fully aware of what he is paying at the gas pump and the supermarket;

e) and, finally, we should remember that Jack Kennedy noted not only that "the rising tide lifts all the boats," but also, as he smirked privately to friends, "when the police raid a house, they take all the girls."

Real estate practitioners sometimes forget how deeply their fortunes are tied to those of the general economy. A good place to begin such a discussion is with capitalization rates, or the ratio between a property's income and its price.

49

A net cash flow as free and clear of $100 with a cap rate of 10% gives a property a price of $1,000. If the cap rate drops to 5%, the price of the same income flow rises to $2,000. When cap rates "revert to their historic mean," those prices will decline accordingly.

From 1987 to 2001, cap rates of U.S. office buildings, shopping centers and rental housing complexes generally were in the 8% to 9% range; by 2007, cap rates had plummeted (in some markets to 5% or less) and prices soared.

The cause was detailed in Tony Downs' perceptive book, *Niagara of Capital*, which describes the massive flow of capital into real estate after Alan Greenspan in 2003 dropped interest rates to 1% and kept them there. For 31 consecutive months, the base inflation-adjusted short-term interest rate was below zero. The result was, in Downs' words, "an unprecedented disconnect between conditions in commercial space markets, where rents and occupancies were falling, and conditions in commercial property finance, where prices soared on well-occupied buildings with good cash flow."

To compound matters, just as a global savings glut, particularly in Asia, poured foreign funds into the U.S., Wall Street's huge increase in securitization of debt of all kinds gave lenders an unrealistic sense of confidence in the very real risks they were facing; and rating agencies' AAA approval of subprime packages added fuel to the fire.

These reinforcing factors pushed cap rates to their recent lows which history tells us cannot be sustained. Last year when Harry Macklowe bought a package of office buildings from Blackstone for $7 billion, with a $5.8 billion short-term loan from Deutsche Bank and $1.2 billion from the Fortress Investment Group, his $50 million on top controlled a lot of bricks and mortar. Today, with Deutsche Bank pressing for return of its loan and no buyers in sight for the package at $6 billion, life looks different for all concerned.

At the moment, U.S. real estate markets are all but frozen, but most observers believe it will probably take about 18 months for them to return to normal fluidity. At what cap rates, and at what sales prices, one can only guess.

U.S. housing markets present a similar picture, with a universal feeling that they are over-priced and over-mortgaged.

As Professor Shiller documents in his thought-provoking book, *Irrational Exuberance*, real U.S. home prices, which traditionally rise at the rate of inflation, increased 52% between 1997 and 2004, much faster than incomes rose. From 1985 to 2002, he points out, "the median price of an American home rose from 4.9 years' per capita income to 7.7 years' per capita income."

Nationally, home prices have dropped about 10% since last Spring, and Professor Shiller said recently that he thinks we could see home prices in gradual decline for five years or more. An authority on the psychology of financial decision-making, he is a firm believer in business cycles.

Some observers believe that during the next three to five years, house prices could fall as low as their 2001 levels, which in some regions would show huge losses. Goldman Sachs recently proclaimed that home prices in California are overvalued by 35% to 40%. Once home prices in a region fall by more than 20%, even borrowers with solid credit and mainstream mortgages face serious problems. Subprime borrowers will have long since been in extremis, with their mortgagees in trauma.

Government assistance efforts to date have focused on lenders; homeowners present a more difficult problem. Widespread home ownership is a desirable goal, but not all purchasers can afford to own houses; and no one feels much sympathy for speculators who bought condos or second homes hoping only for a quick and profitable flip.

Some economists fear that the subprime problem may be the earliest manifestation of a deeper credit bubble involving high yield bonds, commercial mortgages, leveraged loans, credit card and student loan debts and—the big unknown—credit default swaps. These instruments, meant to insure bond holders against default, currently cover some $45 trillion, yes trillion, in investment portfolios, up from $1 trillion in 2001.

If the Bernanke/Paulson team can maintain stability and confidence in the integrity of our financial system, these challenges can be met. Otherwise, the possible scenarios are too painful to contemplate.

When I recently asked Larry Summers, former Secretary of the Treasury and former head of "that other place," if he was worried about credit default swaps and the other huge, opaque financial vehicles, he replied, "Yes, worried, but not panicky," by which I assume he thought they could be dealt with in due course.

At some point, the world's increasingly complex financial structure— with an estimated $500 trillion dollars in opaque derivatives that are unanalyzed, unregulated and barely understood, and recently created multi-billion dollar Sovereign Wealth Funds— that can be applied to political as well as economic goals—must be subjected to mature and thoughtful discussion and prudent regulation.

Eventually, when we come through our current cyclical problem, the next U.S. President can then face our zero national savings rate, large and continuing domestic and foreign account deficits, weakening dollar, huge and pressing infrastructure needs, our unfunded Social Security obligations, painful dependence on foreign oil, and national income inequality at its highest level since 1929. (I assume health care and environmental problems will be tackled first.)

Just as a heroic Paul Volcker faced up to the ramifications of the "cheap money" policies of Arthur Burns, so a new Paul Volcker will in turn have to face up to the problems left by Alan Greenspan; and life will resume.

In time, the world will right itself; and the real estate economy will revert to its historic "mean," that is, house prices rising by roughly the rate of inflation, and income-producing real estate with cap rates reflecting the risk/reward ratios of medium quality bonds.

In the long run, the sound strategies of thoughtful investment managers like Yale's incredible David Swenson and of "value" investors like Warren Buffett will be proved correct, of course. But in the long run, too, new financial bubbles will eventually arise and will eventually burst.

Robert Shiller, who more than any other economist writing today understands the impact on business cycles of herd psychology and "animal spirits," writes admiringly of his mentor, Prof. Charles Kindleberger, author of the classic, *Manias, Panics and Crashes: A History of Financial Crises.*" Kindleberger, in turn, admires and cites Charles Mackay's *Extraordinary Popular Delusions and the Madness of Crowds*, which describes the South Sea Bubble, The Dutch Tulip Craze, John Law's Mississippi Schemes and similar explosions.

If only our bankers, brokers and hedge fund types had read those books!

As for today's second question, that of our individual careers and the lives we lead, I would like to recommend two books that should be required reading for everyone in our field. The first, by Buzz McCoy, is called *Living Into Leadership—A Journey in Ethics*. The second is by William J. Poorvu and is entitled *Creating and Growing Real Estate Wealth—The 4 Stages to a Lifetime of Success.*

These two volumes are by men of character and competence who are giants in our field and whose wisdom is widely admired and respected. They discuss the importance not only of deals but of relationships, of investment not only in one's financial capital but also in one's human capital through appropriate training and experience; and they discuss your role in your career field and in your community.

In pragmatic terms and by practical examples, they echo the ancient Roman Tertullian, who said, "Any calling is noble if nobly pursued."

Study these books and—along with a good sense of values, a happy family and a Yale education—they will help you not only to make a living but to make a life.

Yale Alumni Real Estate Association
April 4, 2008

QUO VADIS REDUX (PART II)

Earlier I discussed the factors leading up to our current economic turmoil. Foremost among them, were the Federal Reserve's policy of keeping interest rates too low for too long; the debased home mortgage lending standards introduced by President Clinton's housing officials and maintained by those of George W. Bush; and the system-wide failure to conduct proper risk assessment.

Events in the months since have confirmed my thesis that the bursting of the U.S. real estate bubble would result in pressures on capital markets which would, in turn, weaken financial institutions, which would then affect U.S. economy of employment, consumption, savings, home foreclosures, bankruptcies, etc. Left unchecked, these mutually-reinforcing factors in due course would have serious international repercussions.

I was concerned at: a) the high leverage of financial institutions in a period of declining asset value; b) the large number of AAA-rated loan portfolios consisting of mortgages to borrowers whose incomes were insufficient to cover debt service; c) the widespread confusion between a "liquidity crisis" and an emerging "solvency crisis"; d) the fear that a financially-exhausted public would be unable to maintain appropriate levels of consumption; and, e) that inflationary pressures would preclude the Federal Reserve from applying traditional "cheap money" actions to stimulate the economy.

No quick fix could prevent the turmoil from lasting longer than Ben Bernanke's forecast of an improving 2008 second half and a recovery in 2009.

Is the "end of the world" coming? No. As Adam Smith noted, "A nation has a lot of ruin in it"; an economy can take a lot of pounding and its citizens can absorb a lot of pain yet still function.

The U.S. economy has prodigious strengths, and our institutions and people are resilient. Our housing prices nationwide have already dropped substantially since the high—some 15%—although they still have far to go (perhaps another 10%) on the road back to sustainable values and market equilibrium. Of the estimated five trillion dollars of phony "value" created by the recent bubble, some $2 trillion has already evaporated.

The bull market in stocks that began in 1983, when the Dow Jones was at 1,163 continued until October of 2007, when the Dow Jones hit 14,198. No one could claim that, in the inevitable decline, the gains would all be given back.

Our strengths are a given; but our failure to anticipate and to forestall the economic trauma will cause anguish to many.

How long-lasting our problems are will depend on our reaction to them. In the 1990's Japan refused to acknowledge its difficulties (also triggered by a real estate crash) and they lasted for several years. U.S. officials were slow to understand what was happening; but when, in March of 2008, Bear Stearns notified the Federal Reserve Friday of its impending bankruptcy, our Fed and Treasury leaders worked throughout the weekend to arrange a buy-out of Bear Stearns by JP-MorganChase. The 'weekend improvisation' involved the Fed intervening with public money for a non-bank financial institution for the first time since the Great Depression. When an action is unprecedented, it establishes precedent; and 'moral hazard' is a legitimate fear. For example: Alan Greenspan has recently said, "There is no credible argument for bailing out Bear Stearns and not government-sponsored enterprises like Fannie Mae and Freddie Mac."

Fed Chairman Bernanke, who told a banking conference in June 2007 in South Africa that "the troubles in the subprime sector seem unlikely to seriously spill over to the broader economy" moved nine months later to forestall the failure of Bear Stearns which would have created an international catastrophe. Bernanke remembered the failure of Austria's Bank Creditanstalt and its role in the Great Depression.

Today, policy wonks quibble over whether we are in a 'recession' in a manner that recalls Bill Clinton's comment, "It depends on what your definition of the word "is" is."

U.S. consumer confidence is at its lowest level in 30 years; an estimated 10 million U.S. families have negative equity in their homes. Home foreclosures, auto loan and credit card defaults and bank failures are at frightening levels; and the Federal Deposit Insurance Corp. is at its most over-extended position since its creation in 1933. Sophisticated observers are convinced that after the November 2008 elections, the National Bureau of Economic Research will confirm the recession.

Will the recovery pattern be in the shape of a U, an L or a W? Only a few Panglossians have hopes of a swift V-shaped recovery.

What is to be done?

The answers lie in: a) short term governmental actions; b) medium to long term governmental actions; c) financial institution regulation; d) rating agency regulation; e) governmental housing policy; and f) bursting bubbles.

SHORT TERM GOVERNMENTAL RESPONSE.

A U.S. public with little personal savings, seriously declining home values, heavy credit card and auto loan debt, and increasing fear of unemployment, is unlikely to spend cash grants from the government. That is why the $168 billion government stimulus program had so little impact, with only 10% to 20% of the rebate cash being spent, the rest going into savings or debt reduction.

Had that same money been allocated to states and municipalities for immediate expenditure on mothballed infrastructure projects, not only would the economic stimulus impact have been greater, but instead of more garden furniture, cosmetics and sports equipment, we would have had improved roads, bridges, water levees, airports and so forth to show for the money.

Yes, we need "Son of Stimulus," but for public capital projects rather than personal consumption. The U.S. Department of Transportation estimates that every $1 billion in highway investment creates 47,500 new jobs and generates more than $2 billion in economic activity. Plus a safer, happier country.

MEDIUM AND LONG TERM GOVERNMENT RESPONSE.

The U.S. economy (public and private) has focused on borrowing and consumption rather than on savings, investment and production.

This is not sustainable, and the sooner we face that, the less painful will be the transition.

To generate major economic activity in the medium and long term, we must turn to infrastructure and alternative energy sources. This means massive governmental expenditures to maintain, restore, improve and create the public physical facilities that underpin our national well-being. Highways, bridges, dams, airports, harbors, water levees, mass transit programs, new energy facilities of various kinds— public investment in all of them is needed to stimulate the economy and to improve our quality of life.

Across the country, there are some 600,000 bridges of which 25% are in below acceptable state, according to the Federal Highway Administration. The American Society of Civil Engineers has put price tags on the necessary repair bills, but points out that America today invests only 2.4% of our GNP in infrastructure compared with Europe's 5% and China's 9%.

Given our clogged ports, our airline flight delays that cost at least $15 billion each year in lost productivity, and the hours wasted in rush hour commuting, public support for infrastructure programs should be enthusiastic. Congestion on roads costs $78 billion annually, in the form of 4.2 billion lost hours and 2.9 billion gallons of wasted gasoline, according to the Texas Transportation Institute.

Historically, we have clear precedent, from Thomas Jefferson's support for canals and roads in 1808 and the national railroad mania in the mid-19th century to Dwight Eisenhower's Highway Act of

1956, which created our interstate system. Today, the rest of the advanced world is building high speed trains, but our only version runs between Boston and Washington on an outdated and inadequate track.

The case for investment in alternate energy sources needs little comment. The U.S. consumes one quarter of the world's oil while possessing less than 3% of its oil reserves; we spend $700 to $800 billion a year importing the difference. Cutting consumption and producing alternative sources of energy like solar, wind, hydroelectricity and biofuels are no longer optional, but mandatory.

Seventy-seven percent of France's electricity today comes from nuclear power, and the United States must rethink the nuclear question.

Infrastructure spending and alternative energy spending can supplement consumer spending in the short to medium term as engines for economic growth; in the long term, our helping to meet the consumer needs of the growing Chinese and Indian middle classes will keep our economic engines running.

In the U.S., personal consumption constitutes 70% of GNP; in China it is below 40%, but in time it will certainly rise. That will help us.

When the Chinese buy more cosmetics, for example, they will probably buy more American brands.

FINANCIAL INSTITUTION REGULATION

The U.S. competitive free market financial and economic system has demonstrated its dynamism and its flexibility. To continue to function well, however, it requires public support and participation that are only gained by embracing the concepts of disclosure, transparency, accountability, and fairness.

The investing public has little idea of its exposure to risk because of institutional 'off balance sheet' transactions and the degree of leverage prevalent in the financial community. The public has little comprehension of the risks of the derivative instruments it owns, directly or indirectly; and it understands little about the workings of hedge funds.

Our government officials have been remiss in permitting opaqueness throughout our financial system. Fresh regulations are overdue in balance sheet and risk disclosure, required liquidity and capital-to-loan ratios; we need more effective disclosure rules about self-dealing and short-selling.

Government regulation of non-banking institutions is now front-burner, since the 'too big to fail' premise implies possible government bail-outs; bailout responsibilities should include regulation.

An alternative is not to let institutions get "too big"; today, giant entities like UBS and Citigroup are considering "restructuring."

Creative destruction, the great insight of Joseph Schumpeter, should not be forgotten. Recessions—and the financial failures and bankruptcies that follow—are part of the mechanics by which a free market system revives itself.

Direct government intervention should be rare, and only used where public interest is the over-riding consideration; it should include financial penalties and loss for the shareholders and company officers; and it should require "pay back" provisions for the return of public funds on the model of the Resolution Trust Corporation of the 1990's.

Fannie Mae and Freddie Mac shareholders and officers should not benefit from government bail-outs, and public policy should be firmly against 'private benefit, public loss.'

One problem is the disparity in accounting standards and disclosure and trading practices around the world. Financial globalization will demand accounting standardization, and appropriate solutions are long overdue.

RATING AGENCY REGULATION.

The AAA bond ratings given to toxic subprime mortgage packages should excite outrage.

Only after unwary lenders suffered severe losses from reliance on defective ratings did the Security and Exchange Commission take notice. In July 2008, the SEC released a scathing 37-page report charging that major rating firms flouted conflict-of-interest guidelines and considered their own profits when rating securities at levels higher than risk exposure justified.

"Who shall guard the guardians?" asked the ancient Romans; there is no easy answer.

Individuals of character and professional expertise (Paul Volcker and Gerald Corrigan come to mind) should be impaneled to recommend changes that will not stifle the financial industry, but will protect the public.

GOVERNMENT HOUSING POLICIES.

The belief that housing values would invariably rise underlay 100% home mortgages to borrowers whose income was insufficient to cover debt service.

With the encouragement of the Clinton and Bush administrations, the percentage of U.S. families owning homes rose from the traditional 62% to 64% to nearly 70%; when the housing bubble burst, some 10,000,000 families found the equity value of their homes was below zero. The majority of those homes had mortgages written in 2005, 2006 or 2007, with little or no down payment required, with unverified borrowers' income and with "teaser," below-market interest rates that were not sustainable.

Now that the chickens have come home to roost, we must realize that not everyone can afford to own a home and that some should rent instead.

Canada has had no subprime debacle because Canada requires substantial down payments from mortgage borrowers and solid indications that borrowers can pay debt service.

Denmark requires that mortgages remain on the balance sheets of the issuers, eliminating the moral hazard of selling off the risks to others. The moral, says George Soros, is that when your own money is at risk, you tend to be more careful.

BURSTING BUBBLES.

Thirty-five years ago an economist named Hyman Minsky (who

believed that free markets are inherently unstable and crisis-prone) described five stages of a credit cycle: displacement, boom, euphoria, profit-taking and panic.

Minsky, his disciple Charles Kindleberger (author of *Manias, Panics and Crashes: A History of Financial Crises*) and Kindleberger's disciple, Yale Professor Robert J. Shiller (author of *Irrational Exuberance*) all understand the role of emotion and psychology in economic decision-making, unlike conventional wisdom, which holds that economic decision-making is rational, markets are efficient, and the Tooth Fairy arrives on schedule.

Those wishing to understand how our system operates should be familiar with concepts like 'discounted future value,' 'price elasticity,' 'bond yield curves' and the like. But they should also be familiar with the works of Minsky, Kindleberger, Schiller and their predecessor, Charles Mackay, author of the classic *Extraordinary Popular Delusions and the Madness of Crowds*.

The American model of a competitive, free-market, loosely-regulated economy has shown the world how it can stimulate the energy and creativity of a dynamic public. The tightly- controlled, rigidly-planned economies of Joseph Stalin, Mao Tse- Tung and Fidel Castro pale by comparison and are now, in Trotsky's phrase, "in the dustbin of history."

An exploding Chinese economy, however, indicates that in the 21st century we may see competition between democratic capitalism in the West and autocratic capitalism in the East.

Over time, each of these pragmatic societies may take on some of the trappings of the other, with more individualism, privacy and free choice in the East and more large scale government intervention in the West.

How will the game play out? As Chou En Lai said in the 1960's of the impact of the French Revolution, "It's too soon to tell."

The Wharton Journal
August 19, 2008

TOWARD A NEW BLACK AMERICAN NARRATIVE

The ancient Greek philosopher Heraclitus could have been speaking of African Americans today when he noted that "you cannot step into the same river twice," since the river keeps changing and you keep changing. Evolutions in America and in black Americans merit more discussion than they have received. The time has arrived for a new black American narrative, one that looks forward rather than backward, that acknowledges the growing diversity among blacks in America. With each decade that passes, the challenges for American blacks are the challenges for America.

America's increasingly pluralistic and ever-evolving society faces severe problems. Some, like our current economic turmoil, are short-term; others, such as educational inadequacies, diminished employment opportunities and unhealthy economic disparities, are longer term; some, like deep poverty, seem intractable, for whites and blacks.

Large pockets of persistent and concentrated poverty, in which successive generations of disadvantaged children have diminished "life chances," are a charge against a society whose founders thought of us as a "city on a hill" and a "light unto the nations." Ideally, in the 21st century, that society should provide job opportunities for those individuals prepared to fill them; and their children should have the opportunity to rise as high as their ability and effort permit.

The inner cities of America's north and the rural hollows of the south, New Orleans' depressed Lower Ninth Ward and Appalachian Kentucky and West Virginia, and the Yazoo Delta backwaters of Mississippi, the poorest of the 50 states—all have large numbers of those, white and black, trapped in a self-perpetuating cycle of despair, marked by widespread semi-literacy, fatherless children, drug abuse and criminality. This is not a race-specific phenomenon, but the racial discrimination faced by poor blacks adds another dimension to the problem.

In this period of national economic stringency, when compassion seems to many a luxury we cannot afford, helping disadvantaged young people to escape poverty and enter the mainstream of American life should be seen as a prudent investment in our national future. This is not "eating cake today" but investing in our national "seed corn for tomorrow." No short term results are likely; but the sooner we begin the better.

Our national challenge is to determine specific steps that should be taken by people of good will to bring our national practices into better alignment with our national ideals, dealing with continuing poverty whose causes are structural and behavioral.

A full and accurate picture of African Americans today presents striking contrasts, with a more multi- faceted social and economic spectrum than is generally realized.

Black astronauts and astrophysicists, college presidents and billionaires, admirals and generals, CEO's of the Fortune 500 and Pulitzer Prize authors, multi-millionaire athletes and leading entertainment celebrities, distinguished intellectuals and innovative entrepreneurs, world-class opera singers and nationally known chefs—are indicators of dramatic good health, as are increasing numbers of black mayors, governors, congressmen, Cabinet officers and, of course, our President. Annual sales by minority-owned businesses grew to $1 trillion by 2007; before the current economic crisis, those businesses had been growing at a compound rate of 10% per annum, three times the national average. On college campuses throughout the nation blacks are prominently represented as students and faculty. Every public opinion poll portrays great intergenerational changes in mindset from old to young among whites and blacks on subjects ranging from integrated employment to racial intermarriage.

The other side of the coin tells a dramatically different story. Heart-breakingly high numbers of black school dropouts, a substantial and continuing black/white academic achievement gap and off the scale teenage pregnancies. HIV/AIDS cases and criminal incarcerations tell of a segment of society gone off the rails, with painful ramifications not only for the black world, but for the country at large.

Between these extremes, numbers of working class, middle class and immigrant blacks are being steadily absorbed into the American mainstream, increasingly judged, as Martin Luther King, Jr. wished, not by the color of their skin, but by the content of their character.

Yet those at the bottom remain on the outside looking in.

With the years ahead presenting the prospect of fewer jobs and those remaining requiring ever greater training and skills, with automation and globalization posing severe threats to American unskilled labor, the economic prospects for our submerged groups, white and black, are frightening.

Technology is polarizing our society, severely dividing the educated and the less educated. The possibility of economic wastelands and social despair in the new information economy must be faced. It is bad for individuals, bad for regions and bad for the nation. But lives can be changed, and with appropriate education and productive careers, tax eaters can become taxpayers, and everyone benefits.

We must recognize our widespread national failure to acknowledge the existence of areas of persistent poverty, in which millions of our fellow citizens are not really part of the 21st century world. Our reluctance to take effective steps to mitigate the pre-conditions underlying those problems represents the greatest failure of American society today. There is blame enough to go around to indict many players in this disastrous socio-economic game— academics, social leaders, political figures across the spectrum and well-intentioned but foggy thinkers of all sorts.

Most social scientists, still cowering from William Ryan's unfounded, but devastating attack on Daniel Patrick Moynihan for discussing the alarming rise in black single births, have precluded serious discussion on black subjects. Timid academics seem petrified of being unfairly labeled "racists." (William Julius Wilson has led a movement to reappraise Pat Moynihan, pointing out that Moynihan's report, The Negro Family: The Case For National Action, was "an important and prophetic document.") That Moynihan was himself a poor, working-class child deserted by a father of whom he had no memories and that Moynihan had profound sympathy for fatherless children, seems never to have been understood. Far from blaming the victim for a "tangle of pathologies," he wrote in 1965 of the pressing need for additional help for the inner city because "Negroes today are a grievously injured people who in fair and equal competition will by and large lose out."

In academia today, the subtle interplay of race, social class and gender, especially the complex relationship between social culture (behavior) and economics, is avoided like a "third rail" of social discourse, with a few exceptions. A fear of violent youths by middle class whites, Asians, Latinos and blacks is a taboo subject. Few observers have been willing to acknowledge the thorny problem of high- achieving black students ridiculed by black classmates for 'forgetting your roots', thinking like oreos (black on the outside, white on the inside) and not acting authentically black, a phenomenon that has arisen since the integration developments of the 1960's. John Ogbu and Roland Fryer have written thoughtfully about this.

A misguided concept of "racial pride," and fear that acknowledgment of problems will fuel prejudice, have stymied constructive discussion by many in the black community. "There comes a time when silence is betrayal," said Martin Luther King, Jr.; silence can be destructive when people need help and it is not forthcoming. Successful African Americans have important roles to play in helping inner city residents rise, but hiding problems is not one of them.

Prominent black demagogues usually look backward, rarely around them, and never forward, ignoring the remarkable progress that much of the black world has made, and also ignoring the factors that made such progress possible. The counter-productive message of victimization and militant despair sends the wrong signals to inner city youngsters, whose conclusion is "Why try?" when the message should be constructive, pointing the path toward personal progress in a complex world. Some observers believe that demagogues serve a constructive role by highlighting ills that might still be overlooked; others believe they have a vested interest in keeping alive a sense of hostility and divisiveness. One hundred years ago Booker T. Washington said: "There is a class of colored people who make a business of keeping the troubles, the wrongs and the hardships of the Negro race before the public. Some of these people do not want the Negro to lose his grievances, because they do not want to lose their jobs."

Many of the more responsible black spokesmen today imply that disadvantaged inner city blacks are like corks floating on the waves, unable to play a part in their own advancement and dependent on government programs to create viable futures. They seem to feel that it will 'give comfort to the enemy' to suggest that some problems may stem from inside rather than outside. Sociologist Orlando Patterson and journalist Bob Herbert are notable exceptions to the "always blame others" school.

Intolerance, prejudice and bias continue to exist in many quarters in America today, even as 'color consciousness' recedes dramatically among the young. Widespread housing discrimination persists, bank borrowing is more difficult for blacks, and what is widely believed to be blatantly discriminatory treatment by police (seen as hostile) is a continuing source of black outrage. Integration of the workplace has not yet been matched by social integration; and just as black college students usually eat together (by choice) in college cafeterias, so white country clubs, dinner parties and social gatherings rarely include blacks. This limits the opportunity for social and professional "networking" so important in today's world.

We know that 72% of all black births today (well over 80% in some postal zip codes) are to single mothers, and that children from fatherless homes (white and black) account for 63% of all youth suicides, 90% of all homeless and runaway children, 80% of rapists, 71% of all high school dropouts and 70% of all juveniles in state-operated institutions. Yet when Barack Obama urged a black audience to greater parental involvement, Jesse Jackson was heard on tape charging him with "talking down to 'ni----s." When Bill Cosby famously called on black parents to devote more time and resources to their children, he was attacked throughout the black world with a vehemence that continues to this day, with some claiming he betrayed black America. Virtually no one objectively addressed the specific points he raised. Simplistic thinking prevails almost everywhere, with white racism or an unfair lack of black employment cited as the problems, with little further discussion.

We know that black women have college graduation rates higher than those of black men and that children of black immigrants (Caribbean and African) outperform in public schools the children of native born American blacks, but no one asks why, or why 78% of black families had two parents in 1950, but only 38% did in 2010. Similarly, when discussing Latinos, no one asks why, in New York today, the children of Puerto Ricans perform worse than do those of Dominicans or Mexicans, or why the suicide rates of young Latinas are so high.

Levels of educational achievement are rarely factored into discussions of black/white differentials in income or in prison incarceration, but we know that today a young black male science graduate married to a black female science graduate will likely have a total lifetime income comparable to that of his white counterpart. And we know that the prison incarceration rates of black college graduates do not differ markedly from those of white college graduates.

Some 68% of Asian 25-34 year-olds hold more than a high school diploma in America today in contrast to 44% of whites and only 26% of African Americans. Not surprisingly, Asian median income is higher than that of other ethnic groups. What one group can achieve, others can, too. If, as predicted, 80% of future new jobs will require knowledge of math and science, young people must be prepared. With rising educational levels, income will follow.

Half a century after Rosa Parks refused to move to the back of the bus, our society has come a long way. We still have far to go; but today, academic achievement, professional excellence and recourse to law are likely to be more productive in achieving economic and social goals than mass demonstrations or civil protest.

Personal preferences in taste and lifestyle are compatible with the standards called for in a well-functioning pluralistic society, but those standards must be accepted by those hoping to rise in the mainstream of such a society.

In the 21st century, the hostility, nihilism and alienation of inner city oppositional culture—now deeply ingrained—leads down a blind alley, as opposed to full participation in mainstream American life and culture increasingly possible with education. The social progress America has achieved in the past five decades has been formidable; our challenge is to extend it into the future.

Liberals tend to emphasize structural forces (primarily economic and racial). Many think of school tracking (grouping students by test results) and objective tests for police and firefighters as "laissez faire racism." They attribute low verbal ability of inner city children to segregated neighborhoods rather than to home influences and they feel that poverty makes for fatherless children rather than the other way around. Some observers feel liberals are excessively protective of dysfunctional teachers and disruptive students.

Conservatives, while reluctantly acknowledging the structural problems, tend to be unsympathetic to human failings and problems. They minimize difficulties and handicaps and emphasize individual responsibility for self-improvement, encouraging incentives for effort and rewards for performance. Both sides grope for solutions, but no "quick fix" is in sight.

Constructive discussion should begin with an examination of the problems of employment, education, mass prison incarceration, narcotics in the inner city, social class and social culture, which I will address in reverse order.

SOCIAL CULTURE

Ever since Max Weber's *The Protestant Ethic and The Spirit of Capitalism* appeared in 1904, followed by Edward Banfield's *The Moral Basis of a Backward Society* and Robert Putnam's *Making Democracy Work* (on cultural differences between Italy's North and South) and, more recently, Thomas Sowell's *Race and Culture*, it has been clear that a society's social culture (beliefs, values, attitudes, etc.) is reflected in its practices regarding hard work, honesty, seriousness and thrift—of money and of time—(Weber) and of trust, cooperation, moderation and compromise (Putnam). The absence of looting by the Japanese after their recent devastating earthquake is a clear example of distinctive cultural influence.

The Chinese attribute their relative success to Confucian values like emphasis on education, diligence, merit and reflecting well on the family. Jews traditionally attribute theirs to the high value they place on literacy, family cohesiveness, individual responsibility and a focus on the future.

Conversely, those cultures, like the nomadic Arabian, that focus on the past and present rather than on the future, that show distaste for work, belittle individual initiative and personal savings and have a fatalistic approach to life, do not do well. In oil-rich Saudi Arabia today, the government presses affirmative action programs for the hiring of Saudi youth over foreign workers, since Saudi employers complain that young Saudis lack a 'work ethic' and a 'time sense' and that they display little self-discipline or personal initiative. Nearby Oman, on the other hand, has surged into the 21st century, thanks to a 40-year intensive drive to give modern education to all its children—boys and girls—along with 'modern' values.

Cultural relativists today, not wishing to hurt feelings or affront ethnic pride, refuse to acknowledge that some cultural approaches are more effective than others in promoting well-being.

Other thinkers—seeing our pluralistic society always in flux—understand the importance of inculcating in early childhood the values and attributes necessary for full participation in a globalized, competitive, high tech world. (*Culture Matters*, by Harrison and Huntington, should be required reading for all undergraduates.)

The "cool pose" culture of America's inner cities reflected in the destructive lyrics of 'gangsta rap' and the air of defiance of inner city street youth; the senseless murder of blacks by blacks in areas with hand guns too easily available; narcotics - burdened inner cities where two parent families and high-achieving students are exceptions; an atmosphere of such physical danger and psychological terror that traumatized children in largely segregated schools are unable to achieve their potential— this is the world in which large numbers (perhaps a third) of black children live today, with diminished "life chances" and few social institutions to help them. Ironically, prison-inspired clothing styles and thought patterns expressed in gangsta rap are working their way into mainstream culture; and graffiti, traditionally considered as visual vandalism, is in Los Angeles today considered a valid form of artistic expression.

There is no one way to live today, no single proper code of values and conduct. But the disadvantaged children I refer to are not able to choose other ways of life, and a well-functioning society should make other life choices possible for them.

Obvious socio-economic disparities among blacks increasingly belie the idea of a monolithic community with similar characteristics and goals and a common agenda, with only two or three designated spokesmen. Black identity based chiefly on memories of oppression and victimization will be harder to maintain in an increasingly pluralistic and integrated society. In Harlem, the epicenter of New York's black community, census figures show that in the last decade the white population has grown from 2% to 9.8% and the black population shrunk from 61.2% to 54.4%. In another example, over half the black students in Ivy League colleges are not descended from American slaves, and some 48% of blacks living in Miami today are West Indian. The Pew Research Center reports that 22% of black men who married in 2008 married non-black women, up from 15.7% in 2000 and 7.9% in 1980.)

In time, personal identity — how we define ourselves— will involve more complex factors than skin color or ethnicity. With social culture decoupled from skin color, educated inner city children will be able to walk through doors increasingly open to them as individuals rather than as stereotypes.

Those "falling between the cracks" will remain a problem, but they, too, must be encouraged to look forward, not backward, and to envision satisfying and fulfilling roles in the American mainstream.

SOCIAL CLASS

The most useful and practical discussion of social class is Edward Banfield's brilliant relating class to one's time sense. Those at the bottom of the social ladder barely think past the current week. A slightly higher group can think through the end of, say, the fruit-picking season; and the next higher group can think a few years beyond that. Middle class mindsets (regardless of income or ethnicity) understand the value of education, a stable home, a professional career, financial savings and a future for their children. Upper middle class types make provision for their grandchildren, establish family businesses and contribute to charities benefiting a broader public than themselves; in general they identify with longer term goals and the well-being of their communities. The relationship between finances and mindset is complex—a semi-literate basketball star worth millions usually may have a different value system than a college- trained school teacher married to another teacher.

Inculcating in children a sense of their promising future, of the value of relating well to others and following the rules, of deferring gratification, of respecting authority and of preparing for an important and satisfying career is something that every parent, regardless of income or ethnicity, should do, difficult as it is in a hostile environment. School can help, but the primary influence is the parent in developing a child's self-control, curiosity and sense of self. Black churches and community leaders, along with black publications and black radio and black TV programs must take the lead in changing inner city child-raising practices, pleading with young girls not to have babies until they have completed their education, and convincing young men to assume responsibility for the children they father. Above all, they must help young men understand that by dropping out of school, they are condemning themselves to lives of despair. We must shout to children from the rooftops; "The more years you spend in school, the more you earn!" And to their parents, that each additional year of high school lessens the chance of prison by 11%.

Inner city boys must be helped to realize that manhood is not defined by joining a gang, fathering multiple children out of marriage, serving time in jail or dealing in drugs. Young men who feel hated, scorned, feared and ignored must be helped to understand that they can earn the respect they crave by positive, not negative and self-destructive actions. Real men earn a living, are responsible fathers and are involved in their community. And this they must learn at home, ideally from parents or relatives. The daughter of a teenage single mother who herself becomes a teenage single mother represents hardships for all involved, and we must help that mother break the cycle, thereby improving the long term prospects of the family.

We need practical steps such as requiring the legal name of the father on a newborn's birth certificate (the practice in England) and requiring a mother to name the child's father to claim State child-care benefits. A young man may think twice about fathering children for whom he has continuing legal and financial responsibility.

It may "take a village to raise a child" but that is in addition to, not instead of, an involved and supportive parent.

Narcotics In the Inner City

Leaders of church, school, community groups and government must make clear that those involved in the drug trade are evil people destroying their young—not heroes because they are beating the system; not objects of admiration because of their clothes, cars and jewelry, but evil people whose goods are acquired from the misery of their community and the enslavement of our children.

An aroused and involved public— in a cooperative relationship with the police— should make the elimination of drugs the highest priority of community life.

Much more could and should be done by government. By treating "use" of narcotics as a health problem and "sale" of narcotics as a criminal problem, we can deal more effectively with each. Sweden, with one of the lowest drug usage rates in the western world, invests heavily in prevention and treatment as well as in strict law enforcement, trying to reduce both supply and demand.

Intensive drug education efforts aimed at the very young; widespread, no-nonsense blood, urine and sweat testing for drugs; low cost treatment for addicts and severe punishment for dealers—will reduce recruitment to drug abuse, will induce abusers to change and will reduce the supply of drugs.

Greater police sensitivity in finding drug sellers— working closely with local community leaders to identify dealers (as in Boston) rather than conducting random searches that open police to charges of "racial profiling"— would be more effective operationally and more publicly acceptable, helping to heal the breach between the black community and the police.

Unfortunately, the police have failed to make clear that crime prevention is their goal, and that arrests are only a means to that end.

Fear and dislike of the police in the inner city is one of our greatest problems, and solving it is one of our greatest challenges. Whites have no idea of the outrage middle class blacks feel when they are arbitrarily stopped by police. DWB—"driving while black"—is how blacks term the non-violations for which police stop them.

Corrupt, brutal or racially discriminatory acts by the relatively few police "bad apples" must be hunted down and eliminated so that public confidence is restored and necessary police/civilian cooperation encouraged. Black police groups like the Guardians Association and 100 Blacks in Law Enforcement should be invited to be more active and more visible in spreading the word that violence and crime hurt everyone.

Indefensible acts like the brutalizing of Abner Louima set the stage for demagogic distortion of a tragic police error in the case of Amadou Diallo. Automatic weapons in the hands of a nervous plain- clothes squad of the NYPD Street Crimes Unit, confronting what they believed to be an armed marauder, had terrible consequences; and our entire society lost in the encounter. Diallo, an innocent but frightened immigrant reaching for his wallet or cell phone, was mistakenly killed (his family received $3,000,000 in settlement); the community was in turmoil, and the Street Crimes Unit was disbanded. The question to be pondered is whether the notoriously crime-ridden Soundview Avenue area of the Bronx is now safer.

"Justice must be done and must be seen to be done," says English Common Law; we must find a way to achieve both, with the police and the inner city community on the same wave length. An "oppositional culture" hurts everyone.

MASS PRISON INCARCERATION

With imprisonment rates for black youths vastly higher than that of whites, and with almost as many black men in prison as in college, the beleaguered public of the inner cities is crying for help. (13% of the U.S. population is black but comprises 49% of U.S. prisoners.)

Some part of these horrendous numbers is due to the disparate punishment practices for crack cocaine (used by blacks) as opposed to powdered cocaine (used by whites). The 1986 Anti-Drug Abuse Act mandated that 5 grams of crack bring the same 5-year prison term as 500 grams of powder cocaine. How unfair it is for Lindsay Lohan and Paris Hilton to get mild slaps on the wrist for what would send a young black man to prison for years, destroying his future and ruining his family. Recent revisions in the sentencing law will presumably change this.

Decriminalizing marijuana (like alcohol after Prohibition) may or may not be a good idea, but lessening the penalties for possession of small amounts would have a dramatic impact on the incarceration rates of young black men who are caught disproportionately by "stop and frisks" that often ignore white students, drivers, etc.

On the other hand, we know that some 90% of murdered blacks are killed by other blacks, and that although blacks constitute 24% of New York City's population, we are told (although estimates differ) that blacks committed 68% of all murders, rapes, robberies and assaults in the city last year. Harlem and Bedford-Stuyvesant lead all New York City precincts in reported rapes.

One question is how to prevent such crime; a second question is how to reorient our dehumanizing prison system to rehabilitate prisoners into productive citizens rather than recycle them into 'repeat' hardened criminals unlikely to re-enter the mainstream. The recidivism rate in New York State is currently 81%.

U.S. prisons have become warehouses for human failures that prevent some crime by isolating potential malefactors, but do little to turn criminals into productive citizens. We do not get good value for the $70 billion a year we spend on prisons.

Incarceration of juveniles— except for the all-but- hopeless cases— should be in facilities more like schools and hospitals than like zoos to contain animals, in which physical abuse by violent offenders and sometimes by prison guards is routine and where counseling is inadequate. Many juvenile prisoners are low risk young men battling addiction or mental illness who would be better served by community facilities near their homes with counseling services for the prisoner and the family. Experience shows these to have much lower rates of recidivism as well as much lower costs; but this change of practice is fought by the politically powerful Public Employees Federation, the union representing rural prison workers fighting for their (counter-productive) jobs. The State of Missouri's Juvenile Rehabilitation Program is the most promising in the nation, redirecting troubled lives, averting future crimes and, yes, saving tax dollars. New York would do well to replicate it.

Among adults, first offenders should be kept apart from hardened criminals and exposed to the education and vocational training that would keep them from returning to jail. Literacy and job training for prisoners is the most fruitful investment our society can make, along with proper treatment for drug addicts. Appropriate vocational training of prisoners for skilled blue collar jobs would be an immense plus for everyone, a win-win game, since pastry chefs, cabinet makers, plumbers, electricians, TV repair men, etc. are in short supply, and computer specialists will always be employed.

For convicts leaving prison, job counseling and short term economic support would help to reintegrate them back into society and keep them from returning to criminal activities. Newark, NJ, with a recent $2 million federal grant and $3 million in private funding, is trying imaginative new ways of helping released convicts to readjust successfully to civilian life.

There is a growing movement in many states to repeal or amend lifetime voting bans for convicted felons. Some five million Americans, mostly black, are disenfranchised, even when they have gone on to lead crime-free lives.

No discussion of crime in America can avoid the subject of the easy availability of handguns. In 2009,
2.4 million pistols and revolvers and 5.4 million guns overall were produced in America, leading to a firearm homicide rate 20 times higher in the U.S. than in other leading countries and 43 times higher for males ages 15 to 24.

Tougher controls on handguns (a quarter of which, police say, are owned by teenagers or younger) must be on everyone's agenda. Pat Moynihan once proposed (perhaps jokingly) prohibitively high taxes on bullets for handguns. We need more such creative thinking.

EDUCATION

Education is the true Civil Rights issue of our day. It is the great equalizer, the only 'magic bullet' we know of to bring submerged groups into the economic and social mainstream. Education does not guarantee a job, but it dramatically improves the odds.

Most of our education theorists today focus on "teaching" (what someone does at the blackboard) rather than on "learning" (which takes place in the head of the student). Our schools seek immediate, short term test results rather than encourage the self-motivated, life-long learning habits that produce an educated public. Critical thinking, problem-solving and the ability of students to communicate effectively and to cooperate with peers seem to have been lost, as have knowledge of the past and of other cultures. We are not providing our children with the tools they need to compete in the global economy and to lead full lives after work.

Although Finland and South Korea spend less on education per child than we do, their children consistently outperform ours in international evaluations. Those nations are proud of their career teachers, who are well prepared in pedagogics and in subject matter as well. Each of those countries has a longer school day and a longer school year than we do, as well as universal and more intensive preschooling; and each encourages greater parental involvement in the child's education. Their teachers are regarded as highly-qualified "professionals" rather than protected "workers"; and they are respected because they merit respect. Needless to say, bad eggs among teachers and students are routinely weeded out.

Our current establishment mantra proclaims salvation through higher pay for teachers, smaller classes, better physical school facilities and higher incomes for parents. Interestingly enough, the only college class in the history of the Nobel Prizes to produce three Nobel Laureates in one college class was not from Yale or Harvard, Oxford or Cambridge, but from New York's City College Class of 1937. The teachers were underpaid, class sizes were large, physical facilities were shabby and most of the parents were sweatshop workers from the Lower East Side. The students, however, were motivated young people who valued literacy, thought critically and planned for the future; and their dedicated public school teachers came from the highest, not the lowest, academic percentiles of their own college classes. (Higher salaries would be needed today to attract their equivalent.)

To change results we must give up looking for a "quick fix" and focus on what the educational process really is. We must change the mindset of students by changing the mindset of their parents. Parents must be helped to value education and to stimulate children from birth by speaking with them, reading to them, exposing them to books, encouraging questions and inculcating high aspirations and a sense of the future. They should encourage their children to spend more time on reading and homework and less on TV and computer games, and they should take an active interest in the child's school progress. Every child should have a public library card and be encouraged to use it and to become familiar with children's programs at the city's museums and libraries (learning chess helps, too). Ronald Ferguson's studies of the educational achievement gap have focused attention on the crucial role of a child's home environment.

Parents should demand the highest quality in their children's teachers (regardless of ethnicity), because the issue is not jobs for teachers but learning for students. Michelle Rhee achieved remarkable results in Washington, DC by firing incompetent teachers regardless of ethnicity, and history will side with her, not with the teachers' unions who opposed her firings. The unions also fought against her desire for appropriate credentials and higher pay for teachers of high school math and science, teachers whose current expertise in such subjects is low and whose ability to inspire their students to pursue science or engineering careers seems nil. Correlation is not causation, of course, but higher teacher science qualifications seem to relate to higher student science achievement.

Inner city children should be encouraged to feel as proud of their academic achievement as of their athletic prowess, buoyed by the praise of parents, teachers, neighbors and role models. Far from feeling disloyal to their friends for taking school seriously and not acting cool, they should be encouraged to feel that their academic success reflects well on themselves, their school, their family and their community.

Pride and shame—powerful motivators for us all, but especially for adolescents—must be harnessed to socially productive, not destructive goals and actions.

Hours spent on S.A.T. test prep, not "hanging out" with friends;

following the rules of others, not making your own; saving available money, not spending; self-discipline, not unfocused freedom; thinking of tomorrow, not playing around today—these are choices a young person should make, for they determine the long term quality of life and reflect the shared values of those succeeding in our common civic culture.

Can this be achieved? Successful examples abound— from Geoffrey Canada's Harlem Children's Zone to the 99 KIPP schools in 20 states across the country to eye-opening HEAF (the Harlem Educational Activities Fund), 100% of whose Harlem children graduate from high school and over 90% of whom graduate from four-year colleges, in contrast to a national rate of under 60%. (A third of HEAF students go on to post-graduate education, and HEAF-sponsored inner city chess teams have ranked No. 1 in the United States.) Prominent public school examples are the Davidson Magnet School in Augusta, GA; the Amistad Academy in New Haven, CT; the M Street School in Washington, DC— all high poverty, high minority, high performing schools whose students rank above the national norm.

All these principals and teachers "talk the talk and walk the walk." Inspiring and encouraging the best in their students, they have also learned to deal with disruptive ones whose "acting out" keeps others from learning.

It is a brute fact of life (not widely understood by middle class America) that survival on the tough streets of the inner city requires one code of conduct, while entering and rising in the national mainstream requires another. As Elijah Anderson points out in *Code of the Street*, fear, suspicion and present-mindedness reflect one social code; self-confidence, trust and looking ahead, reflect the other. Constant noise, frequent violence and aggression, thin-skinned anger and resentment prevail in one world; quiet, self-restraint and adaptability prevail in the other. Maintaining direct eye contact, normal in the middle class world, is seen in the inner city as a hostile challenge requiring an aggressive response.

Sensitive and knowledgeable teachers can help students learn the difficult art of functioning in both worlds. This is hard and it is easy to see why many children do not succeed in adjusting to life with different value systems. Until they do, they will be seen as interlopers in the mainstream world. We must help them.

As for public vs. private vs. charter schools, Alexander Pope put it clearly: "O'er forms of governance let fools contest; whate'er is best administered is best."

EDUCATION

A motivated, educated, socialized young person (regardless of ethnicity) will have the tools with which to compete successfully in a competitive, high tech, globalized world. As Nobel Laureate James Heckman points out, by increasing an individual's "human capital" we increase society's "human capital."

Sadly, the retrenchment by government at all levels— federal, state and municipal— will have a serious impact on black employment. Blacks are disproportionately employed by government or by services such as healthcare that are underwritten by government. Dismissed workers without special skills will be hard pressed to find replacement employment.

Engineers, chemists and other technically-trained personnel are hired upon graduation at high salaries—yet blacks are dramatically under-represented in our technical schools. The military is widely seen as the most color blind and meritocratic sector of American life, yet middle class, not inner city blacks are attracted to it, in part because of the G.I. Bill college benefits. Small retail activities, a traditional avenue of upward mobility for poor immigrants, have little appeal for black inner city residents. Micro-lending, so effective overseas, could be explored domestically, since inner city would-be entrepreneurs chronically lack "start-up" financing and working capital.

Many call for a new Marshall Plan to help the inner city, but they forget that the original Marshall Plan was successful because the Germans and Japanese at the time were able to make constructive use of our help. America's Alliance for Progress, the counterpart program for Latin America, achieved little, largely because the culture of the region was not conducive to development. Haiti, for example, which was an economic and social disaster in the past in spite of billions of dollars of U.S. aid, may continue to be one, regardless of future aid. Here at home, Lyndon Johnson's well-intentioned "War on Poverty" turned out to be not a war but a skirmish, and we didn't win it; we lost it. Benefits went to service providers, not to service recipients, leaving those on the bottom virtually untouched. In New York City today, an estimated 30% of children are living in poverty.

Our inner cities need financial help, but they need social help even more. Our challenge is to break self-perpetuating cycles of poverty and hopelessness and to replace them with vistas of upward social and economic mobility made possible by education.

CONCLUSION:

The classic black American narrative — reacting to victimization, disenfranchisement and marginalization by angrily pounding on closed doors—is becoming less a subject of current events and more one of history.

A new 21st century black narrative— of achievement by taking advantage of unfolding opportunities—may be a constructive 'self-fulfilling prophecy.'

Immigrants from Africa and the Caribbean, who come to America voluntarily because of the prospects it offers, take advantage of those opportunities, as do many native- born black Americans. Too many others, influenced by a heritage of legal servitude, Jim Crow laws and the KKK, will require time and positive experiences before they can profit from the new realities.

Most African Americans who play the game according to the currently accepted color-blind rules are making their way in the American mainstream and are major assets to our society. Those who, for a variety of reasons, are out of phase with currently accepted civic norms are suffering terribly and are destined to continue to do so, regardless of governmental programs designed to help.

Fifty years ago, black challenges were largely legal, and were dealt with by Brown vs. The Board of Education and by Voter Registration Acts. From here on, the challenges will be largely cultural, and the solutions more complex.

The civil rights victories of 1964 and 1965 resulted from the efforts of literate, articulate, impressive people like Thurgood Marshall, A. Philip Randolph, Bayard Rustin, Walter White, Roy Wilkins and, of course, Martin Luther King, Jr.—educated people who thought of themselves as members of W.E.B. DuBois' Talented Tenth, dedicated to the uplift of black America. Stokeley Carmichael ("smash everything western civilization has created") may be giving way to W.E.B. DuBois ("I sit with Shakespeare and he winces not...arm and arm with Balzac and Dumas...I summon Aristotle and Aurelius.")

As Henry Louis Gates, Jr. has written, "When I was growing up in the fifties, the blackest thing a smart colored boy or girl could be was a doctor or a lawyer, not a baseball player or an entertainer. Far too many of our people have lost their understanding and grasp of this, the cardinal principle of black success from slavery to freedom."

With Colin Powell in the past and Barack Obama in the present, let us hope Cory Booker and Deval Patrick point the way to a pluralistic future in which talent and skill, motivation and effort— not skin color— determine achievement. The successfully-integrated U.S. military is a model. Harvard Law School Dean Martha Minow writes, "Clear commitments to uncompromising standards of performance, combined with multiple opportunities for education, training and mentoring, are important elements of the army's success with racial integration."

Experience demonstrates that focusing on the wholesome development of children—giving them hope and indicating realistic paths toward achieving their hope—is the most effective way to advancement. This can best be achieved by the tough-minded involvement of government, public groups and private citizens for the benefit of all children, regardless of ethnicity. Inculcating in young people a desire to achieve their potential and a willingness to pay the price in personal trade-offs are first steps in the rise to leadership in American society.

Frederick Douglass, born enslaved in 1818, self-educated, and one of the greatest figures America has produced, closed his autobiography (1881) with the observation, "If the time shall ever come when we shall possess in the colored people of the United States a class of men noted for enterprise, industry, economy and success, we shall no longer have any trouble in the matter of civil and political rights." No one has said it better.

Yale University
February 8, 2011

MY BROTHER'S KEEPER

All modern societies should provide effectively for public well-being; and as our systems converge, we must learn from each other how best to respond to our common problems.

All societies provide in some way for the destitute and distressed, provide vehicles for health and education and support culture and the arts, but nations pursue these goals differently depending on their customs, traditions and beliefs.

Government, the marketplace and private philanthropy play a part; determining the appropriate role for each deserves thought. The strength of government lies in its ability to enforce its dictates; the strength of private philanthropy lies in the diversity and creativity it encourages; the strength of the marketplace is that it reflects what the public is willing to pay for.

A visitor from Mars or Venus in 2006 might think that Americans ask too little from their government, that Europeans ask too much, that each could do better in utilizing the marketplace for the common good, and that private philanthropy is an under-utilized tool for filling the gaps left by the other two.

In nations with a history of strong central government, a dominant church and a hierarchical society with an energetic aristocracy, government traditionally assumes responsibility for the public good, its costs underwritten by taxation.

Established custom has permitted Europeans to believe that payment of taxes absolves them of further responsibility to their fellows, and that the government is their "brother's keeper"; but, as the recent growth of European philanthropic activity demonstrates, that is changing.

Reliance on government persists, of course. Today, in France, for example, it is taken for granted that most of the Louvre's expenses are paid for by the government, as are pre-school services and primary education. In Italy, the staffs of La Scala and La Fenice are virtually employees of the government.

But a younger "frontier society" like the United States reflects different traditions and social assumptions. Our continent, settled by 17th and 18th century Europeans with no strong central government, with no state religion and no established aristocracy, called for different responses.

If American pioneers wanted a church or a school, they had to build it; if they wanted hospitals or roads or courthouses, they had to construct them.

Since raising the rafters of a barn could not be done by a farmer alone, he had to call on his neighbors for help; and he, in turn, helped them. The festive party he gave for his neighbors on the barn's completion lives on in the phrase "raising the roof."

This pattern of voluntary association of private individuals for mutual help continued;   by 1831, Alexis de Tocqueville wrote, "Whenever at the head of some new undertaking you see the government in France, or a man of rank in England, in the United States you will be sure to find an association [of private individuals"].

America's tradition of involved individuals and limited government persists; today, no one is surprised to find that, for example, private sources provide 87% of the budget of the Art Institute of Chicago and 96% of the Cleveland Orchestra budget, or that private individuals like me are still battling to persuade our federal government to underwrite the cost of universal pre-school education.

The three sources of social support—government, the marketplace and private philanthropy—bear close examination.

First, Government:

Traditional American wariness of government is reflected in our widespread popular preference for decentralized power over centralized, private over government support; and when government support is indicated, indirect subsidies over direct.

Indirect support for housing, for example, is given through tax exemption for home mortgage interest payments; indirect support for religion is given through tax exemption for religious institutions; and indirect support for the arts is given through tax exemption for cultural institutions.

Indirect subsidies permit government support without moral or aesthetic judgments, which Americans do not like their government to make for them; and these subsidies have stimulated creativity and diversity.

Tax exemption for gifts of art to museums at current market values with no capital gains tax paid are attacked by some as "windfalls for the rich"; but most of us prefer to think instead of the Rembrandts, Giottos or Jackson Pollocks, now in American public collections.

This American system—of providing public goods through private philanthropy encouraged by tax exemption— works well for middle and upper income Americans, but works less well for poor and lower income groups.

Our research universities and art museums are among the world's finest, but health care and child care for poor Americans are below European standards. That some 15% of Americans are without health insurance is a national disgrace, and it is not clear when this will be rectified.

Prospects for eventual federal government support for universal pre-school education are better, because recent studies demonstrate clearly that pre-schooling is an excellent public economic investment, yielding a high financial return as well as important social benefits.

If federal funding of pre-schooling does take place, it will be an interesting demonstration of the American preference for governmental aid to benefit society at large, rather than to provide compassionate help for those in need.

Europe today presents a different picture: here, active governments take more and give more than their American counterpart, especially in matters of culture and of help for the poor. In a period of emerging economic stringency, will this model still be economically feasible?

Berlin's three separate opera houses, Dutch government warehouses filled with contemporary paintings that no one seems to want, and France's government-imposed 35-hour work week raise questions about what a nation's economic priorities should be.

When aging and retiring workers require more government expenditures paid for by taxes on a smaller and younger labor force, hard choices will be faced by many governments.

In the years ahead, more government involvement in health and education seems likely in America; and some governmental pullback in support for culture seems likely in Europe.

The second area of social support is The Marketplace:

In health, education, social welfare and culture, the roles of government and philanthropy vary. What is untouched by them is left to the marketplace, which allocates resources to provide what the public desires and can pay for. Subsidies may tilt the balance in one direction, taxation in the other, but the preference of the cash-paying consumer rules.

For example, European opera lovers note the large amount of Verdi and Puccini that New York's audiences demand; French filmgoers usually vote at the box office for taxed American films over government-subsidized French movies and for pornographic films in spite of the punitive VAT taxes they carry. When French films try to please the public rather than the critics, they, too, do well at the box office.

In matters of health care, housing and education, America's middle and upper income groups are well-served by privately-supplied services they can afford to pay for. Our problem is that the poor are not well served. "Private affluence and public squalor" is how John Kenneth Galbraith described American life in his 1958 book *The Affluent Society*, and although conditions are somewhat better today, our government has far to go to meet European standards for its poor.

The American hope is always that the poor will in time enter the middle class, but conditions can be painful in the interim.

The third area of social support is Private Philanthropy:

Private philanthropy is perhaps the least understood and least appreciated leg of the "public support" triad, particularly in Europe. It meets needs that the marketplace and government leave unfilled.

The accepted American definition of philanthropy is "voluntary giving, voluntary service and voluntary association for the benefit of others." Distinct from "charity," which is help for the poor, philanthropy's goal is improving the "quality of life" as one sees fit.

Although the U.S. government spends our tax money as politicians or bureaucrats decide, it is through philanthropy that we give or do as we wish so long as it is seen as for "the public good." Our President may oppose stem cell research, for example, but some private universities pursue it anyway.

This year Americans will spend approximately $300 billion (equal to about 10% of our federal budget and over 2% of our GDP) on causes ranging from saving whales to curing AIDS in Africa, from building university research laboratories to sponsoring productions at the Metropolitan Opera, from providing scholarships for disadvantaged minority students to preserving neglected historic landmarks.

The rich donate buildings or endow named professorships, the poor give to their churches, but the majority of Americans give, serve or solicit for some not-for-profit cause; and smaller gifts are frequently the most creative and effective. On death, it is customary for rich Americans to leave charitable bequests, and the names of Ford, Rockefeller, Carnegie, MacArthur and that reclusive American, Henry Wellcome (benefactor of the Wellcome Trust, England's largest foundation), live on through the foundations they created.

Our federal government permits the sums thus contributed to be deducted from taxable income. In recent years many other nations have started to permit tax deductible gifts to approved organizations (Sweden being a notable exception). Tax exemption procedures abroad, however, are often complex and discouraging, unlike American tax laws (and now British laws) which are designed to encourage giving.

Europeans claim, mistakenly but repeatedly, that "Americans give because of the tax advantage"; but American income taxes were first introduced in 1913, long after the American philanthropic pattern had been established. In Europe, the new Picasso Museum went to France because of favorable tax arrangements, and similar arrangements could be explored by others.

We Americans are proud of our philanthropic sector. If all private philanthropy were abolished and that $300 billion were added to federal revenues, few think that the quality of life in the U.S. would be improved.

The majority of Americans believe that governments are best at catching thieves, putting out fires and fighting wars, but that other activities are performed more effectively by non-profit or free market entities. The Jeffersonian notion of limited government— "that government is best which governs least"—is reinforced by the American belief that government is inefficient.

NGO's (non-governmental organizations) are seen as more creative and innovative than government, less tied to precedent, more responsive to public needs and wishes and, above all, as more competent and cost effective. "Saving as many lives as possible at the lowest per capita cost possible"—Bill Gates' goal—reflects philanthropic, not governmental, thinking. Philanthropy has its weaknesses, but they are widely seen as fewer than those of government.

At all income levels, Americans give voluntarily of their time, effort and money to a degree unheard of in Europe. For example, there are few U.S. elementary schools, public or private, without a Parent Association through which parents raise funds to provide supplies or services to schools; but the formation of such groups is relatively recent in Europe.

One fundamental aspect of American philanthropy is donor recognition; although most Europeans decry this practice and find it embarrassing, Americans cannot imagine philanthropy without it.

When the Reverend John Harvard died in Cambridge, Massachusetts in 1638, leaving to the local divinity school 800 pounds sterling and his library of 400 volumes, in gratitude the school renamed itself "Harvard College.

When, eighty years later, Elihu Yale donated goods sold for 560 pounds sterling to the Collegiate School of New Haven, Connecticut, the school was promptly renamed "Yale College," even though Elihu Yale had not been in America since childhood and was never to return.

(On a personal note, this June, at our 55th college reunion in New Haven, my Yale Class of 1951 collectively donated to the Yale Alumni Fund $64,764,127, with contributions coming from 90% of all living classmates. Yale is a private institution, but over 20% of the alumni of America's state-supported universities contribute annually as well.)

Johns Hopkins of Maryland, when he died in 1873, left one million dollars to be divided among the members of his extended family, but he left an unprecedented seven million to found America's first research university and teaching hospital. Hopkins would have understood—and loved—Warren Buffett's comment, when asked, after he announced his $37 billion gift to Bill Gates' foundation, what provision he had made for his family.

Buffett's answer thrilled the nation: "I have always wanted to give my children enough to do anything, but not enough to do nothing." Americans identify with the worker bees of the hive, not with the drones.

Brown University, Duke, Cornell, Vanderbilt, Stanford and Rockefeller Universities are among the many other institutions named for their founders or major benefactors.

American museums list on their walls the names of major donors, and major tax-exempt organizations publish Annual Reports listing the names and gift levels of donors, even the most modest.

"Vulgar," "ostentatious," and "crude" are words sometimes applied to American fundraising techniques; but Americans, the most pragmatic people since the ancient Romans, reply, "Yes, but they work." If Europe wishes to replicate American philanthropic success, it should consider finding ways to praise and encourage donors while embarrassing the rich whose names are absent from the lists.

Philanthropic peer pressure from friends, neighbors and business associates is non-stop; invitations to testimonial luncheons, dinner dances, theater parties, auctions and rock concerts assault us; a daily avalanche of charity mail fills our mailboxes. And, yes, "it works."

Harvard University's endowment is over $26 billion, Yale's is over $16 billion and Princeton, Stanford and the University of Texas each boasts over $12 billion. Fifty-six American colleges have endowments of over a billion dollars; this year alone, 22 U.S. universities have each announced fundraising drives of over one billion dollars—Columbia, $4 billion; the University of Virginia, $3.3 billion; Yale, $3 billion; New York University, $2.5 billion; and even the municipally-financed City University of New York is seeking $1.2 billion from private donors.

In the 21st century, when intellectual capital is more important for a nation's international competitiveness than physical or financial capital, private philanthropy has an important role to play in higher education.

Our superb M.I.T.'s or Cal Techs not only educate and perform research; they also set high standards that public institutions strive to meet, and everyone benefits.

Cynics question the motives of donors, and those motives are indeed complex. Professional fundraisers cite many reasons for philanthropic giving:

a) Common Sense and Enlightened Self-Interest—it helps the community, of which the donor is a member;

b) Religious Imperative—God wills us to help others;

c) Good Investment—society gets a good return on funds expended; the donor gets prestige and enhanced social standing.

d) Fun—socialites organize dinner dances, theater parties, raffles, etc. and enjoy working with friends on such projects;

e) Altruism—generosity, benevolence and selfless giving feel good and are spiritually rewarding;

f) Repayment— school and college alumni, former hospital patients, etc. feel that they have benefited from the institutions and that they "owe" something in return;

g) Family Tradition—inheritors of wealth and members of prominent families feel loyalty to institutions.

The degree to which individuals define themselves and their values through their giving is sometimes overlooked by professionals. "I am what I give" is a more common belief than is generally realized.

The profound sense of mission of George Soros, a "one man Marshall Plan," who has already given over 3 billion euros to European philanthropies and has pledged to them his remaining 5 billion euro fortune; the hardnosed practicality of Bill Gates, whose fortune is willed to his foundation and who demands a dollar's worth of result for each dollar donated; and the imaginative involvement of Michael Bloomberg, New York City's billionaire mayor, who on completion of his term in government will devote his imagination, his energy, and his $6 billion dollar fortune to full-time philanthropic activities— are, of course, in a special class.

Others abroad are following suit. Indian billionaire Anil Agarwal recently announced his country's largest ever donation of a billion euros to found a university in his native province; Li Ka- shing, Asia's richest individual, has announced that he is bequeathing one-third of his 15 billion euro fortune to his foundation. Richard Branson of Virgin Atlantic; the founders of Google; and Ted Turner are among those announcing huge pro bono gifts. They are the living embodiment of Andrew Carnegie's dictum that creators of great fortunes should apply the same thought and attention to disposing of their riches as they did earning them.

But it must be remembered that it is not only the rich who give; John D. Rockefeller tithed from his very first pay check; Michael Bloomberg's father, who never earned more than $11,000 a year, discussed his charitable giving with his family at the dinner table; and most Americans contribute some time to pro bono activities.

Securing philanthropic contributions is an accepted career field now— involving part art and part science— and American fundraising professionals focus on the basic motivations I have described. Such professional fundraising is just beginning to appear in Europe.
To increase European voluntary giving, not only should tax laws be simplified, but traditional cultural patterns of public praise should be re-examined.

England bestows knighthoods on major philanthropists; France, the Legion of Honor; America awards Honorary Doctorates; but encouraging all citizens to feel proud of their contributions is an important step in increasing those gifts.

In Italy, a good start would be to identify "la bella figura" with philanthropy and to convince the public that its contributions will be spent honestly and productively, with accountability for income and outgo equal to any other investment.

The introduction of a prestigious "Lorenzo De Medici Award," to recognize outstanding philanthropy, presented by the President of the Republic at a major ceremony, could help change attitudes. Here in Milan, an award for private patronage of the arts could be named after Ludovico Sforza, the sponsor of Da Vinci's Last Supper.

In New York's "Little Italy," the Feast of San Gennaro, a joyous 11-day street fair, annually attracts over a million attendees and raises support for parochial schools, activities for the elderly, and other projects of the Archdiocese; such fundraising fairs could be replicated in the mother country.

For smaller fundraising events, Beppe Severigni suggests that they celebrate the family and Italian cuisine, and that they be conducted with great style.

Fundraising professionals know that those who donate to philanthropic causes, those who work actively with them and those who solicit funds from others, are "psyching themselves up"; and every effort is made to involve participants in these mutually- reinforcing activities.

94

In New York David Rockefeller, Brooke Astor and Arthur Ross are well-known examples. Another is Lewis Cullman, who has personally contributed some $250 million to New York charities, is a tireless solicitor, an activist Board member and author of an excellent treatise, How to Succeed in Fundraising by Really Trying, which can be found on www.LewisCullman.com.

In Europe and America, large fortunes are increasingly in the hands of what Warren Buffett calls the Self Made Man, as opposed to the Inheritor; and the Self Made Man is more inclined to donate his money.

"There must be more to life than having everything" is their frequent discovery; and the satisfaction, the pride—and, yes, the prestige—of commendable philanthropic contributions are high on the list of goals of wise creators of new fortunes, who increasingly realize the destructive potential of huge sums left to their families.

Skillful encouragement of major gifts is a slow process that in the United States is usually conducted by professionals. First, they establish a relationship with the prospective donor; next, they educate the donor about the organization and encourage identification and involvement with it; then, they encourage a modest gift whose effectiveness is demonstrable and for which appropriate appreciation is expressed.

They help the donor conclude that his or her next major gift will achieve something the donor believes is important and from which the donor will receive satisfaction and pride. Finally, the professionals help select the appropriate person to suggest (or ask for) that major gift.

When the gift has been pledged, the donor is acknowledged and celebrated, rewarding the donor and encouraging others.

Private philanthropy—in addition to, not instead of, government expenditures—has earned an important place in modern life, with material benefits to society and psychic benefits to donors.

In conclusion, while government and marketplace mechanisms can be improved, private philanthropy, from donors large and small, is the area most open to expansion, especially in Europe. In some cases the American model may be useful; in others, new vehicles, such as the great new Italian banking foundations, may evolve. And we are likely to see in Europe more private institutions such as Milan's excellent Bocconi University or Rome's respected LUISS University.

The creation of large private fortunes—and the prospect of huge inter-generational wealth transfers— give Europeans today the opportunity to reintroduce into public discourse the concepts of "noblesse oblige" (or perhaps "richesse oblige") and "obedience to the unenforceable". It has already started.

The medieval and Renaissance cathedrals that are the glory of Europe could be matched in our day by secular cathedrals of education and culture financed by today's private fortunes.

Then Europe's rich would be able to answer the Biblical question, "Am I my brother's keeper?" with the proud reply, "Yes, I am!"

Fondazione Cariplo Forum on Philanthropy
Milan, Italy
October 19, 2006

LITTLE ACORNS, GREAT OAKS

Ever since the shock of the Soviet launch of Sputnik in 1957, Americans have been concerned about the international standing of our educational system; and ever since the 1983 release of the report A Nation at Risk, Americans have been painfully aware of our educational failures.

In the "post American World", authorities like Nobel Laureate James J. Heckman tell us that the most effective step we can take to improve our international economic competitiveness is to devote sufficient resources to high quality, universal preschool education.

Businessmen, academics and military leaders agree that effective preschool education for all our children is not just a matter of generosity or compassion, but of national self-interest.

To the traditional arguments of "fairness" (letting all children begin life's race from the same starting line) and "social benefit" (preschooling produces better citizens), business groups like the Committee for Economic Development add that good preschool education is sound economic policy, returning to society many times the dollars invested. Economic studies show a 10% to 16% internal rate of financial return, along with dramatic "social" returns. A New York State study shows a return of seven dollars for every dollar spent, and a Brookings Institution study suggests that between 2008 and 2080, $59 billion spent on quality preschooling would generate $400 billion in added tax revenues and diminished expenditures.

Higher secondary school and college graduation rates with less remediation; fewer teen pregnancies, less crime and imprisonment; increased incomes with high taxes paid are all results of good preschooling; and the favorable impact on our skilled and productive national labor force is beyond computation. A diminishing income gap between our richest and poorest citizens would also result.

A child who enters first grade with self-confidence undermined, with curiosity and desire to learn dampened, a child who has never heard English spoken correctly, who has never been read to or even seen books, who has never learned to relate comfortably to others—such a child is a challenge to us all. But we do know how to meet that challenge with effective early education!

The age from three to five or six is crucially important in a child's development, in helping evolve a sense of self, in developing a sense of right and wrong, of creating EXPECTATIONS that guide behavior and a way of looking at the world for the rest of that child's life.

The most successful and effective preschool programs differ markedly from the worst, which are merely glorified baby-sitting exercises. Desirable programs expose children to committed and dedicated teachers with extensive vocabularies and a proper command of language, who conduct programs with favorable teacher/student ratios, up-to-date teaching materials and activities that involve and train parents (yes, good parenting can be taught!). In addition to preparing a child to read, write, count and think, these programs also stimulate a child's self-control, curiosity and self-confidence.

The five-year old who learns to wait patiently for his or her turn, who learns to share toys, who learns to appreciate justified praise, who learns to ask questions and to express ideas and opinions, who learns that "cause" leads to "effect" will become a 35-year old who will be a "taxpayer" not a "tax-eater," who will be an effective employer or employee, a desirable neighbor and a citizen leading a productive and fulfilling life.

In the United States today, when one third of all students (half of all minority students) drop out of high school; when 2.2 million prison inmates give us a national incarceration rate among the world's highest, remediation has proved to be expensive and often futile. On the other hand, prevention has been shown to be possible and cost effective. High quality preschooling is a key factor in prevention.

The best studies show that early childhood education should be a career field for qualified teachers with a bachelor's degree and appropriate child development training; a career field that must be rewarded with salary and benefits equal to those of elementary school teachers if it is to attract and retain career teachers of caliber.

The quality of teaching is the key factor in education; class size, ethnicity, location, physical facilities and parental poverty pale by comparison. To achieve our goals, we must attract and retain preschool teachers of skill, knowledge and commitment and compensate them accordingly.

"Teaching" is part art, part science; but its goal is "learning" for all students.

What should we—educators, non-profit spokespersons, civic minded laymen—be doing?

First, we must try to understand the problems in all their complexity—economic, social, political.

For example, trade unions—whether coal mining, automobile production or teaching—traditionally represent the economic interests of their members, not necessarily the best interests of the public. In education, we often find teachers' unions demanding lifetime tenure; promotion based on seniority, pay scales reflecting years served rather than professional merit, "end-loaded" pension and benefits arrangements which are stacked against the young entrant to the field to the benefit of the grizzled veteran, worst of all is the impossibility of removing teachers of demonstrated incompetence. These conditions are legitimate areas of public concern.

Educational policy, too, is important. When Clemenceau observed that "war is too important to be left to the generals," he could have been speaking of the classroom.

Oakland, California's embrace of "Ebonics" is an example; another is the widespread refusal to permit the differential pay scales necessary to attract chemists, physicists and mathematicians to high school teaching. Still another problem is occasional teacher insistence on using the whole word method of reading instruction only, rather than the effective phonics approach to learning to read as well.

The public must make clear to legislators that we are willing to pay the taxes that underwrite the necessary expenses that high quality preschooling involves.

High quality, universal preschooling is an idea whose time has come. As Oliver Wendell Holmes noted, however, "The mode by which the inevitable comes to pass is called "effort."" I hope the American public is prepared to make that effort!

Channel Thirteen
Conference on Early Education
December 10, 2008

SPEAKING WITH IRAN

T ruth is stranger than fiction, it is said, because fiction must
stick to probabilities, but truth need not.

And so it came to pass that a superannuated, New York-
based, Jewish real estate man emerged as a spokesman for American
values on Iranian national television.

What began as an intellectual lark soon became deadly serious as
I found myself aware of the profound misconceptions that each society had of the other.

Knowing and understanding the other's positions (and negotiating strengths and weaknesses), seeking areas of mutual interest, adju-
dicating differences when possible and negotiating compromises—are
desirable; and meaningful communication—which has been totally
lacking—is an important first step.

What can be achieved by a single individual with a marginal role
cannot be determined; but the prospect was challenging and I plunged in.

For over two years I participated by telephone from New York in
English language current events discussions which are broadcast live
from Tehran in late evening to the Iranian public and by satellite to
an audience abroad.

Subjects range from breaking political events in Iraq and Iran, activities of the United Nations and of the Arab League, censorship, the
role of women in the Islamic world, events in Israel and in Saudi Arabia, and, of course, Iran's nuclear development program.

The program's moderator is neutral, my fellow participants—usually leading Iranian academics and government officials or anti-U.S.

policy Americans and foreigners (Noam Chomsky and the Vice President of Iran were on a recent program)—defend Iranian government positions; and I defend the U.S. against charges of hypocrisy, insensitivity, brutality and evil.

What has emerged from these discussions, from my meetings with Iranian academics, journalists and government officials, and from my reading, is a picture of Iran today that differs from conventional wisdom.

First, far from being a monolith, Iranian society is deeply fractured. Although the political leadership refers to the U.S. as "the great Satan," the Iranian public, especially the young born since the clerical take-over in 1979, until recently admired and respected the U.S. to a degree unparalleled in the Islamic world. The majority of the Iranian public (some estimates run as high as 80% to 90%) is opposed to mullah domination of Iran's political and economic life, a domination which has led to economic stagnation and a degree of corruption staggering even by comparison with the Shah's regime. Common sense dictates that conveying a vision of a better life for the Iranian people is a more effective means of increasing the gap between the government and the public than threatening military action.

Some fraction of the top leadership— size unknown but fanatic in intensity—may actually seek a nuclear Armageddon, to be followed by the presumed arrival of the 12th Imam and universal peace; another fraction, devout but rational, espouses worldwide expansion of Islam but without war; and a third fraction, pragmatists, may seek only Iran's well-being. The strength of their respective influence on the Supreme Leader—who calls all the shots—varies from time to time.

The revolutionary generation of fervent Islamists currently in control is aging, however; and the nature of Iranian leadership five years hence is unknowable.

Second, Mahmoud Ahmadinejad—unexpectedly elected President in a process that stringently limits and controls the selection of candidates— was in no sense a conventional popular choice in the

102

Western sense; he is widely feared as a "loose cannon" even by Iran's top leadership.

His aggressive position on nuclear development in the face of what is seen as Western bullying has touched a responsive chord of national pride even among the young, who despise him; as usual, an outside threat solidifies domestic support.

Ahmadinejad's intemperate statements, which no one can control, are an embarrassment to many of his colleagues, but his ability to act is strictly controlled by others.

Third, because of assassination or imprisonment of opposition voices and the imposition of a climate of menacing fear and because of a governmental structure giving total political control to a small coterie of senior Islamic clerics, governmental leadership rests in just a few hands.

An unelected Supreme Leader, an unelected Council of Guardians and an unelected Expediency Council have control of all aspects of government and the institutions of the republic. Widely held in contempt, they rule, not by respect or admiration, but by fear.

Fourth, to the majority of the highly nationalistic Iranian public, nuclear weapons per se are of little importance, but national prestige, the ability to play an important role in regional affairs and, above all, security arrangements that protect them from invasion or even domination by "outsiders" are paramount.

Events in Iraq, coupled with repeated U.S. talk of "regime change," have convinced Iranians that the U.S. threat to Iran is real and imminent.

Fifth, current economic and social conditions in Iran are a continuing disappointment for Iranians, even with recently enhanced oil revenues. Unemployment is high, inflation rampant, the stock market in turmoil, domestic investment low and the jobless rural poor are flooding the cities. More than a million young Iranians enter the labor force each year, while fewer than 400,000 jobs are created annually; and the "brain drain" of educated and well-trained Iranians is high and increasing.

Ahmadinejad's campaign promise to divert more resources to the poor has not been realized; his recent announcement of Iranian financial aid to the Hamas government of Palestine has brought public demonstrations demanding that the funds be spent instead for the poor in Iran.

Economic performance is Ahmadinejad's weak point, appeals to national pride his strong point.

Sixth, Iran's moves toward the development of nuclear weapons and the means to deliver them are unquestionably real. If they are not stopped, the only question is at what point they will become a "clear and present danger" that, for the safety of the rest of the world, must be neutralized, regardless of cost or ramifications.

Where does all this leave us? Opinions vary, but here are mine:

a) Iran and the U.S. are two nations whose economic and geopolitical interests should rationally dovetail; they are heading toward conflict due to ideological differences about popular democracy and about "separation of church and state," but, above all, about the Iranian leadership's messianic views reflected in state-supported international terrorism and the development of nuclear weapons and the means to deliver them.

The key question facing the West is in whose favor time is working.

If Iran's Islamic fanaticism will in time be a spent force, as many believe, working strenuously to forestall the development of Iranian nuclear weapons in the short run by negotiation should be the West's over-riding concern.

If the Islamic messianic movement continues to broaden and strengthen, other strategies must prevail.

b) One staunch Republican, Richard Nixon, neutralized the threat from Mao Tse Tung by demanding a change of "actions," not "regime," and peace prevailed. Another staunch Republican, Ronald Reagan, neutralized Mikhail Gorbachev by demanding a change of "actions," not "regime," and peace prevailed. Eventually, of course, in each case "regime change" did occur, but not through outside military action.

104

The constantly-reiterated American goal of "regime change" in Iran may be the key factor in preventing progress in changing "actions," since everyone in Iran considers America determined to overthrow the regime. There is general consensus that "giving in" to the U.S. on anything will merely encourage the U.S. to demand more and more concessions.

Iran's ambassador to the U.N., a polished and eloquent diplomat of the old school (reminiscent of Brasidas, the charming and articulate foreign spokesman for ancient Sparta) insists that Iran is reasonable and is ready to negotiate all issues; but we do not know for whom he speaks. At this stage, we should pursue his offer (without deferring powerful international actions to compel Iran to end nuclear weapon development).

c) Offering face-saving "carrots" of major and compelling economic incentives (such as membership in the World Trade Organization), including internationally guaranteed availability of nuclear fuel for Iran's peaceful purposes, and offering appropriate, internationally-backed security guarantees giving Iran real and effective protection against U.S. invasion, could change the nature of current negotiations.

In return, the West could require a nuclear nonproliferation agreement with enforceable and verifiable provisions that would preclude the subterfuge and trickery the Iranians have practiced in the past.

The offer of such a Grand Detente—bringing Iran back into the community of nations—should include an end to Iran's state-sponsored terrorism abroad and a "stand down" on the Israeli question, but it must also include such economic inducements and security guarantees that it would be seen not as a defeat for anyone, but as a victory for all concerned.

The offer of such a package would demonstrate to the world and to the Iranian public that the American President is not the psychological counterpart of the Iranian President, which is what many throughout the world believe him to be.

Threatening Iran tends to unify that nation behind its leadership;

offering major economic and security benefits could help drive a wedge between the government and the Iranian public.

With $51 billion of exports and $48 billion of imports last year, Iran does not want to be an international pariah. Its need for foreign capital investment and technical know-how to modernize and upgrade its petrochemical sector is desperate, if only to stop wasting the $2 billion a year worth of natural gas it is burning off or to end its need to import gasoline because its refineries are inadequate.

The reply made by opponents of a Grand Détente proposal is that the Europeans have hinted at it in the past and they have been rejected by the Iranians.

In reality, the good faith of the U.S. is questioned because of its insistence on "regime change," and our offers have heretofore not been considered real. A Grand Détente— involving all major international and regional powers, European, Russian, Chinese and Arab, as well as U.S.—is not the same as U.S. offers to discuss a specific problem.

d) In the final analysis, it may be that real negotiations are not possible and force may be necessary to neutralize an Iranian nuclear threat.

In such case, international economic force in all its many forms should be applied before military force is resorted to; both for practical reasons (it may work) and to gain international support for subsequent military action.

e) These, too, are "the times that try men's souls," and we must seek the least bad option.

May 11, 2006

TALLEYRAND ENTERTAINS METTERNICH

AT THE CONGRESS OF VIENNA

F irst of all—a confession.
   What may superficially appear as a gastronomic tour de force
   is in truth a statement on the stark contrast between American
diplomatic techniques in the 20th century and those of the French in
the 19th. Secondarily, this is an evening of homage to Talleyrand, the
prime exponent of la diplomatie gastronomique, and to Carême, the
greatest single name in the history of French cuisine, who so ably
aided and abetted him.

The Congress of Vienna was one of the most important political
gatherings in the history of Europe, and also the most splendid. From
a political point of view, as Henry Kissinger wrote of the statesmen at
the Congress in his doctoral dissertation, "Their achievements were
not inconsiderable: a period of peace lasting almost a hundred years."

From a social view, Duff Cooper wrote that, "The Congress that
assembled at Vienna in the autumn of 1814 attracted to that city all
that was most brilliant in Europe. Not only did the leading statesman
of every country attend, but in most cases the reigning princes accompanied them. The royal palace at one moment lodged two
emperors and as many empresses, four kings, one queen, two heirs to
thrones, two grand duchesses and three princesses. The flower of European nobility, the richest, the most distinguished, the most beautiful, all who played any part either in the political or in the social
sphere flocked to Vienna.

"There was an endless series of balls and banquets, hunts, shooting parties and musical rides. There were theatricals given by the most celebrated performers of Europe, with others performed by aristocratic amateurs. There was a medieval tournament; masked entertainments were frequent, and glamour was lent to them by the knowledge that any mysterious stranger might be the ruler of a vast kingdom, that any domino might conceal a queen."

In the political sphere, Talleyrand's personal achievement was described by Kissinger (no admirer) as gaining for his defeated nation "the end of the isolation of France and the recognition of its equality." While his colleagues were carousing, Talleyrand's shrewd intellect was in overdrive. When the Turkish ambassador dropped dead suddenly after midnight revels, Talleyrand was widely reputed to have pondered, "What did he mean by that?"

In the social and gastronomic sphere, Louis Madelin of the Academie Francaise writes, "Talleyrand arrived at Vienna on September 23rd; hardly a week went by before everyone knew that none could surpass him in the luxury of his receptions and in the excellence of his hospitality."

Now, to the heart of the matter. Was there a relationship between the two?

In this age of American diplomatic defeats we have had one president who gave heartburn to his foreign visitors with spicy Texas barbeques, and another who proudly presented Georgia specialties such as catfish, grits and okra. Would history have been different had the food been better? Unsubstantiated rumor has it that Kennedy's missile crisis triumph over Khrushchev was planned over superb White House dinners presented by chef René Verdon, but that his disaster at the Bay of Pigs was hatched in Hyannisport over beer and burnt hot dogs.

Seriously, though, at peace talks in our time, such as Panmunjom, American diplomats have been known to focus on the shape of the table, while Talleyrand concerned himself with what was on the table. American diplomats seek policy instructions; Talleyrand, when offered help at Vienna, replied in official documents to King Louis XVIII, "Yes, sire, send more saucepans!" Is it conceivable that an American would say that?

Our own Dr. Kissinger's pages on Metternich, Castlereagh, etc., are extremely detailed, but in his entire 332 pages the word "cheese" never appears; yet several journals and memoirs of the period document a lively discussion during the Congress when Lord Castlereagh praised English Stilton, Nesselrode spoke for Emmenthal, Falk for Holland's Edam and Alvino for Italian Strachino. Talleyrand was silent until a courier arrived with the very Brie de Meaux we share tonight. As French historian Jean Orieux describes it on page 468 of *Talleyrand—The Art of Survival*, "The brie rendered its cream to the knife. It was a feast, and no one further argued the point. No diplomatic victory was too small for Talleyrand."

Was omission of this incident an oversight on Kissinger's part, or a subtle philosophic point he was making?

As with eating, so with drinking. Considering our New Year's Eve alcoholic consumption in the relatively puritanical 1980's, one can only guess about pleasure-mad Vienna in 1814. In fact, things got so hot that the Russian headquarters in an art-filled palace actually burned to the ground one night. But Kissinger very drily notes, "On 31 December Castlereagh and Metternich proposed that henceforth Talleyrand participate in meetings of the Big Four. Ipso loquitur; the thing speaks for itself!"

Then again, how much objectivity can be expected from one who has never acknowledged the influence of America's growing taste for Szechuan cooking and dim sum on the Nixon/Kissinger initiative in opening China?

One final significant point concerning Talleyrand and an ancient but rapidly dying art is illustrated by a story that was widely circulated in his day. A young visitor once downed a glass of Talleyrand's rarest and most expensive brandy in a single gulp, causing the older man to say, "Sir, the first thing you should do is to take your glass in the palms of your hands and warm it. Then shake it gently, with a circular movement, so that the liquid's perfume is released. Then raise the glass to your nose and breathe deeply." "And then, my lord?" asked the young man. "And then, sir," replied Talleyrand, "you replace the glass on the table and you talk about it." Duff Cooper makes the same point, writing, "We owe to Lady Frances Shelley the following account of a meal at Talleyrand's home. During the whole repast the general conversation was upon eating. Every dish was discussed and the antiquity of every bottle of wine supplied the most eloquent annotations. Talleyrand himself analyzed the dinner with as much interest and seriousness as if he had been discussing an important political question."

Who knows if the recent Geneva summit conference could have resolved the "star wars" question had Reagan and Gorbachev discussed sauces along with satellites and mousses along with missiles?

It is in the spirit of such discourse that we present tonight's dinner. But I cannot close without a few words about Talleyrand's great chef, and our dinner tonight â la façon de Carême.

As one whose stated goal was "to raise his profession to the level of an art," Marie-Antonin Carême was the unrivaled leader of the great classic French cuisine, for which he prescribed the recipes, menus and kitchen techniques in a monumental series of cookbooks and commentaries. One of his specialties was the pièce montée, great constructions of sugar, marzipan and the like in ships, castles, Greek temples and so forth. We like to think that he would have been pleased with our pièce montée tonight in the exact form of the New York Public Library's neo-classical Fifth Avenue home, prepared using the building's original architectural plans.

At the Congress of Vienna, Carême complained that the local meats were deplorable, but that the game was excellent, especially the partridge; so that, of course, determined our main course. Turbot he called the royal fish and poularde à la Reine a noble presentation dish. La gelée was almost his trademark and the gateau Nesselrode was named for the Czar's Foreign Minister, a handsome young fellow whose affairs were the talk of the Congress.

The caviar would have been in honor of Czar Alexander himself

110

and the foie gras for Castlereagh, who loved it; the consommé, with its julienne of celery root, veal and leeks, was one of the 299 soups Carême was credited with inventing.

Of the wines, Metternich is represented by the sekt from his ancestral estates; for one of the reds we chose a Rothschild, in recognition of Nathan Rothschild's successful efforts at the Congress on behalf of the civil liberties of European Jews. The second red, Romanée Conti, was known to be one of Talleyrand's personal favorites. We close with a Chateau d'Yquem, the wine of Michel de Montaigne, who, in a well-ordered universe, would be the patron saint of diplomats, writers, enthusiasts of the table, indeed, of civilization itself.

Dinner for The New York Public Library
December 10, 1985

RETURN TO SINAI

It is heartwarming to return to Sinai Temple, the scene of so many events of importance in my life and that of my family, moments of happiness and of sadness that give resonance to life.

Whether thinking of Sunday School or Confirmation, whether seeing in my mind's eye Rabbi Kagan officiating at my Bar Mitzvah, my wedding, or at the funeral of my father, I realize how many of my own spiritual rites of passage are connected with Crary Avenue. So it is a particular pleasure to play a part in the celebration of the 70th anniversary of the Congregation.

These 70 years span the most turbulent in the history of the Jews. It begins with the massive Jewish immigration to the United States at the turn of the century, continues through Hitler and the Holocaust which obliterated the vital world of eastern European Jewry, continues through the re-founding of the State of Israel and its victories in four wars of survival, and continues to this very day when we find Israel still fighting for physical survival and Diaspora Jewry girding to meet the challenge of prosperity and toleration as successfully as it did the challenge of hatred and discrimination.

Of all the events of the period, however, one that is emerging may be as important to the future of world Jewry as any of them, and that is the gradual, but, I believe, real emergence of a new creature on the world scene – a product equally of the Hebrew tradition and the American setting, an individual equally proud of Thomas Jefferson and Judah Maccabee, equally at home with Walt Whitman and Martin Buber, with Ralph Waldo Emerson and Abraham Joshua Heschel.

113

The American Jewish community has achieved an un-paralleled level of material well-being, prestige, and influence; virtually all the doors of our society are open to it; its challenge is to choose among acculturation, assimilation, and disappearance or a new Golden Age of spiritual evolution, accomplishment, and contribution.

It is interesting to note that 1906, the year of Sinai's founding, was the year of the largest Jewish immigration to the United States and the year of the worst Cossack raids on Jewish villages in Russia. In Fiddler on the Roof, the exodus from Anatevka took place in 1906, as did the founding of the American Jewish Committee "to prevent infraction of the civil and religious rights of Jews in any part of the world".

Just one year later, the United States won its first Nobel Prize, and it was won by a Jew – Albert Michaelson.

From 1899 to 1914, U.S. government figures record 1,532,690 individuals arriving at Ellis Island and declaring themselves to be Jews.

A poor, bedraggled lot, only 7% had at least $50 or more; 38% had less than $50; and 55% had no money at all. 70% stated that they paid for their journey with money borrowed from relatives.

What were these immigrants like? In 1906, the British author H.G. Wells stated that he thought America was making a horrible mistake by admitting them. They would never, and these were his words, "be more than a semi-literate, urban peasantry."

On September 1, 1908, the New York City Police Commissioner, Theodore Bingham, raised a storm of protest charging New York's Jews with control of the criminal underworld, and stating that, although Jews constituted one-fourth of the general population, they made up one-half of the criminals.

Seventy years later, simple facts and numbers tell a different story. America's Jews make up under 3% of the population, but consistently win over 20% of the National Book Awards and Nobel Prizes, buy an estimated 25% of all "trade books" published in the United States and constitute nearly one-third of the incoming freshman class of every Ivy League college. The college entrance rate of American Jewish youth is approximately 90%, compared with 40% for the nation generally.

This 3% of our population today includes the Secretary of State, Attorney General (of the U.S. as well as New York State), the Mayor of New York, the Chairman of the Federal Reserve Board, and the President of DuPont. The head of Notre Dame University not long ago openly asked a conference of Catholic educators, "Where are our Einsteins, Oppenheimers, and Salks?"

Yet our plays, books and poems, our folklore, and our comedians would still have us believe, as one observer put it as recently as 1960 that, "psychologically Jews are still in exile, marginal people with an undiminished sense of estrangement, an unbated sense of otherness." Writers still write of American Jews as aliens on the margin of culture, uprooted, displaced, persons who do not quite belong.

I maintain that the opposite is true. In America, where the majority consists of minorities, where each is free to follow his bent and seek fulfillment, the American Jewish community may emerge with a vitality, stability, and continuity unequalled in history.

It is up to us to make sure that our institutions, our customs, our traditions, and our mindsets are cast in such a way as to make Jewish continuity and survival not merely possible, but likely.

Using the resources of our synagogues, our Jewish community centers, our Hebrew educational system, and our nationwide charitable network, we must inculcate in succeeding generations not just the best of American tradition, but the best of Hebrew tradition: compassion and tzedaka, the love of learning, the sense of family, justice, and, above all, the sense of mission imparted by the Covenant of Mount Sinai.

If we succeed, we will produce finer Jews and finer Americans, but most important, finer human beings better able to lead satisfying, productive, and spiritually enriched lives.

In 1907, one year after the founding of Sinai Temple, Rabbi Israel Friedlander, a professor at the Jewish Theological Seminary, offered his fellow Jews a vision, and it is the ideal note on which I end:

"...when we thus try to penetrate the mist that encircles the horizon of the present, a vision unfolds itself before our mind's eye, presenting a picture of the future American Israel. We perceive a community great in numbers, mighty in power, enjoying life, liberty, and the pursuit of happiness...adding a new note to the richness of American life, leading a new current into the stream of American civilization; not a formless crowd of taxpayers and voters, but a sharply marked community, distinct and distinguished, trusted for its loyalty, respected for its dignity, esteemed for its traditions, valued for its aspiration, a community such as the Prophet of the Exile saw in his vision: 'And marked will be their seed among the nations, and their offspring among the peoples. Everyone that will see them will point to them as a community blessed by the Lord.'"

Looking forward to the next 70 years, I pray that with luck and effort, our children and our children's children may see his words come true.

Sinai Temple, Mt. Vernon, NY
70th Anniversary Celebration
September 17, 1976

116

ST. CRISPIN AND THE MOTT HALL SCHOOL

Members of the Mott Hall School's Class of 1999—heartfelt congratulations on this happy day, one that will be long remembered.

It is the year that your elementary school chess team journeyed to the national competitions at Phoenix, Arizona and came in Number One in the United States; the year that your Junior High school chess team entered the national competitions at Columbus, Ohio, and also came in Number One in the United States; the year when the founding coach of your chess teams won designation as the first African-American International Grand Master in the history of chess; the year when the reading ratings released this month showed your fourth grade ranked Number One in all of New York City; the year you graduates earned admission in record numbers to New York's most competitive and meritocratic public high schools; and on and on.

One day in high school or in college some of you will study Shakespeare's play Henry V, where you will read in stirring verse of the pride and honor of those who triumphed over fierce odds at the battle of Agincourt on St. Crispin's Day. Although this is not St. Crispin's Day and I am certainly no Shakespeare, the sentiments are much the same.

Despite limited resources and against the odds, in the face of hardship and struggle, you, too, have triumphed. Mott Hall has no auditorium, no real gymnasium, and, until private donors supplied it, no outdoor playground.

But if you are short on physical facilities, you are long on spirit!

117

You have cultivated high aspirations and self-confidence, disciplined attitudes and the capacity for sustained hard work that invariably lead to high achievement.

Sustained and encouraged by your families and by outstanding school leadership that prides itself on bringing out the best in its students, you have achieved wonders.

Now, as you go on to high school and then to college, we hope that you will keep alive in your hearts and minds the vision that this wonderful school has labored to instill in you—a desire not only for schooling, but for learning, leading not just to a job, but to a fulfilling career, not merely to earn a living, but to lead a life that is productive and satisfying.

Graduating students of Mott Hall, we will follow your lives with encouragement and high hopes, confident that you will continue your trajectories of growth and development, and that you will demonstrate to the world what you are capable of achieving.

To those of us who have tried to be helpful, you have eloquently echoed the words that Winston Churchill addressed to the U.S. Congress in World War II, "Give us the tools and we will do the job."

You are doing the job!

And we are so proud of you.

God bless you all!

Commencement,
Mott Hall School
June 14, 1999

LEADERSHIP FOR THE SEVENTIES

In the early days of the French Revolution, the Marquis de Lafayette was having a drink in a Parisian café when someone burst in, shouting, "Where is that mob going?" Lafayette polished off his drink, pulled on his jacket, and said as he headed for the door, "I don't know, but wherever it is, I have to get there first, because I'm their leader!" That, of course, *is* one form of "leadership," following from the front, as it were, capitalizing on the views of the moment and using them for one's own ends.

Another type of leadership is that of the monarch who "reigns but does not rule," or his counterpart in everyday life who delights in the perquisites of office, but shirks the responsibilities and whose goal is not to rock the boat, to alienate as few people as possible, and to leave his office much as he found it.

A third form of leadership is that of the dictatorial "knock-their-heads-together" approach that can work in some situations but that is clearly out of phase in this age of participatory democracy.

There *is* one other style of leadership, however, that is not only in keeping with the times, but gives hope of being the most effective, especially for the Jewish community.

It is the theory of leadership that presupposes a thoughtful, aware, and concerned constituency serviced by "spokesmen-guides" who see their role in several lights: to delineate and clarify significant issues; to present for consideration feasible alternatives; to articulate the views of the group; and to formulate and implement programs of effective action that reflect a rational consensus.

119

Leadership is a process of communication and change that cannot be conducted in isolation; it requires interaction *with* the group as well as *for* the group, where the leader, in Erik Erikson's words, "tries to solve for all what he cannot solve for himself alone." If, as many believe, lack of effective analysis of our problems is our most pressing concern, then the leadership task is clear.

In this age of over-simplification, when complex subjects are discussed in banner headlines with all the loss of subtlety implied; when, in all areas, we are encouraged in unrealistically high expectations of performance that in our more mature moments we know cannot be met; when novelty is the order of the day and the "new and plausible" is automatically preferred to the "former and probable" – the role of responsible leadership is more difficult, more thankless, and, sadly, more necessary.

These are the problems of leadership in our *time* rather than of any given organization or particular field. For this is the day when some of the nation's very best mayors, such as Lee of New Haven or Cavanaugh of Detroit, and many first-class university presidents, such as James Perkins of Cornell, have walked away from their jobs in despair; they could not face the impossibility of providing responsible leadership to a constituency that prefers the expedient placebo to the more-difficult, more-expensive, and longer-range solution which has a higher degree of eventual success.

Constituencies of today tend toward impatience, but also toward the extreme position; today's leader, would-be or actual, is under pressure to declare himself Pollyanna or militant, with any intermediate stance considered a "cop-out".

But the problems will not evaporate because they are ignored or mistreated; they will be dealt with successfully or not, and the constituency will benefit or not. It has been said that in science there are neither rewards nor punishments, only consequences. It will be the thankless role of contemporary leadership to bear the blame.

What are the major problems that the American Jewish community faces and how can its leadership be most helpful? On the one

120

hand, there are the problems of American society with whose well-being the American Jewish community is inextricably bound; on the other hand, there are those of the world Jewish community, with whom segments of the American Jewish community identify in various ways and degrees.

In either case, leadership may be most effective, not by taking stands on specific issues, but by helping to formulate attitudes and clarifying underlying concepts. Whether through the general press or the Jewish-oriented press; through conferences, debates or forums; through existing organizations or new ones; through the synagogue or the community center; or, most likely, by the use of all of these, the American Jewish community must be helped to understand the nature of the pressures and influences being brought to bear on them which affect their value systems, their lifestyles, their physical surroundings, even the very nature of their existence.

All progress involves change, but not all change leads to progress. The time has come to review the basic assumptions underlying a number of specific issues.

For example, one's thoughts on the real but ignored conflict between the current interpretation of "equality" and the traditional interpretation of "justice" on the other will determine one's attitude on many inter-group questions such as "benign quotas," professional standards, educational testing procedures, etc. No one can doubt that objective standards and objective testing are under fierce attack today. Ironically, it used to be the *conservative* who opposed objective tests for college admission, etc., on the grounds that there were factors more important than intelligence, and the result was the "quota system"; today, it is the *radical* who is on the attack, but that does not make the argument any more logical. If specific tests have a recognizable bias that does not screen for a meaningful characteristic, that specific test should be discarded, but *objective testing* should not be. Let us rethink the concepts of equality and justice.

Another key issue is the virtually undiscussed question of socioeconomic class; it is pressing because of its confusion with the question of color. In the Forest Hills, New York, subsidized housing controversy, for example, politicians insisted on discussing the difficulty in terms of race, whereas local residents insisted on discussing the problem in terms of schools and safety.

Socioeconomic class differences *do* exist in our society and are reflected in differences in lifestyle, motivation, time-sense, and many other ways. Lowest-class, working-class, and middle-class groups have different ideas of what they demand from a school system, and it is not a sign of bigotry for a middle-class group to fight hard for maintenance of high standards.

Sociologists are just beginning to realize that Jews consider the quality of a school system a key factor in their choice of residence; faced with declining quality in schools, they just pick up and leave.

Before the Berlin Wall went up, it used to be said that the East Germans "voted with their feet." Well, the mobility of Jews in fleeing our troubled central cities has been greater than that of Italians, Irish, and other groups; it was due to changes in the school system; in retrospect it would have been in everybody's best interest to fight the school question through and to have them all remain in the city.

Another question whose implications are starting to plague us is the one put by Shaw in the mouth of Eliza Doolittle's father in *Pygmalion* when he discussed the "deserving" versus the "undeserving" poor. Should access to public housing be a right or a privilege, should welfare payments be in cash or in kind, and how do we treat the "crisis ghetto" syndrome (what is best for the resident dysfunctional family and what is best for the city as a whole.)
A careful and sophisticated analysis of the question of poverty must be made; we must differentiate specifically between the aged or the handicapped or the tragedy-struck and those who are not only dysfunctional themselves but destructive to others. Remedial programs helpful for the one are almost useless for the other; and the failure of many well-intended programs threatens to destroy those that have worked or that could work in a different context.

The determination of "national priorities" is a lively issue; one's judgments will be influenced by one's attitude on the proper balance between what Galbraith calls public and private goods. We must think about cost/benefit ratios and "lesser of two evils" situations. It isn't enough to discuss Consolidated Edison supplying electricity to New York City only in terms of the Storm King Generator's harm to the Hudson River: or only in terms of the thermal pollution of a nuclear plant in Jamaica Bay; or only in terms of polluting smokestacks along the East River; or only in terms of high tension wires bringing power from faraway areas; or only in terms of a power shortage which will black out the city, cut off summer air-conditioning, stall subways underground on stifling days, etc.

Political leaders whose attention span seems to extend only from election to election can beg such questions, but leadership must help the public to face the problem of such trade-offs realistically.

The question of community control and local home rule is a variant of the same problem. Airports, museums, hospitals, bridges, community centers, and similar facilities concern all of us and their placement must be thought through by all of us. Each of us knows where they shouldn't go, namely on his own street corner, but none of us knows where they *should* go, except usually some place involving cost to be borne by higher taxes which we refuse to pay.

We are in danger of becoming a society in which "veto power" is so widespread that any vocal group can stop an action while almost no coalition of groups can *start* one. We risk a creeping paralysis of public will, another alternative to effective action.

The deterioration of our central cities continues apace. Jews have traditionally been the country's most enthusiastic city-dwellers; they have more to lose from urban decay and the most to gain from urban resurgence. Jews have not so much willingly gone to the suburbs as been driven from their preferred city. Even in suburbia, the Jew seeks the urban virtues of convenience, comfort, and cultural and social opportunities. In a survey of housing preferences taken among suburbanites near Philadelphia several years ago, it was found that after the children were grown, almost all of the non-Jewish parents wished to remain in their single-family homes while the majority of Jews intended to return to urban apartments.

Recent city problems may have changed the pattern somewhat, but there is little doubt that safe, clean, vital cities would re-attract vast numbers of suburban Jews.

Some think that urban problems can be solved by better public relations and more cheerful publicity, King Canute and Dr. Coué to the contrary. In all likelihood we will wait until some major city like Newark or St. Louis actually goes bankrupt before we realize that a Gordian Knot problem requires a Gordian Knot solution. There are those, I among them, who believe that central cities can regain health by shifting financing of local education from the municipal property tax to the state income tax (with the burden falling on those best able to pay), by the federalization of welfare costs and benefits, by zoning and land use changes that re-distribute the poor from dense concentration in central cities to dispersion throughout the region and, finally, by regional solutions to regional problems.

Whatever the solutions they will come about only when an informed citizenry demands them; and Jews have a vested interest in taking the lead.

Another area for rethinking is the controversy between separatism and integration, whether rich and poor, black and white, Jew and non-Jew; the subject of ethnicity and the melting pot must be reexamined.

In today's fluid, yet pluralistic society, sensitivity and common sense should focus on differentiating the significant from the trivial.

Leadership must be positive and guide its constituency in these days of troubled inter-group relations. We must try to achieve a "color-blind" society that recognizes the legitimate concerns of the Black as much as it does that of the Jew. Failing that, we may see our society destroyed.

Housing must be integrated, schooling must be integrated, employment must be integrated. And we must strive to see these goals achieved without lowering standards.

124

All these are problems that concern all of America's 200 million people, but we Jews are among those 200 million and we cannot be like the fellow in the leaky rowboat who refused to help bail out because the leak wasn't under his seat. John Donne has answered that for all time and we cannot ignore the tolling of his bell.

Of specifically Jewish concern, however, is what the thrust of Jewish philanthropic efforts should be in the future. New York's Federation of Jewish Philanthropies empaneled a special commission to discuss it, and its recommendations, if implemented, would require a budget far greater than can realistically be raised; selectivity is needed.

In the early days of the 20th century, Jewish hospitals were necessary not only to treat the Jewish sick but to permit Jewish doctors to enter the field of medicine. Jewish social welfare programs were financed largely by successful members of an earlier German Jewish migration and were aimed at what was frequently the physical conditions and destitution of later Easter European immigrant groups. Jewish education was considered the province of the cheder and the synagogue, while Jewish cultural survival seemed assured and was manifest in a thriving theatre, press, social clubs, burial societies, political organizations, and so forth.

Today, the outpatient departments of most Jewish-sponsored hospitals serve many more indigent non-Jews than Jews; downtown Jewish community centers are faced with constituencies fleeing to suburban havens; Jews themselves have access to virtually all the social institutions of our society; and the role of government has expanded to embrace areas that were once the preserve of private philanthropy.

In considering the future we must face the question of how we relate to our own needs and to the needs of the larger community of which we are a part.

One school of thought holds that there is no such thing as a Jewish swimming pool, gymnasium or surgical operating room, and that these should be sponsored by general public funds for general public use. Another school holds that, just as Yale and Harvard were Congregationalist contributions to American life, and Bryn Mawr and Swarthmore were Quaker-sponsored, but available to all, so the Jewish community should support its share of first-rate institutions benefiting the general public. This is essentially the outlook of Brandeis University.

A third view holds that so long as there are Jewish poor, aged, and handicapped who are not adequately cared for by other means, the Jewish community should remedy the deficiency.

But virtually all would agree that Jewish cultural survival, as opposed to physical or theological survival is in grave danger through ignorance; and that creative leadership is called for to meet the challenge.

The community center is the logical vehicle for this purpose, and its support justifies a handsome share of all the talent, energy, and money we can find.

In a time when alienation and despair seem widespread, when family bonds have become tenuous, when so many lack motivation and goals, when life appears aimless and even our physical surroundings seem to lack human scale, the inculcation of Jewish cultural values in congenial settings justifies anything we can do to add meaning and grace to the lives of those who share it.

These are not problems unique to contemporary Judaism; Thoreau's observation about the lives of quiet desperation led by those around him is echoed in André Malraux's comment that "other people are much more unhappy than one thinks," and neither statement would seem novel to the writer of the Book of Ecclesiastes.

If ever the Jewish community center field had meaning and value, it is today; and in the reevaluation of philanthropic priorities, advocates of the community center must speak loudly and clearly of their concerns.

Also, the continuing relationship of the American Jewish community to Israeli and foreign communities must be thought through in constructive ways.

In the case of Israel, one can say that rallying around a nation

126

under military attack and in danger of physical obliteration is one thing; creating a long-term, mutually productive relationship between two stable, separate entities is another.

Our relationship with non-Israeli Jewish communities abroad deserves imaginative thought; Jews in Russia, but also in Europe and Latin America, will look increasingly to American Jewry for guidance and assistance on a scale and of a nature much different from the past. The recent European interest in the American Jewish community center movement and local efforts to replicate it are indicative; and we must be prepared to take full advantage of this opportunity to forge new bonds with co-religionists abroad.

In all these concerns, whether national or international, whether on specifically Jewish or more general questions, our leadership must be bolder, more thoughtful, more willing to stand and be counted than ever before. We have passed the point where raising money for worthwhile causes is sufficient to discharge our obligations. Our leadership must be willing to ask difficult questions and to encourage informed and searching debate.

Solutions to the problems call for a lowering of hysterical voices and an increase in the level of sophistication we bring to these complex questions.

Our leadership, our spokesmen-guides, must encourage us all not to be satisfied with superficial responses, but to dig deep into the problems, to demand more of ourselves and others.

In the final analysis, it all gets back to Hillel, who laid it on the line, "If I am not for myself, who is for me? If I am only for myself, what am I? If not now, when?"

Keynote Address
1972 National Jewish Welfare Board Biennial
April 12, 1972

THE ROTHSCHILDS CELEBRATE WATERLOO

As one of a number of festive events taking place tonight in support of Jewish historical preservation, what is more appropriate than a formal dinner commemorating the most remarkable family in modern Jewish history.

This unique "mishpocha" created immense wealth and applied it to living well and to dispensing unparalleled charitable benefactions. The Rothschilds were accepted in high society, yet never forgot or failed to celebrate their Jewish origin and identification. Its members endeavored to lead lives of satisfaction for themselves and for the benefit of the society of which they were a part and the tradition from which they sprang.

We have chosen to celebrate this extraordinary family with a composite dinner acknowledging their greatest single coup, Nathan Rothschild's "scoop" on the Battle of Waterloo and the staggering windfall he scored as a result.

Beef Wellington, a dish created by the great chef Carême in honor of the battle's hero, was the logical choice for the main course; its accompanying wine has long been identified with the family.

The preceding dish, Sole Montefiore, was a family favorite named after a Rothschild family connection. Its accompanying wine is identified with Prince von Metternich, a close family friend whose political successes dominated Europe in the first half of the 19th century.

The salad and cheese, also accompanied by a Rothschild wine, are in honor of Gutele, the family matriarch; the dessert, the classic Soufflé Rothschild, is paired with a present-day Rothschild sauterne.

129

The climax of the meal, an 1815 vintage famous as 'The Waterloo Port,' is accompanied by walnuts which were a favorite of the family's founder.

Mayer Amschel Rothschild and his five dynamic sons had achieved wealth and fame long before 1815, primarily through their dealings on behalf of Prince William of Hesse, the sale of whose Hessian troops to the British in the American Revolution helped him become the richest ruler in Europe. And the Rothschilds' financial services to the British government against Napoleon gave them yet more gold, influence and power. By 1815, the yellow and blue armbands of their private couriers, their private ships and even carrier pigeons, were recognized throughout Europe.

The results of Waterloo reached Nathan Rothschild even before they reached the British government. Leaning against his favorite pillar at the London Stock Exchange, he ostentatiously sold British government securities, creating a financial panic in the belief that Napoleon had won. When prices hit bottom, only minutes before the official news arrived, Rothschild repurchased a huge quantity for a song, carrying off the financial coup of the century. We can only assume that Nathan's dinner that night was a festive one.

Carême, chef to Prince Talleyrand and later to the Rothschilds themselves, was preparing a feast in honor of Wellington when he heard that the victor of Waterloo would be delayed. The beef, already half-cooked, was hastily pulled off the fire. When the Duke finally arrived, Carême spread the partly-cooked beef with foie gras, covered it with pastry dough and popped it back into the oven, as we have done tonight.

The accompanying wine, (Chateau Mouton Rothschild 1982) is described by Robert Parker as one of the greatest wines he has ever tasted.

The first course, Sole Montefiore, is named for Sir Moses Montefiore, who, in 1812, married Judith Cohen, Nathan Rothschild's sister-in-law. Nathan so promoted the young man's career that he was able to retire in 1824 with a great fortune. Montefiore thereupon spent the rest of his life aiding Jewish causes in Palestine and throughout the world. The accompanying Schloss Johannisberg 1989 is from Prince von Metternich's own vineyards.

Tonight's salad and cheese course is named for Gutele, Mayer Amschel's wife, the mother of five remarkable sons and herself a shrewd businesswoman. When she was in her early nineties and someone wished that she would live to 100 she replied, "Why should God take me at 100 when he can have me at 94?" The 1976 Chateau Lafite Rothschild accompanying this course is described by Parker as the best Lafite of the 1970's.

Accompanying the Soufflé Rothschild is Chateau Rieussec, a sauterne vineyard acquired by the Lafite Rothschilds in 1984. Parker calls the 1988 Rieussec a "winemaking tour de force."

Our final offering, the treasure of our cellar, the Waterloo Port, speaks for itself.

With the possible exception of the Fuggers in the Middle Ages and the Medicis in the Italian Renaissance, no family in recorded history has lived with such amplitude, with such a charitable record, and with such familial loyalty and mutual support as the Rothschilds.

Professional activity, family and charity have been their common vocation for 200 years; and one could do worse! We are confident they would smile on Eldridge Street.

Dinner for the Eldridge St. Project
April 28, 1993

MESSAGE, MESSENGER, AUDIENCE

"Friends, Romans, countrymen, lend me your ears. I come to bury Caesar, not to praise him. The evil that men do lives after them. The good is oft interred with their bones. So let it be with Caesar."

That's how Shakespeare opens one of history's greatest speeches. What a beginning!

"And gentlemen in England now a-bed shall think themselves accursed they were not here, and hold their manhoods cheap whilst any speaks that fought with us upon Saint Crispin's day." That's how he ends another of the world's most memorable orations.

"I know not what course others may take, but as for me, give me liberty or give me death." Patrick Henry's ending is part of our national heritage.

That is how great speeches are constructed. A strong beginning, a convincing middle and a rousing end, delivered with conviction by a speaker with authority, whose goal is to convince an audience open to persuasion. At the moment, this seems a lost art.

The speeches at this year's Republican and Democratic National Conventions—with the exception of Bill Clinton's rousing performance and a few others—reflect what has happened to public speaking in America. Angry polemic, gracelessly expressed, delivered to already-converted partisans, is standard fare.

A nation moved by Lincoln at Gettysburg and by FDR's fireside chats, by Jack Kennedy's asking what we can do for our country and by Lyndon Johnson's proclaiming that "We Shall Overcome" deserves better.

133

Effective public speaking is not rocket science. Twenty-five hundred years ago Aristotle observed that credibility ("ethos"), logic ("logos") and emotion ("pathos") underlie all good speeches, and that vivid images and appropriate use of figures of speech will reach the hearts and minds of a targeted audience.

Few of us are called upon, like Winston Churchill in 1940, to revive the self-confidence of a nation, or like Joan of Arc, to encourage one's compatriots while being burned at the stake. We may be Father of the Bride or Maid of Honor, eulogist at a funeral, commencement speaker or recipient of an honor; the basic rules remain the same.

Suiting the talk to the occasion is common sense ("decorum" the ancients called it), but many a Best Man does not realize that the bawdy joke well-received at a Bachelor Party is in poor taste at the Wedding; or as Mitt Romney discovered, the 47% comment that went over well with 'true believers' was a disaster before a broader audience.

Good delivery—what Demosthenes called the first, second and third requirements for a great speech—has become rare in American life. Nine out of ten mumble to the front row rather than boom out to the back row. Many nervously speak quickly before an audience rather than use the slower pace that experts recommend. Good speakers employ judicious pauses for emphasis and dramatic impact, raising or lowering their voices as indicated.

Some techniques used by experts can be dangerous for amateurs. In the Carter/Reagan presidential debate, for example, when Carter leveled his fiercest attack, Reagan chuckled, threw his head back and said, "There you go again!" The audience exploded with laughter, and the election was over. An amateur should not try this.

Debates, essays and speeches are different art forms. The Mitt Romney who bored his public with his Convention acceptance speech energized them at the first Presidential debate, while the reverse was the case with President Obama. Ronald Reagan and Bill Clinton excelled at both forms, while neither could write a decent essay.

When, in the Spring of 1963, our friend Bayard Rustin invited my wife and me to have dinner with him and Martin Luther King, Jr., we had been deeply moved by reading MLK's extraordinary Letter From Birmingham Jail, one of the most powerful and eloquent missives of all time. Denied stationery in his cell, King poured out his thoughts on toilet paper and in the margins of newspapers, while Birmingham Police Chief Bull Connor (a name out of Restoration Comedy) turned fire hoses and police dogs on non- violent protesters.

King's letter was a reply to eight white clergymen who called his actions "unwise and untimely." King's evocation of St. Paul and of Socrates, Aquinas and Martin Buber— his citing Shadrach, Meshach and Abednego's refusal to obey the laws ofNebuchadnezzar—and his portrayal of the terror and despair of black children throughout the South, should be required reading in every American school.

When we gave our contribution to help plan the Washington protest later that summer, I feared that bringing together vast numbers of civil rights activists and southern police could result in a counterproductive riot. The Reverend was certain that the tone would be spiritual. His 'I Have a Dream' speech became one of our nation's greatest orations.

'I Have a Dream' has been called the most important and influential speech of the 20th century. Addressing a transfixed audience, standing resolutely, his back to the Lincoln Memorial, King began his speech with "Five score years ago, a great American, in whose symbolic shadow we stand today, signed the Emancipation Proclamation."

What a man, what a setting, what an opening!

After evoking the Declaration of Independence and the Constitution as "promissory notes," he declared that America had defaulted, the check had come back marked "insufficient funds"; and he proclaimed (like Amos in the Old Testament) that he would not be satisfied until "justice rolls down like waters and righteousness like a mighty stream." He went on to describe his dream ("deeply rooted in the American Dream"), echoing the powerful resonance of the Biblical Isaiah. He cited "My country 'tis of thee" and finished with the old

Negro spiritual refrain "Free at last! Free at last! Thank God Almighty, we are free at last!" The nation responded by supporting Lyndon Johnson's Civil Rights legislation.

In the classical world, Aeschines warned the Athenian Assembly of threats from Philip II of Macedon, and everyone commented on how eloquently Aeschines spoke. Demosthenes then rose to give his Philippic, and the Assembly shouted, "Let us march against Philip!"

Studying memorable speeches can be educational as well. The greatest secular speech of all time, Pericles' Funeral Oration as reported by Thucydides 2,600 years ago, conveys ideas we would do well to ponder today.

Think of our Millionaires' Congress: Pericles says, "Advancement in public life falls to reputation for capacity, class considerations not being allowed to interfere with merit; nor does poverty bar the way. If a man is able to serve the state, he is not hindered by the obscurity of his condition."

Consider the mega yachts of hedge funders on the political Right, as Pericles notes, "We cultivate refinement without extravagance and knowledge without effeminacy; wealth we employ more for use than for show." How many on our political Left could dispute his point that, "The real disgrace of poverty is not in owning to the fact but in declining the struggle against it."

Lou Gehrig's "Farewell to Baseball," at which I cried as a young boy, expressed a modesty, a gratitude for the good things life had given him, that is unthinkable from our gladiators of today.

Studying failures—or lost opportunities—may be even more helpful to mistake-prone amateurs. Studying great "saves" can be instructive, too. Richard Nixon's emotional "Checkers" speech, for example, effectively ended talk of the embarrassing "Nixon Scandal Fund."

The failure of Obama's advisors and "handlers" to prepare him adequately for the first debate will be notable in political history. David Axelrod, Obama's chief advisor, noted after the debate, "The president showed up with the intent of answering questions and having a discussion. Romney showed up to deliver a performance, and he delivered a very good performance." As Reagan's speech writer, Peggy Noonan, said years ago, "A speech is part theater and part political declaration".

When Axelrod was asked why Obama did not address Romney's "47 per cent" gaffe, he replied, "The president obviously didn't see the appropriate opportunity." The appropriate opportunity? Obama's opening statement could have been, "Governor Romney is concerned about some of us; I am concerned about all Americans, including the 47 per cent."

My suggestion would have been: "We have started the recovery from the disaster we inherited; with your support we will finish it."

Michelle Obama's Convention speech was widely praised, and the audience came away feeling that this good woman loved her husband. Necessary but not sufficient. I would have added to her remarks: "The man I live with may look calm, but he spends sleepless nights over our casualties in Iraq and Afghanistan, and agonizes over students who can't find jobs and unemployed workers whose insurance is running out."

Martin Luther King, Jr. wrote his own sermons and speeches. John F. Kennedy's were written by Ted Sorensen, Ronald Reagan's were by Peggy Noonan, Barack Obama's by Jon Favreau. Franklin Roosevelt corrected his own, but the first drafts were written by skilled writers like Sam Rosenman, Robert Sherwood, Archibald Macleish and others. If you get help for a major talk, or have someone prepare a draft, you are in good company. But writing your own material can not only be fun, but also educational. E.M. Forster's comment, "How do I know what I think until I hear what I say?" expresses it clearly.

Plunge in and write your own; but remember Aristotle's "ethos," "logos" and "pathos"; Cicero's "decorum"; Demosthenes' "delivery"; and the one attribute of all great speeches—say something worth saying!

Burstyn Memorial Lecture
Hunter College
October 15, 2012

DATA/KNOWLEDGE/WISDOM

What can an experienced practitioner say that would be useful to graduate students entering the field of real estate?

The platitudes of the textbooks are valid—that's why they are platitudes—but financial turmoil has changed the business landscape enough to require new perspectives. The day of one, two or even three employers over a career is ancient history.

Until World War II, the joke ran that when the president of the Pennsylvania Railroad retired, they hired a new office boy; and everyone else moved up one step on the corporate ladder.

Today, some of you will move from real estate to corporate life to finance to entrepreneurship to consulting to government to heaven knows what.

You are likely to have many employers and your knowledge and skills must be as portable as your pension benefits or health care provisions.

The half-life of the techniques and practices you learn in your formal education grows ever shorter; and your practical education (flowing from experience) must prepare you for challenges not yet on the horizon. It should be taken for granted that all students can read with understanding, write clearly, think critically and analytically, and speak effectively on their feet or in conference. But they should also question, question, question.

When the Greek philosopher Heraclitus observed that you cannot step into the same river twice, he meant that you keep changing and the river keeps changing. Add what economists call "exogenous factors" (say, an earthquake changing the course of a river) and you get an idea of what you may face over your professional career.

Let's start with "you," proceed to the "river" and finish with the "earthquake."

Before grappling with answers, start with the right questions: what kind of person do you want to be, what kind of life do you want to lead, how do you want your spouse and your children and your neighbors to think of you, and what kind of obituary would you like to have? Are you the kind of person you admire and respect?

Recent polls show that 75% of U.S college seniors have as their life goals a) making a lot of money, and b) becoming widely known.

Angelo Mozillo, the disgraced former CEO of Countrywide Financial (the nation's largest originator of sub-prime mortgages) is more widely known today than he or his family would like; but as Countrywide went down in flames, Mozillo walked away with nearly $200 million. Some of you might be content with that Faustian pact while others would not.

Ken Lewis left a troubled Bank of America with nearly $100 million, as did Kerry Killinger leaving desperate Washington Mutual; Stanley O'Neal left Merrill Lynch with a "golden parachute" worth a reported $250 million. Even the heads of Fannie Mae and Freddie Mac walked away from their respective wreckages as multi-millionaires. If any of the aforementioned has offered to give anything back, I have yet to hear of it.

These men made a lot of money; they are widely-known; but what do they see when they look in the mirror?

Michael Lewis' excellent book *The Big Short* (which should be required reading at all business schools) describes in detail how John Paulson made $6 billion, at a time when three million U.S. households are expected to be foreclosed in 2010, up from 2.8 million in 2009.

Current hearings indicate that the packagers, sellers and "shorters" of the credit default swaps and collateralized debt obligations knew exactly what they were selling and what they were "shorting." Daniel Patrick Moynihan's 1993 essay Defining Deviancy Down describes the moral climate in which this took place, where the Goldman Sachs defense was essentially that "everybody does it." The phrase "the banality of evil" comes to mind. These are not new problems— Trollope described them in England, Balzac in France.

In a system that rewards transactions, but rejects responsibility for its consequences, a system that rewards the "ups" but does not penalize the "downs," is it surprising that gross distortions occur?

Top lawyers today are often regarded as clever "hired guns" for amoral clients, and top accounting firms are often seen as "shills" for obvious malefactors. Professor William Simon of Columbia Law School has drawn a scathing picture of the shenanigans of his legal colleagues in The Market for Bad Legal Advice. The rating agencies— Moody's, Fitch, Standard and Poor's— that gave AAA ratings to toxic securities issued by their clients, have all but escaped notice. The ancient Romans said "caveat emptor"— let the buyer beware— but we should have progressed beyond that.

All persons entering the business world should ask how they would have reacted in these situations. On a more modest level, each must ask whether lying on a resume to get a job or to help your company once you have one is acceptable. Some people believe that MBA has come to stand for "Me Before Anyone"; others hold themselves to a higher standard. They want to learn—not the tricks of the trade—but the trade itself.

In one's professional life as in one's personal life, I suggest that to be trusted, you must be trustworthy, to be relied upon, you must be reliable. The values you learned as a child are clear. You must determine when, where and how they are to be applied. Each of us is responsible for his own actions. Learning how to say "no" with tact; knowing in advance what can and what cannot be compromised; understanding that when in doubt, we should ask, discuss, ponder—are the positions of wise and honorable people.

Abraham Lincoln once reluctantly agreed to give a private interview to a sleazy fellow who was an important contributor to his political party. Lincoln talked of the war, but the man asked for confidential information on Army contracts, for which he was prepared to pay a large sum. Lincoln kept talking, and the man kept increasing his offer, until Lincoln said, "Sir, I must ask you to leave because you are getting too near my price." A wise man, and a good man.

Lincoln and Mozillo each, in Thoreau's phrase, marched to the beat "of a different drummer." To what beat will you choose to march?

Now let's turn to the "river" into which you will be stepping, because the business world will keep changing throughout your professional life.

"High tech," a phrase to older people, must become an obsession with younger people. The rate of change in communication and computation is such that "looking around you" is not enough; you must learn to "look ahead."

Multi-disciplinary activities will be an increasing fact of life; it will not be enough to master one field. Anyone hoping to rise professionally must become a generalist as well as a specialist. No "royal road," no single approach, no list of books to read will suffice. Each must meet the challenge personally, but it must be met. One book everyone should read, however, is the classic on negotiation, *Getting to Yes*, especially the important chapter entitled What if They Use Dirty Tricks.

Yes, the river will keep changing; but with a well-deserved reputation for character and competence—doing the right thing and doing it well—your head will stay above water.

The third factor—the "earthquake"—is one of which each of us must be aware. The likelihood of future major economic turmoil— more serious than that of 2008-2010— is greater than conventional wisdom acknowledges.

For the past forty years, the U.S. debt-to-GDP ratio has averaged around 40 per cent. This year it will exceed 60 per cent, and by the end of the decade it is projected to be 90 per cent, approaching our record of 110 per cent after World War II. The ramifications are (or should be) frightening, considering a day when potential lenders either balk at buying our bonds or charge excessive rates of interest to do so. Some observers, like the International Monetary Fund, point this out, but few people seem to be listening.

A crisis is lurking in the woods, and the various scenarios will be played out in your lifetimes, if not in mine. Never forget that in the story of the boy who cried wolf, the wolf eventually came!

We have seen how the Japanese economy paid a severe price for failure to face their banking problems; and we have seen how Greece suffers from its failure to acknowledge unsustainable deficits.

Given a U.S. Congress in which one political party resists any increase in taxes and the other resists any decrease in expenditures; and given the power of banking lobbyists to stifle meaningful financial reform, economic pain appears to lie ahead.

Our situation recalls the 19th century British schoolmaster who wrote to a duchess, requesting permission to cane her incorrigible son. The duchess replied, "Reginald is a very sensitive child. If you beat the boy in the next seat, Reginald will get the message." Unlike Reginald, our Congress does not seem to be "getting the message" of Japan or Greece.

Can we change quickly enough to avert impending difficulties? Unlikely, in the short run.

The recent U.S. Supreme Court decision on campaign financing and free speech has opened a Pandora's Box. The embarrassing correlation between trial lawyers' political contributions and Congress' failure to include in the Health Care Bill provisions on medical malpractice suits hints at what's in store. The "nine old men and women" seem to have forgotten that the Lord's Prayer does not say, "Let me be good." It says "Lead me not into temptation," and our cash-strapped campaigning legislators may not have the character to resist the blandishments of lobbyists.

We may soon need a new Paul Revere to shout "Our creditors are coming, our creditors are coming!"

Given the changing "river" and the possibility of "earthquake," how should one react? At the end of his life, Charles Darwin took issue with the phrase "survival of the fittest," and preferred the phrase "survival of the most adaptable." Adaptability may be your most useful attribute.

Smothered by data, our challenge is to organize that data into usable knowledge, and hope that our knowledge is transmogrified into wisdom. Wisdom is the ability to make proper choices and to anticipate their consequences.

If I could wish anything for you, it would be that you achieve the wisdom you need to help you make wise choices throughout your careers.

NYU Schack Institute of Real Estate
April 22, 2010

PAT MOYNIHAN, WHERE ARE YOU WHEN WE REALLY NEED YOU?

Daniel Patrick Moynihan, whose ideas and career we celebrate tonight, was a brilliant, erudite and complex thinker whose lessons we would do well to remember.

In an age of widespread 'tunnel vision,' he brought to his deliberations the knowledge of institutions of a political scientist, the understanding of cultures of a sociologist, the time sense and perspective of a historian, the appreciation of data and numbers of an economist, the love of teaching of a professor, the values of a philosopher and the hard-nosed appraisal of realistic possibilities of a vote-counting politician.

Moynihan viewed cities through the lens of a master urban planner, and transportation as a regional planner, studied architecture with the eye of an aesthete and historian, and approached the subject of traffic deaths as an epidemiologist.

A true polymath, Moynihan could have echoed the great Max Weber's irritable reply to a questioner, "What am I, a cow, that I must have 'a field'?"

As a shrewd observer of government, he understood the destructive potential of misused 'secrecy'; and he understood that the U.S. military build-up of the 1980's was as much designed to starve our other government expenditures as it was to frighten the Russians.

Pat felt deeply the crucial importance of a stable family, since he himself had been a middle class child fallen on hard times because of a deserting father. He never forgot the role government scholarships played in his own undergraduate and graduate degrees and foreign study.

As a wit, a coiner of the apt phrase ("defining deviancy down" among the best) and a true son of Blarney Castle, he delighted academic and political audiences.

Above all, as a Roman Catholic and FDR New Deal style Democrat and proud member of an ethnic minority, he never forgot who he was or what he stood for. That, simply stated, was an incorruptible devotion to the common good.

The Moynihan prescience was legendary; some have called it his ability to 'see around corners.' After the collapse of the Soviet Union, for example, Henry Kissinger sent him the brief note, "Dear Pat, Your crystal ball was better than mine." And his ability to spot promising young people and to advance their public careers was remarkable.

Our cars now have seat belts and padded dashboards because of him, and Washington's Pennsylvania Avenue is now a source of national pride rather than embarrassment, because of him. With 72% of American black babies born this year to unmarried mothers and with an increasing number of white babies being born to unmarried mothers, Pat's 1965 study, "The Negro Family: The Case For National Action," is at last being recognized for its inspired insights.

Pat was profoundly hurt by his professional colleagues' failure to support him on the Moynihan Report. He understood the ancient Greek word "parrhesia" as "speaking the truth even at great personal risk"; but he frankly never anticipated the public firestorm or lack of professional support. Pat being Pat, he probably reflected on a similar lack of support for Giordano Bruno as he was being burned at the stake, or of Galileo when he was forced to retract.

As U.S. ambassador to the United Nations, he fervently defended American values, with the U.S. often "in opposition." He vigorously and eloquently attacked the concept of "Zionism is racism," to the dismay of old State Department hands who felt he was always 'rocking the boat.'

146

A lover of the appropriate quotation, Pat would probably have described our current Congressional performance on the economy in William Butler Yeats' lines, "The best lack all conviction, while the worst are full of passionate intensity."

When I first visited Pat's study in the schoolhouse in Pindars Corners, I thought of Michel de Montaigne in his tower study; when I looked out the window of the Moynihans' Washington apartment, I recalled the shabby souvenir shops and fast food stands B.M. (before Moynihan). When I taste curry, I think of the memorable party Liz and Pat threw in India to celebrate the 500th birthday of the Mughal emperor Babur (whose garden Liz discovered). When I pass Pat's favorite corner luncheon table at the Century Association, I recall his almost apoplectic anger one day at the just-released health care bill that Ira Magaziner had prepared in secret hearings for Hillary Clinton. Over 1000 pages long and fearfully complex, its provisions would devastate New York's great teaching hospitals, Pat raged. He felt the bill was doomed to failure, and he bemoaned the fact that an important opportunity would be lost.

The fundamental importance of education was a major Moynihan belief, and he studied the subject carefully. James Coleman's 1966 landmark report, Equality of Educational Opportunity, blazed fresh trails; its impact stayed with Pat permanently. Coleman's thesis, backed up by massive statistical analysis, demonstrated that money was but one of many complex factors influencing education.

Pat remained skeptical of glib theories unsupported by detailed research; he would have cheered Diane Ravitch's courageous change of positions when research demonstrated that the excessive emphasis on charter schools and the simplistic reliance on standardized test scores advocated by the No Child Left Behind program (and previously supported by Ravitch) had become counter- productive.

Honest and dispassionate analysis of appropriate data should be the bedrock of the social sciences, Moynihan felt; he would have been proud to see this year's Daniel Patrick Moynihan Award go to Diane Ravitch.

Our society, that values vitamin pills over the full, well- balanced meal, keeps looking for an educational equivalent— some cheap, instantly-effective elixir that will transform dysfunctional children into Nobel Prize winners. We haven't found one yet.

We refuse to acknowledge what a fiercely complex subject education is, how many factors are involved and how little we really know about them.

In 1967, for the Carnegie Foundation, Diane studied the fiasco of the Ford Foundation's intervention in the Ocean Hill/Brownsville controversy. This resulted in her classic 1974 volume The Great School Wars. She later studied the history of educational fads and enthusiasms across the 20th century. The dozen books she has written (and others she edited), her term as Assistant Secretary of Education, and her countless papers, conference appearances and blogs have stimulated thinking throughout the field. Her research is rigorous, in keeping with the Moynihan Dictum, "Everyone is entitled to his own opinion, but not his own facts."

I am certain that Pat would have been delighted to award this year's Moynihan prize personally to Diane Ravitch.

American Academy of Political And Social Science
June 2, 2011

FIGHTING ALLIGATORS

VS. DRAINING THE SWAMP

The American philanthropic enterprise began as "charity," aid to the destitute, the handicapped, the orphan. It evolved into "philanthropy," support for a broad array of non-profit institutions and services and into research into "root causes" of varied social problems.

Today, and in the years ahead, the challenges of a complex world require more complex and sophisticated responses— locally, nationally and internationally.

Among the unsolved problems I present for your consideration is a new one, one that must be addressed by America's "third sector," the conscience of our society.

We are engaged in a war of ideas, in a battle for world opinion— not in a clash of civilizations, not in a conflict of medieval theologies, not in a war of economic imperialism, but in a contest between totalitarianism and the liberal democratic values of free thought and expression, secularism, tolerance and critical inquiry.

It is a war we are in danger of losing. Unlike battles of military hardware, in which America is pre-eminent, the battle for hearts and minds requires a degree of wisdom, conviction and sophisticatio beyond what our national leaders seem able to muster. "Realist" weapon systems are important, but "idealist" philosophic underpinning may be more important.

While our government focuses on the short-term goal of combat-

149

ing terrorism, or "fighting alligators," the philanthropic sector should focus on the long-term goal of "draining the swamp," or helping dysfunctional, hostile societies evolve into peaceful, economically successful and cooperative members of the world community—for their benefit and for ours.

At the moment, prospects seem dim; but the dramatic turnaround of China after Mao, of Eastern Europe and/or Russia after the end of the Cold War, of the so-called Asian Tigers in recent decades, have involved cultural change of similar magnitude. Today, with the Middle East in flux, advances in electronic communication—in news media, computers and the Internet—mean that governments no longer have a monopoly on communication.

At a moment in history when fanaticism and destructive technology are converging, as 9/11 demonstrated so tragically, thoughtful people should approach the challenge of international and cross-cultural dialogue with a sense of urgency.

Feelings of national grievance and resentment against Americans throughout the world, justified or not, have an explosive potential that must be faced, analyzed, and, where possible, defused. Societies that feel defensive, humiliated and beleaguered must be reassured.

An American public, encouraged by its geography, history and favorable economic situation to regard the rest of the world as customers or suppliers, must learn that our future, our physical well-being, and even the existence of our major cities, are not so assured as we believed, and that political ferment elsewhere is our problem, too.

The world's poor and disenfranchised—not only in the Middle East, but in Latin America, Africa and Asia—question what place the modern world holds for them. They wonder if economic well-being, dignity, a sense of identity, personal freedom and a better future for their children are possible for them. We must reassure them that liberal democracy is the best way to achieve their goals.

In the Arab world where 280 million people are mired in a web of social, economic and political problems complicated by, but not caused by, theological questions, America has important self-interest

150

in helping this significant faction of mankind emerge from chaos and enter the 21st century.

The 1.2 billion people of the Muslim world include those in Turkey, Indonesia and Malaysia; these are countries which are politically mature and advancing economically and at the moment seem to pose little threat to the world, although the al-Qaeda network in those countries is active and expanding, and we can count the growing number of its victims.

The Arab world is a different story, and it is an immediate and present danger to others.

Significant change there can come only from within; the role of "outside" entities should be limited to support and encouragement; change must take place gradually, in ways sensitive to culture and tradition. The role of the West in general and of America in particular can be positive in what we do and don't do. Helping to bring the Arab world peacefully into the world community should be on the agenda of American educational institutions, foundations and philanthropic donors.

Two important United Nations-sponsored documents present the problem clearly: the Arab Human Development Reports of 2002 and 2003. These reports, hailed by Time Magazine as "the most important publications of the year," were prepared by a panel of distinguished Arab experts. They spell out in detail why the Arab world has fallen so far behind, and why its alienated, frustrated and enraged young people, unvoiced and powerless, are lashing out destructively.

The prime cause, according to these reports, is the "freedom deficit"; the region is the world's least free, and has the lowest level of public participation in government.

The second cause is the dismal state of education and diffusion of knowledge in the Arab world.

The third is the exclusion of women from meaningful participation in Arab society.

And the fourth is the isolation of the Arab world from the international trading community.

The ramifications are heartbreaking, and are reflected throughout the Reports by citations showing, for example, that while Muslims constitute some 20% of the world's population, they produce fewer than 1% of the world's scientists, or publish in Arabic few non-religious books each year. Only 1.6% of the Arab population has Internet access, compared with 68% in the U.K. and 79% in the U.S.

These underlying factors create an atmosphere in which fervent religious fundamentalism, paranoid conspiratorial theories and a desire for violence are manifest. The best discussion of this is still Eric Hoffer's classic, *The True Believer.*

Addressing these problems in the Muslim world in general and in the Arab world in particular is a pressing concern for us all. We must help America and the West to a fuller and sounder knowledge of all aspects of the Muslim world, not praising or condemning, but understanding. Ambrose Bierce's century-old comment that, "War is God's way of teaching Americans geography" is timely.

We should help American Muslims demonstrate to the world how one can live a valid Islamic life without conflict within a larger democratic society.

Since the Arab-American Muslim community is influenced by Saudi Arabian money, and extremist elements are visible and vocal, those Muslims who reject extremism and desire peaceful integration with American society need support from the wider community.

Edward Gibbon pointed out that in ancient Rome, the public thought all religions were equally true, the philosophers found them equally false, and the administrators found them equally useful. Perhaps all three groups were right.

To increase Arab exposure to the best the West has to offer we must strengthen and improve institutions like the American-sponsored universities in Beirut and Cairo. We must help to create or expand institutions like the United World Colleges, headed by Queen Noor and Nelson Mandela. We should make imaginative use of emerging
information technologies to help the Muslim world modernize with-

out becoming westernized. And we should encourage and support those who embrace non-violent accommodation with modernity. These people must be found— in the present oppressive climate they are unlikely to come forward.

American philanthropy can play a constructive role in strengthening those institutions, groups and individuals working to reconstruct the Muslim world. It can help them reconnect with the positive aspects of a distant past such as the Golden Age of the Abbassid caliphate, when Muslim scientists, philosophers, artists and educators sparkled in one of the great cultural flowerings of all time. For five glowing centuries, until it was destroyed by the Mongol hordes of Genghis Kahn, a society stemming from the teachings of the Prophet of Mecca and Medina rivaled the greatest civilizations of mankind.

Then, Muslims remembered that the Prophet said, "The ink of scientists is equal to the blood of martyrs"; then, Muslim thinkers were proud of their familiarity with the best of the world's cultures; then, it was taken for granted that science and knowledge belonged to all mankind and that intellectuals' borrowing and lending benefited everyone. What the Muslim world had once, it can have again.

Today, the suicide bomber is mistakenly viewed by the world as the quintessential Muslim. We forget how recent a development violence is in the Arab world. When people note that nearly a million Jews left or were expelled from Arab countries after the creation of Israel in 1948, they forget that those Jews lived peacefully in those Arab countries for centuries. Before WWII, one-third of Baghdad's population was Jewish.

The current espousal of violence and killing of innocents by militant fundamentalists may end in time, as it will with the Chechnyans in Russia, the Tamil in Sri Lanka, the Basques in Spain and the IRA in Ireland; but the greatest disservice Muslim totalitarians have performed for the Islamic world has been to disdain education and substitute religious indoctrination and rote memorization of a few Koranic texts.

Financed by Saudi oil revenues in the belief that backing the Wahhabi mullahs will ward off political upheaval, or by Libyan money, the madrassas preach hatred. No math, no science, no foreign languages or literature are included in curricula heavy with diatribes against everything foreign.

Edward Said, a sympathetic Arab intellectual, wrote, "We need a qualitatively different knowledge based on understanding rather than on authority, uncritical repetition and mechanical reproduction."

But if Saudi or Libyan funds can be influential, so can American charitable funds—to different ends.

To the extent that education that stimulates curiosity and critical thinking as well as imparting knowledge—can be brought to the Muslim masses, a positive impact is possible.

Primary and secondary education are local concerns, but proper training of teachers and the provision of appropriate secular educational materials can be provided on a larger scale.

Today, we forget what the Jesuits have always understood: the importance of inculcation of values in early childhood.

That some al-Qaeda bombers have American college degrees is not a reflection of faulty university training, but of poor moral training as children; and that must be remedied.

The cost will be great, but the rewards will be immense.

Helping the Muslim world to rediscover a "usable past"—a creative constructive past—and helping it reject simplistic fanatics are tasks to engage the best thinking and resources of the American philanthropic sector.

Throughout the Muslim world there are thoughtful individuals who wish to modernize but not westernize Islam; they deserve support in their struggle against those who would return Islam to the Bedouin culture of the seventh century, but this time with weapons of mass destruction.

Throughout the world, battles rage over how to protect a society's traditional culture from the homogenization that globalization brings. Mass production of clothing and mass communication of styles have caused teenagers everywhere to dress alike, but their parents resent it when they think alike. We should make clear that modernization does not necessarily mean Westoxification.

American popular culture attracts the foreign young, but repels the old who see it as violent, materialistic and sex-drenched, promoting a value system they deplore. The older generation also fears that modernization mandates a humiliating loss of national identity.

Maintaining national dignity and personal self-respect while modernizing is important in successful adaptation; Americans do not realize how diminishing it is when English displaces the local language, the Beatles displace national folk songs, and teenagers regard their elders as unaware.

A creative tension between modernism and traditionalism—along the lines of Japan's Meiji Restoration in 1868 but without the militarism— can produce a culture that will reflect the best of the old and the best of the new.

Some aspects of modernization—equal participation of women in all aspects of society, and civil rights in its fullest form, i.e. free speech, political rights, free press, etc.—need to be presented not as yielding to "western" influences, but as joining the world's advanced societies.

These are not theological questions but political ones, and they deserve 21st century answers.

The best argument liberals can present is that social justice, social peace, material well-being and children leading fulfilling lives are more likely to be achieved in a modern, tolerant, well-educated society where free choice permits each to select the life he or she wishes to lead.

Helping Arab women educate and liberate themselves is an important way the West can bring light and air to the Arab world. Awarding a Nobel Prize to Shirin Ebadi, a leading Iranian civil rights activist, and giving the prestigious Civil Courage prize to Shahnaz Bukhari, a Pakistani, for her work on behalf of victimized women, send important signals; and they do have an impact.

This month, for example, Morocco substantially liberalized its divorce laws, and Saudi Arabia, which does not permit women to drive a car, recently appointed a woman as Dean of a Saudi university. The winds of change are blowing.

To the extent that many in the Muslim world can envision a future of legitimate aspirations met and positive expectations realized, there is a chance of constructive change.

Many in the West do not realize that there is no single accepted Islamic theology, no one accepted interpretation of Islamic law, no central Islamic authority. There will always be fringe groups who despise us. But just as the majority of the Muslim world today is energized by hate and resentment, so it can, in time, with resources and well- directed effort be galvanized by hope.

We forget how quickly Afghans turned their backs on the Taliban when they were liberated in 2001. The current ferment in Iran reflects growing discontent with the mullahs' mismanagement of the economy; reformist sentiment can be revived and Iran may, over time, evolve into a Muslim society with a secular democracy.

In Saudi Arabia, overwhelmed with fundamentalist Wahhabis, the problems are political, religious and educational; if secular education for the young could be introduced, political and religious change might follow.

With effective political institutions in place and a growing entrepreneurial middle class able to participate in a global market economy, Islamist fundamentalists could function in a liberal society as the Amish do in America or Ultra-Orthodox Jews throughout the world.

What should be the role of American philanthropy in a changing world? Your imagination can be your guide, but recognize that efforts are being made to open these closed societies, to stimulate the free flow of ideas and to create the necessary preconditions for democratic societies.

The Carnegie Corporation, under the leadership of Vartan Gregorian, the Rockefeller Brothers Fund, led by Stephen Heintz, and the MacArthur Foundation, headed by Jonathan Fanton, have begun major efforts to reach out to the American Muslim community and to stimulate dialogue between western thinkers and Muslim intellectuals, academics and professionals in the Middle East.

The EastWest Institute, led by John Mroz, is establishing training centers in Turkey where young academics, journalists, and government administrators in the Muslim communities of the former Soviet Union in Central Asia are exposed to western thinking and managerial techniques.

At the Brookings Institution, the Saban Center's papers and conferences on U.S. relations with the Islamic world are invaluable tools. The Pew Foundation's sponsorship of public opinion polls and the Mott Foundation's varied efforts are important.

Private donors or smaller foundations seeking a worthwhile American vehicle for intervention might consider the Abraham Fund, which brings together Arabs and Jews in Israel; the Boston-based International Institute for Mediation and Historical Conciliation, which performs imaginative and constructive work in many nations; and the Sabre Foundation, also in Boston, which distributes thousands of books to the Third World, and is expanding its donations in Arab countries.

Turkey, a successful secular Muslim state under siege by al-Qaeda, may be a key demonstration project from which others can learn; but "the Turkish model" is not yet a template for replication. The late Tip O'Neill's observation that "all politics is local," applies to the Middle East as well.

Helping the new Muslim "Justice and Development Party's" government in Turkey to demonstrate a liberal balance between secularism, Muslim tradition and democracy; helping it strengthen its parliamentary, legal and educational systems; helping it deal sensitively with questions like Kurdish cultural rights and a well-functioning civil society—will serve as a constructive influence throughout the Arab world.

Academic exchange programs and visiting professorships; use of advanced information technology for educational purposes, such as creating an Arabic version of Sesame Street; the opening of libraries and reading rooms, computer centers and even children's science museums; translation into Arabic and wide dissemination of western documents and texts including the best western textbooks in the humanities and the social sciences are needed.

If the 5,000 princes of Arabia's ruling House of Saud realize that at Runnymede, England's seminal Magna Carta was given not to the common people but to the nobles, who knows what may follow?

If a young Syrian or Libyan reads Thoreau's essay On Civil Disobedience, who knows if its impact will be like that the same essay had on the young Mohandas K. Gandhi, who, in turn, influenced Martin Luther King, Jr.?

A young Tunisian reading Montesquieu or James Madison on governmental separation of powers may be stirred to thought and then to action.

In the Arab world the creation of business schools that inculcate the free flow of ideas, capital and people would be an effective vehicle to spread the message.

Today, virtually all Arab companies are individually or family-owned. Venture capital, perpetuation, limited liability, increased liquidity, risk management, greater exposure, transparency and other benefits from corporate structure are absent. The introduction of public ownership of commercial, industrial and financial entities could transform the region.

The cumulative impact would be formidable.

These "seeding" efforts fall on fertile soil, as reflected in the 350 people arrested recently for participating in Saudi Arabia's first known political demonstrations. Stimulated by a London-based group of Saudis called the Movement for Islamic Reform in Arabia that reaches a growing Saudi audience through the Internet and radio broadcasts, this event may foreshadow what is to come.

Well-intentioned calls for "Marshall Plan" economic thinking in the Arab world ignore the fact that such efforts can succeed only if introduced into societies psychologically prepared to benefit from them. In developing the pre-conditions for progress, American philanthropy can play an important role. Mistakes will be made, and some well-intentioned efforts may prove counter-productive but we must try.

The State Department uses the term "clientitis" to refer to diplomats sent abroad who come to see the world through foreign eyes; that can happen with philanthropic groups, too. Some of the most virulent participants at the recent U.N. Conference in Durban (from which Colin Powell withdrew the U.S. delegation) were heavily financed by U.S. charities.

It is dismaying to see American charitable funds unwittingly underwriting hate speech, disruption and even violence. Responsible donors should know where their funds are going.

We will know we have succeeded when the Arab world boasts of its human capital stemming from education rather than its financial capital stemming from oil revenues, or when a future Prime Minister of Malaysia points with pride to the Muslim Albert Einstein, Sigmund Freud or Jonas Salk.

Today, Finland, with a population of 5.5 million, produces more than all the Arab nations combined. Tomorrow could be a different story.

The French statesman George Clemenceau stated an important truth when he declared that, "War is too important to be left to the generals." By extension, education cannot be left to the educators, health to the doctors, and so forth. The philosophic defense of our society cannot be left to our government leaders who have failed to speak effectively to our friends, let alone our enemies.

Franklin D. Roosevelt in WWII, Woodrow Wilson in WWI, Abraham Lincoln in the Civil War, and Thomas Jefferson at our nation's birth had "a decent respect for the opinion of mankind"; each stated the philosophic case for our cause, and acted on it.

Our government has recently started to "talk, talk, talk" about democratic values, but it has yet to "walk, walk, walk" in the Middle East; and shows no sign of doing so.

Dealing with the short-term threat of terrorist attack is a challenge for governments. Meeting the longer-term challenge may rest on the shoulders of civilians and particularly on the philanthropic world.

We must give the people of the Arab world alternatives to autocratic rule and militant radicalism, changing hearts and minds and creating the pre-conditions for liberal, democratic, secular societies. Societies based on the rule of law and respect for human rights, on the accountability of government officials, on a vibrant civil society, on government transparency to prevent corruption.

We must convey the vision of a peaceful, cooperative, mutually helpful world in which all can play a productive role.

Let us hope that the American non-profit world will rise successfully to that challenge.

Philanthropy Day 2003
Association of Fundraising Professionals
November 21, 2003

JUDAISM - A PERSONAL VIEW

In our age of confidence in the literal, the quantifiable and the scientific, and skepticism about the intuitive, the moral and the spiritual, religion has a difficult time defending its case. Within the broad spectrum of approaches to Judaism today, however, I believe that a thinking person in the 21st century can find a comfortable home. As one at the liberal end of the Reform Jewish scale, I hope to demonstrate why.

Even the least sentimental and imaginative individuals find a need for form and structure in their lives, for goals toward which they can aim, for standards by which they can measure their progress. Many wrestle with questions about the meaning and purpose of life; at the end of the day, they seek a philosophic underpinning for their actions more satisfying than nihilism, the cult of nothingness.

They respond to the aesthetic and emotional impact of ritual and incantation at life's important junctures — birth, death, marriage; and they take satisfaction and comfort in identification with something larger and more significant than self-serving activities. Awed by the Parthenon, Chartres Cathedral, or the Kamakura Buddha, dazzled by Bach's B Minor Mass or Handel's Messiah, they recognize the impact of religious inspiration. God's finger approaching Adam's on the Sistine Chapel ceiling moves everyone.

Yes, superstition, wishful thinking, and traditional practices whose origins are long forgotten are part of all religions. Thoughtful adherents of all faiths select those which they accept, reject, or choose to ignore.

Most who identify themselves as religious believe in some form of Divine Revelation, with varying degrees of personal mystical experience. Others, like the Deists, believe that spirituality and reverence do not necessarily require the existence of a personal God.

Between fundamentalists who feel they know what the Creator said to whom, where, and when, and those who ponder the Unmoved Mover or Uncaused Cause that preceded the universe's Big Bang, there is a broad range.

For those who consider themselves Jews, a particular cluster of attitudes and mindsets, a body of customs and traditions and a characteristic way of looking at life have been a source of philosophic and emotional support over the ages; as an individual, I feel comfortable with that identification.

Theoretically, each of us is born with a clean slate and consciously chooses a religious orientation. In practice, Baptists are the children of Baptists, Buddhists are the children of Buddhists, and Jews say that birth automatically enrolls one in their faith.

By the act of Bat or Bar Mitzvah, however, a youngster on the brink of maturity consciously stands before family and friends and announces a personal desire to become a member of the congregation.

In my case, a liberal Reform rabbi presented a concept of Judaism as a compelling moral and ethical code conveyed by eloquent allegories and metaphors, by beautiful and moving ceremonies, and by life-enhancing practices consistent with human reason. What was communicated to me was the vision of a well-lived life, and I accepted that view without reservation.

In a post-Enlightenment world, however, we should try to understand the "why," as well as the "what," of our beliefs and by reason or rationalization, that effort should be rewarding.

Many religions focus on life after death; liberal Judaism concerns itself with life before death. A sense of "here-ness" and "now-ness" and "ought-to-ness" pervades Jewish thinking. The sage Hillel expressed it in his questions, "If I am not for myself, who is for me? If I am only for myself, what am I?

If not now, when?"

162

Some religions see salvation granted to those with 'appropriate' religious faith or those blessed by God-given grace; liberal Judaism emphasizes acts over beliefs. You are what you do; and Jews believe unequivocally in "free will," which permits you to be precisely the kind of person you wish to be.

Some religions feel that salvation is possible only for their believers; Judaism believes that anyone — regardless of religious belief — who lives morally will "share in the world to come." Judaism has no equivalent of "extra Ecclesiam nulla salus" (outside the Church there is no Salvation) and no predestined "saved" or "damned." There is no Jewish equivalent of Jonathan Edwards' sermon, "Sinners In the Hands of an Angry God."

"Who shall ascend the mountain of the Lord and who shall stand in His holy place?" asks the Book of Psalms. "He that hath clean hands and a pure heart, and hath not sworn deceitfully." In another formulation, the prophet Micah asks, "What doth the Lord require of thee?" and the answer echoes over the millennia, "To do justice, love mercy and walk humbly with thy God."

Other religions believe that God created a world to which we must adjust; Judaism believes that God created the world but deliberately did not finish it so that mankind could help Him finish it. Tikun Olam — "repairing the world" — is a responsibility for each of us. Some interpret this as a call to improve the lot of all mankind, some, as a challenge to be the best individual one can. ("The nightingale sings to the world; the skylark sings to her nest. Who is there among us who can say which song is best?")

Many religions have multiple dogmas and mandatory core beliefs; liberal Judaism gives individuals leeway on most issues, except for the general acceptance of our relationship to God. As Hillel said, "Do not do unto others what you do not wish them to do unto you. That is the Law; the rest is commentary. Go now and study!"

Most other religions proselytize, but Judaism has not been a missionary faith for over fifteen hundred years and the Orthodox even try to dissuade conversion. Jews feel, however, that they have been given a universal message to convey to the world, and that while "it is not for you to complete the task, neither are you free to stand aside from it."

Some religions are xenophobic, hostile or suspicious of strangers. The Hebrew Testament, on the contrary, has 36 separate references to "love the stranger, for you were strangers in Egypt." And when the patriarch Abraham welcomed strangers, he discovered they were angels in disguise.

The sanctity of human life, fundamental to Jewish thought, is expressed in the ceremonial toast "l'chaim" ("to life"), and in the belief that "saving one life is like saving the whole world." Al Qaeda, Hamas and Hezbollah spokesmen claim that they will win because, "You love life, while we are unafraid of death." We must hope that they are wrong.

Judaism's pragmatic approach to philanthropy is reflected in the "tzedakah" ("righteousness" or "justice") of the Old Testament rather than the "caritas" ("love") of the New Testament. Jews are called upon to do the right thing to their fellow man, whether they love him (or even like him) or not. According to Maimonides, Judaism's greatest philosopher, the highest form of charity is to help someone earn a living so as not to require further help and to maintain self-respect and independence.

Study and learning are lifelong Jewish moral imperatives; the synagogue, however modest, is a place of study and prayer. The rabbi is not an intermediary between God and the communicant, but a teacher and scholar; both teacher and student are continually learning. Continuing involvement with the community is another moral imperative; and, yes, you are your brother's keeper.

Home and child-focused family are the settings for most Jewish religious observance, particularly the Sabbath with its expressions of gratitude for what we have received. Life is a joyful experience, appropriate sex is holy (not only for procreation but also to cement the relationship between husband and wife). Jews are admonished that in the afterlife they will be held accountable for every legitimate pleasure and delight

164

that God put on earth of which they did not take advantage.

Asceticism and self-denial have little place in Jewish spirituality; community is built upon the willingness to let the "I" be shaped by the "we"; education is seen as a conversation between the generations. Jews traditionally see themselves as heirs of those who came before and guardians of those who come after, with that attitude reflected in the story of the old man planting a sapling by the roadside with the comment, "I plant for my children as my father planted for me."

Yiddish, the colloquial mixture of German and Hebrew that served as the common tongue of Eastern European Jews, gives insights into the character of its speakers. For example, just as "fair play" exists only in English, "joie de vivre" only in French and "schadenfreude" only in German, so the phrase "schepping nachas" (delighting in the success of others) reflects Jewish values.

In addition to the Torah, which Ultra-Orthodox Jews consider the literal word of God, the Talmud—clearly the work of man— plays an important role in the codification of Jewish practice. With its commentaries (and commentaries on commentaries), the Talmud is Judaism's effort to interpret and make accessible the sometimes opaque, gnomic, sometimes harsh literal statements of the Torah.

Differing interpretations of religious texts are highly valued, and to this day Talmudic students study the opposing views of the House of Hillel and the House of Shammai.

Judaism is a religion in which human beings talk to, argue with and remonstrate with God, as Abraham did before the destruction of Sodom and Gomorrah. Argument (called "pilpul," or pepper) is the primary form of religious discourse—Rabbi "X" says this; Rabbi "Y" says that; what do you think? The Passover Seder emphasizes "The Four Questions."

Talmudic commentaries are sometimes wise, sometimes disputes about questions the non-Orthodox would consider trivial. For centuries, however, these exercises have sharpened the minds and focused the insights of generations of students. Albert Einstein, asked how Jewish students flooded the German universities of the 19th century shortly after Napoleon released them from the isolation of the ghetto, replied, "They had been preparing for their entrance examinations for centuries."

At every Bat or Bar Mitzvah, proud parents and family wait expectantly for the child to discuss the day's biblical text with some fresh insight, some thoughtful comment that displays a creative mind. If Waterloo was won on the playing fields of Eton, perhaps some Nobel prizes have been won at the Bar Mitzvah pulpit.

Experience shows that observance of religious rituals bears no relationship to morality or ethics. Taliban fanatics are not better parents, neighbors or citizens than their secular Muslim neighbors. The same is true of the Haredi (Ultra Orthodox Jews). I think of myself not as a "lax" Orthodox Jew but as one trying to be an "authentic" Reform Jew.

Of course, there are questions:

- Is Judaism a universal religion or a tribal cult?
- Must an ethic and a moral system be based on Divine Revelation, or can it be based on logic and experience?
- How do we account for evil and for the suffering of innocents if a personal God is both omniscient and omnipotent?
- What do we know of life after death, about which the Hebrew Bible (Tanakh) says almost nothing?
- Is thoughtful meditation as acceptable as prayer to a personal God?

Jewish tradition provides some replies, but some questions (such as those raised by the Book of Job or by the Holocaust) we pass in silence. Maimonides states that there is much we do not know and cannot know because we are as unable to read God's mind as a blind person is to imagine the color blue.

Contemplating the fate of the Hittites or the Philistines, the followers of Zeus or Jupiter, and others over the centuries, even skeptical Jews may wonder what distinguishes them from so many others. Some

166

aspects of the Judaic tradition must be so life-enhancing, or have such survival value, or encourage a tenacious communal bonding.

All religions share basic elements — a doctrine concerning God and man and the universe; a moral code for the individual and for society; a regimen of ritual and custom; laws; sacred literature; institutions; and worshippers.

Judaism, in addition, is a religion of memory. It has a sense of history, a distinctive language, and a memory of location that, without parallel in world history, have "brought them home." Two millennia after their political state was swept away, their Temple twice destroyed, their priesthood dissolved and their population dispersed, Jews scattered across the face of the earth still ponder the Jewish experience and reflect on where we have been, where we are and where we are going.

The sense of "chosenness" mentioned in the Hebrew Bible is considered by Jews as a call for us to set an example, to be a "kingdom of priests and a holy nation" and "a light unto the nations." Since God used the Jewish people as His vehicle for communicating His will, Jews feel that more is expected of them.

As to why God chose the Jews specifically, Maimonides said merely that we do not know. Some jokes suggest that after the Jewish experience of the last four millennia, it may be time for Him to choose someone else. In reply to the rhyme, however, "How odd of God to choose the Jews," someone wrote, "It isn't odd; the Jews chose God."

The various branches of Judaism comprise:

ORTHODOXY (which claims to be the most authentic transmitter of the faith), whose approaches range from Ultra-Orthodox (such as those who oppose the State of Israel because men, not God, created it) to Modern Orthodox, who reflect a sophisticated understanding of the relationship between tradition and Biblical injunctions on the one hand and the exigencies of the modern world on the other.

By and large, however, the Orthodox accept the Torah's 613 commandments by which a good Jew should live, including those called "Hukim," for which no known reason is discernible, but which they follow as an act of faith; many are silent about those commandments

167

(such as ones relating to animal sacrifice, smiting the Amalekites, living in agrarian society, etc.) which have lost relevance. In Orthodox practice, women are precluded from participation in much ritual observance and cannot join the Rabbinate; and acceptable co-religionists include only those stemming from Jewish matrilineal descent or from the demanding Orthodox formal conversion.

Ultra-Orthodoxy requires detailed observance of prayer, clothing, dietary restrictions and household practices that are difficult to follow in modern life and whose relevance has been questioned by other Jews. Modern Orthodox identify with Hebrew tradition and theology without feeling the need to dress like 18th century Polish nobles, or to follow many other Ultra-Orthodox practices.

The 93% of American Jews who are not strictly Orthodox regard the Orthodox in varying lights; but the disproportionately large political power the Orthodox wield in Israel (because of its parliamentary system) and the intransigence of Ultra-Orthodox views on many political questions there, are a source of concern to many other Jews. That Reform and Conservative rabbis are not permitted to perform marriages in Israel is a continuing irritant, and the Orthodox desire to control all religious conversions is another.

CONSERVATIVE JUDAISM accepts many of Orthodoxy's strictures with modifications permitting adaptation to mainstream culture. It maintains that "halacha" (religious law) is open to reinterpretation. For example, the Conservative movement has in recent years accepted women into the rabbinate. Today, the movement appears to be moving in two directions, one closer to Reform practices and one back to tradition.

REFORM JUDAISM accepts the spiritual autonomy of the individual. It welcomes women as full religious participants, including membership in the rabbinate. It accepts the concept of patrilineal descent and has different requirements for conversion to Judaism. Significantly, it believes that the Hebrew Bible was written by humans, not God, and that many of its strictures (such as dietary laws) and rituals are not binding today.

RECONSTRUCTIONISM, a 20th century formulation created by Rabbi Mordechai Kaplan, emphasizes Judaism's evolving cultural and communal aspects and repudiates concepts such as "chosenness" and a personal messiah. Rabbi Kaplan also struggled against a supernatural view of God.

SECULAR JUDAISM is a recent development that regards Judaism as a culture rather than a theology, and reflects the growing number of unaffiliated Jews and those who identify themselves as Jewish but non-observant.

Orthodox Jews feel that they represent the prophet Isaiah's 'saving remnant' who will constitute Jewish survival, maintaining the continuity of Jewish tradition and theology. They fear that Conservative, Reform, Reconstructionist, Secular and unaffiliated Jews are on a downhill slide to assimilation and disappearance.

Given the tone of contemporary American life, in which effortless acculturation is a fact of life and Jews have open access to the society at large, in which anti-semitism is declining and the percentage of Jewish intermarriage is over 50%, fears for Jewish continuity are not groundless. Affiliation is a matter of choice today, and some may choose "out."

Absent a virulent domestic anti-semitism which draws people together for self-protection, or the communal fervor and self-taxation called for to restore a homeland in the Holy Land, will extended periods of peace, prosperity, social acceptance and intermarriage accomplish what hatred and pogroms could not?

Is a 'circling of the wagons' exclusionary approach indicated, or should a welcoming hand be extended to the spouses and children of intermarried couples and to the unaffiliated? To maintain Jewish continuity, is renewed emphasis on traditional ritual and observance called for or is the answer adaptation to contemporary life with full acceptance of women and gays in the religious life of the community, less emphasis on ritual and more on good works, etc?

The Ultra-Orthodox approach looks inward and backward, hoping to continue the traditions of the past; the liberal approach looks outward and forward, basing its position on the merits of its case for life enhancement.

a) By any objective index or form of measurement, Judaism's culture helps its practitioners lead productive, satisfying and fulfilling lives;
b) Jewish customs, traditions and religious rituals are emotionally, philosophically and aesthetically satisfying;
c) Liberal Judaism's tenets do not run counter to the logic or experience of the 21st century mind.

The Ultra-Orthodox approach assumes perpetual "otherness"(and the presumed hostility of others), and a sense of "chosenness" for obligations that cannot be dismissed. Some Orthodox, such as the Lubovitch Hasidim, believe that the Messiah may arrive shortly and human action can speed His arrival. The creation of the State of Israel is seen by some Ultra-Orthodox as an intrusion by men on the work of God, but by most Orthodox as a manifestation of Divine fulfillment.

Liberal Jews feel that Jews in an integrated, pluralistic society can be good neighbors who demonstrate their values by good works and good lives, that Jewish customs, traditions and beliefs are life-enhancing and beneficial to society.

Liberal Jews consider the State of Israel the creation of people restoring a homeland which provides a haven for oppressed Jews worldwide. They work and contribute generously toward its well-being and share its aspirations. They are concerned about its welfare and proud of its achievements, but distressed by its failings and flaws (among which is the absence of a written constitution).

American Jews of the post WWII generation identified with Israel's "founding fathers." Abba Eban, Golda Meir, and Teddy Kollek were friends and colleagues with similar outlooks and values. If American Jews today wonder how Israel's founders would regard the country's current leadership, they may also wonder how John Adams, James

170

Madison and Alexander Hamilton would regard the current U.S. Congress.

With every decade, however, American Jews and the Israeli public seem to be heading along different paths. American Jews are confident about the prospects of Jewish life in America, with which they identify. Many find it difficult to understand Israeli politics, and fear that modern zealots might be working against Israel's best long-term interest.

Like relatives reluctant to criticize family, American Jews often do not discuss their misgivings openly. The chief reasons are that they (and their children) are not exposed to the constant dangers Israelis face and they do not want to give comfort to Israel's enemies, who are numerous, worldwide and implacable.

Liberal and Orthodox views differ markedly in many respects. For example, whereas liberals refer to "Israel's West Bank" (real estate that can be traded for peace), the Orthodox refer to Judea and Samaria (a gift from God). The Orthodox see Israel as central to Jewish existence and consider the Diaspora as exile. The liberal American Jew sees Israel as a significant factor of Jewish life, but regards life in a sympathetic Diaspora as independently sustainable.

"By the waters of Babylon, we sat and wept," says the Psalmist. By the waters of the Hudson, this particular Jew is grateful to his ancestors who came to America, the modern "land of milk and honey," where each can "sit under his own vine and his own fig tree and none will make him afraid."

The Orthodox position holds that the Judaism which has survived for millennia should be maintained unchanged "in doing God's work." The liberal Jew says that a Judaism adapted to the exigencies of the modern world can continue because of its life-enhancing value for its believers. As a liberal Reform Jew, I note that in the past 900 years, Judaism in the ghetto or in isolation (whether enforced or self-imposed) produced little of interest to the non-Orthodox Jewish world. The mysticism and numerology of the Kabbalah, for example, which absorb many ultra Orthodox, are considered by liberal Jews in the category of astrology.

In interaction with the rest of the world, however, the 13,000,000 Jews worldwide, less than 1/5 of 1% of the world's population, have won nearly 30% of all Nobel prizes; have produced towering figures such as Einstein, Freud and Marx (Karl or Groucho, take your pick) and have contributed to western civilization, and to American cultural life in particular, out of proportion to their number.

It is true that Jews have been hated by some in the classical world, in the medieval world and in the modern world. They have been disdained by some conservatives, like T.S. Eliot, and despised by some liberals, like Voltaire. Some of the haters, like Martin Luther, hated the individuals because they would not convert; others, like the humanist Erasmus, hated what they stood for. Some of the haters are content to ostracize us socially, others to pillage and victimize us, others to try to remove us from the face of the earth.

The causes of anti-semitism in history are complex: in some cases, it is theological; in some cases, 'fear of the other' who holds himself apart; in some cases, it is demagogic, trumped-up fear of political conspiracy; often, it is resentment at Jewish success, with Jews being scapegoats for the problems or failures of others.

Traditionally forbidden to own land or to farm, Jews were hated as city dwellers; traditionally prohibited from many ways of earning a living, they were hated as money-lenders or as merchants and peddlers.

In *Mein Kampf*, Adolf Hitler charged Jews with being a biologically inferior race who were defiling Germany's superior Aryan race and succeeding in life by unfair means. At the time, Jews were 1% of the German public, but 16% of German lawyers, 10% of German doctors and dentists, 17% of German bankers, and 10% of the musicians in the Berlin Philharmonic. The Jews' passion for education and their exclusion from other fields of endeavor were ignored. Jews also won a disproportionately high number of Iron Crosses in the German Army in World War I. And in Austria, where Hitler was raised, the percentage of Jews in the arts, sciences, and professions was even higher than in Germany.

172

Self-hate and self-mockery, which usually reflect the internalization of others' disdain, are recurring facts of Jewish life. Throughout history, some of the worst anti-Semites have been of Jewish descent— Torquemada of the Spanish Inquisition, Pfefferkorn in medieval Germany, and many, many others.

In New Left circles in Europe and America today, many anti-Semitic Jews can be distinguished from those merely critical of specific Israeli policies or actions by the "Three D's"—Demonization of everything Israeli; Double Standards applied to Israel in the international arena; and Delegitimization of the Israeli state.

Self-deprecating Jewish humor is a healthier response to anti-Jewish feeling. For example, Vice Presidential candidate Barry Goldwater replied, when denied access to a 'restricted' golf course, "Can I play the first nine, since I am only half Jewish?" or Groucho Marx's comment "I wouldn't want to belong to any club that would have me as a member." When faced with negative feelings about Jews, I recall Benjamin Disraeli's reply to Daniel O'Connell's attack on his ancestry: "When the ancestors of the right honorable gentleman were brutal savages in an unknown island, mine were priests in the Temple of Solomon."

The recrudescence of international anti-semitism, expressed in such madness as Holocaust denial, I find bewildering and cannot explain. The fact that a significant portion of the American public does not accept Darwin's theory of evolution or that millions throughout the world still believe the CIA or the Israelis were responsible for the Twin Towers bombing on 9/11, I also cannot explain.

The sad fact is that Jew hatred has existed, does exist and probably will continue to exist, so long as paranoia, envy, resentment and a need for scapegoats and rationalizations for personal or group failure exist. American Black anti-Semitism, in light of consistent Jewish pro-Black support, and current anti-Semitism in Japan, where there are no Jews, are puzzling.

On balance, it is better to be resented for success than pitied for failure; and Jews have traditionally done well thanks to cultural patterns that exalt education, curiosity, independent thinking and competitive achievement.

Are there downsides to traditional Jewish culture? If the ancient Greeks' morally dysfunctional heroes and their lustful, violent and duplicitous gods and goddesses are quintessentially non-Jewish, so, too, are the Greek sense of balance and "moderation in all things" and the Renaissance gentleman's code of graceful, effortless achievement. Castiglione's Book of the Courtier advocated 'sprezzatura' and thought it bad form to try too hard, but the Vilna Gaon and other prominent rabbis were proud of their exhausting twelve hour days of study and debate.

Plato and Aristotle disdained manual labor and commerce, but the Hebrew Bible emphasizes the inherent dignity of labor and the value Judaism sets on work. The great rabbis themselves were laborers, businessmen or professionals, just as Hillel was a wood-cutter, Rashi a vineyard worker, Maimonides a practicing physician and Spinoza a lens grinder. While the Greeks perfected the art of tragedy, it was Judaism that created a theology not of "optimism" but of "hope."

As American Jews become more acculturated and assimilated, they, too, will act effortlessly and gentlemanly and, presumably, become proportionately less productive. In A.J. Gurney's play Love Letters, the WASP father warns his son, "If you keep getting all those A's, people will think you are Jewish!" That may not be the case in the future, since highly motivated Asians increasingly displace Jews in meritocratic rankings. Social grace, manners and etiquette are acquired at a price.

Will Hamans and Hitlers recur eternally? If so, is the price for maintaining Jewish values too steep to pay? Or is America, wonderful America, different? In a nation in which the majority consists of minorities and in which legal walls exist between church and state, one hopes so.

For Jews, America has proven to be the Golden Land of immigrant dreams. Do I hope that my descendants will be part of the continuing American story and that they will remain active and identifiable members of its Jewish community? I do. The challenge is to engage with the world constructively without losing the identity that reflects the best of Jewish tradition.

I hope that as full-fledged Americans, they will attend High Holiday services and Passover Seders, celebrate Bar and Bat Mitzvahs and be knowledgeable about Jewish history, customs and traditions as well as Jewish memories and values such as moral obligation and duty toward the community, reciprocity and trust. I hope that they will care about Israel and its historical associations, that they will be public-spirited, family-conscious, charitable and compassionate, and that they will share the Jewish mindset of curiosity, literacy, individualism and a passion for social justice. (Martin Luther King noted that Jews had provided some 90% of the contributions over $1,000 that he ever received.)

Some laugh at the old saw that "Jews earn like Episcopalians but vote like Puerto Ricans," but many are proud of it; and Jews have always led in liberal causes. For example, until "Black Power" advocates demanded their removal in the late 1960s, the NAACP (founded 1909) was a largely Jewish-dominated organization, with Joel Spingarn Chair from1914 to 1934, with early financial support underwritten by men like Jacob Schiff and Julius Rosenwald, and its early legal efforts supervised by NAACP Board Member Louis Marshall, and later by Jack Greenberg.

Will my form of Judaism be able to survive? I hope so, especially if the intermarried, their children, and the presently disaffected are re-attracted and welcomed by the Jewish community.

Will Judaism continue to encourage a fuller, more satisfying life for its adherents, one that is productive for them as well as for the society of which they are a part? I believe so, and have lived my life accordingly.

One modern definition of "a good Jew" is one whose grandchildren are "good Jews," and I hope my own take note.

To my descendants, I say, along with the Book of Proverbs,

"Behold, a good doctrine has been given unto you. Forsake it not...Its ways are ways of pleasantness and all its paths are peace."

February 2010

HOW TO BUILD BETTER

AND FASTER FOR LESS

Some titles invite skepticism – "Brain surgery for Fun and Profit" and "Making Millions in the Stock Market by Ouija Board" come to mind. My assigned title "Building Better for Less," is almost in that category; it implies that there are tricks one can use to insure an effective building at a low cost.

The truth is different. Sophisticated construction people realize that one rarely gets something for nothing; they ask, "What am I giving up for what I am getting?" Rightly so, for ours is the cost-conscious world of the "trade-off," the quid pro quo. And the greatest waste is always the wrong result for you regardless of cost.

Rather than thinking of "better for less," we should aim at "right for me at lowest feasible cost."

In graduate business schools, they speak of cost/benefit ratios; and I recall former Secretary of Defense Charles Wilson expressing his problem as "getting the biggest bang for the buck."

In real estate terms,

"Would Versailles have passed F.H.A. scrutiny as a planned unit development?

"How were the acoustics of the Parthenon?"

"What capitalization rate did the mortgagee apply to the Taj Mahal?"

These questions give an idea of the trade-off difficulty. High quality of anything and low cost usually do not go together. The ideal for one specific use conflicts with flexibility for multiple use, whether you are selecting wine for a meal, designing public spaces or purchasing what in Army-Navy Stores they laughingly call "the tool of a thousand uses." Lowest first capital cost often means higher maintenance or operating cost later on, and vice versa.

For competent architect or general contractor, the difficulty comes in weighing the trade-offs. In our increasingly complex structures, the penalties for error will become more and more severe.

The owner, or a surrogate, must exercise an owner's function in weighing the trade-offs and in integrating the analysis, planning, design, and construction functions of a project His function, if ignored, will be assumed by default by another entity (architect, G.C., Amateur Building Committee, etc.) that may not be qualified to handle it. The trade-off judgments divide into two categories, those of cost/taste/specific-tenant-requirements, and those of general building determinations.

Taking the latter first, every security man knows that physical security and easy control can be designed into a building or can be designed out; every maintenance man knows that efficient maintenance can be designed in or out; so can noise control, atmospheric comfort, efficient pedestrian circulation, sensible waste disposal, proper elevatoring, and so forth. Best practice indicates that input on these matters should come from security specialists, maintenance specialists, acoustical engineers, etc., and that anyone exercising the owner's function must be prepared to make (and to accept responsibility for) well-considered judgments, balancing the demands of utility, cost, beauty, speed and similar factors.

The elevator program for a building with a single-tenant occupant requiring much inter-floor traffic is different from that of a building with several unrelated tenants; the key factor is not how many people work on each floor, but what their elevator use will be. Escalators, two-or-three-stop hydraulic elevators, private interior stairways, and carefully planned use of elevator "cross-over" floors should be considered.

The H.V.A.C. zoning and control program for a tenant requiring frequent 24-hour use of small areas scattered throughout a building differs from that of a tenant whose great open bays are used on a 9-to-5 schedule.

The waste disposal problems of a building throwing off routine clerical wastepaper differ substantially from those of a building with many eating facilities and the resulting wet garbage. A bank or investment securities firm whose wastepaper baskets might accidentally contain negotiable securities or irreplaceable documents requires a longer 'holding period' than a building with a routine tenancy. The security treatment for such buildings is also important.

The configuration and massing of a building also involves more than zoning and aesthetics. Many a corporate headquarters finds itself in a tall, thin tower with small floors and the high perimeter-to-interior ratio more suitable to a building occupied by smaller firms involved in law, public relations, etc.

The second category of trade-off judgments reflects cost/taste/specific-tenant-requirements, which require the corporate owner or his surrogate to wear separate hats, those of client and of developer.

"How many and what type of amenities can we afford for the money we have?" is one approach; "How inexpensively can we build the building we want?" is the other.

Some give-and-take occurs in all development situations, with the 'quality-first' job usually being scaled down somewhat as the cost estimates roll, while the stark "budget" job is frequently upgraded in the course of letting subcontracts.

An entrepreneurial builder is in touch with his market and knows what his tenants want enough to pay for; in business schools they refer to this as "the discipline of the marketplace." A corporate owner-tenant developing for his own account has no comparable guide, and the result is often an unproductive over-design.

Over-design is as much a pitfall as under-design, and occurs more often than is generally realized. A management group that automatically equates higher cost with higher quality may actually be proud of the gargantuan price tag hanging from the neck of their newly acquired white elephant. It does not necessarily follow that more expensive is better.

This year, for example, because of recent accidents, earthquake precautions and fire safety are on everyone's mind. But common sense need not be thrown to the winds. One financial institution recently announced that the frame of its new 48-story building was between 2 and 3 times the local code requirements. I am not familiar with all the specifics, but either that building is over-designed or there are many unsafe buildings in the city.

One question is whether the same effective degree of protection could have been provided at a fraction of the cost.

In another example, a consortium of banks developed a sizable garden apartment job composed of fully fireproofed, reinforced-concrete, two-story structures. The prime movers were dismayed when the renting public attached little importance to that expensive feature; they were also disheartened when the project was eventually sold at a price that reflected its net cash flow capitalized, with no reflection whatsoever of the development costs.

'Moderation in all things' advised the Greeks 2500 years ago, indicating that even when they had lavish 'corporate headquarters' types hanging around the Agora, contrasting with skin-flint speculative types a few yards away asking a drachma or two less per square foot!

Stating a difficulty is one thing; resolving it is quite another. Since the area for greatest savings is at the onset of the project, in its conceptual stage, the solution lies there, too. It is in selecting or creating the entity that makes the trade-off choices on which the success of the venture hinges.

Some major organizations are equipped to handle the development problems of their home office buildings on an 'in-house' basis, but those are few. Others who contemplate getting involved in new construction would be well advised to:

    a) retain on a fee basis the best construction managements teams available;

b) consider going "joint venture" with a larger, more competent and experienced owner/builder organization; or

c) arrange for "prime tenancy" in a first-class rental building designed from inception with their needs in mind.

The 'in-house' route is the riskiest, and some organizations with high levels of professional 'in-house' talent have chosen the 'joint venture' or 'prime tenant' approach. They work on the theory that they would not like to go to a doctor, no matter how good, who had no other patients.

If 'in-house' works successfully, the organization ends up with the right structure, has made a good investment, and has saved fees. When it fails (which is often the case), sums can be "sunk without a trace" and senior corporate management never really knows what happened. A sense of corporate 'machismo' seems to prevail, and almost every week one hears of another major organization going down the primrose path.

My guess is that those firms whose "in-house" talents permit them to develop successful investment properties should stay with 'in house', the others should run for outside help.

In a construction-management approach, if handled properly, a skilled team of coordinated specialists is involved in the project from conception through to occupancy. The job is treated as an integrated whole. Information-collecting, analysis, planning, design, specification writing, bid analysis, subcontract letting, on-site supervision, what in the space program is called 'mid-course correction;' and final occupant acceptance are scheduled and controlled from start to finish, with trade-off judgments along the way made as wisely as the current "state-of-the-art" permits.

If your job actually receives all that, whatever fee you pay is cheap; if not you have been overcharged, regardless of how low the fee.

A small, but growing number of firms do provide such services; a greater number of firms claim to provide those services, but in fact, do not. The competence of a construction manager is crucial.

The story is told of the patient who was referred to a specialist who

181

charged $100 for the first visit and $25 a visit thereafter. The patient said that for $100 the doctor should be able to guess. The doctor looked at him for a minute and commented, "My friend, you don't need a doctor; you need a veterinarian!"

If a client doesn't give even the construction manager the fullest cooperation and information from the start, the job will suffer; what that client really needs is a veterinarian!

The joint venture role and that of prime tenant can be essentially the same, except that in the former case the corporate tenant is willing to make a real estate investment with chance of gain and risk of loss, the degree of control, planning involvement, etc., can be as much or as little as the parties decide. Once again, the choice of bedfellows is the most important decision the corporate tenant must make, and the best basis for selection is the owner-builder's past track record.

CONCLUSION:
a) Rather than try "to build better for less" we should seek the right building at the lowest feasible cost;
b) The best time to deal with problems is before they arise;
c) The heart of the problem is the exercise of proper judgment in determining complex "trade-offs";
c) Money-wasting over-design is as much a pitfall in corporate building as under-design, although only the company accountant seems in on the secret;
e) 'In-house' development management, outside professional construction-management on a fee basis, joint venture with an investment builder-partner, and use of a major long-term lease to exert leverage on a building to be built, are all feasible approaches. Experience has shown repeatedly that "in house" is the most popular and least effective; in the other cases, the selection of bedfellows is the most important decision to be made.

At all times common sense working with long-term trends and dealing with the right people is your best policy.

182

For those on whom you rely, it boils down to the "Whistler" approach. James McNeill Whistler, you will recall, was the 19th century painter once asked by a rival with what he mixed his pigments to get such remarkable effects. Whistler looked him straight in the eye and said, "Sir, I mix my pigments with genius!"

Such talent is hard to find, but it's worth looking for.

American Management Association Conference
New York
September 27-29, 1972

HOUSING AND THE ELDERLY

When Pruitt-Igoe, St. Louis' prominent public housing development, was deliberately demolished little more than a decade after winning a national award for architectural excellence, the housing industry was forced to face unpleasant facts; not the least, that in housing, "people" problems require solutions as well as "brick and mortar" problems.

The economic plight of the elderly tenant and his need for costly services pose a problem that our society is just beginning to recognize.

There is need for increased public awareness, which could lead to governmental programs by which public, private, and philanthropic strengths could be brought to bear effectively.

At that point, the role of the professional housing manager dealing with the elderly becomes crucial.

In housing for the elderly, physical questions are important – no one minimizes the need for safety-engineered bathrooms, 36-inch wide door-bucks to permit wheelchairs rather than the customary 24-inch width, waist-high electrical outlets to reduce bending, ramps in addition to awkward steps, electric-eye doors, non-skid floors, appropriate illumination and internal communication systems. But the most difficult lessons we have to learn are those that deal with people.

In 1900, those over 65 constituted some 4% of the nation's population; by 1940, the percentage reached 6.8%; today the 23 million men and women over 65 make up over 10% of the nation and, significantly, 16% of the voting age population. Every day 3,000 persons over 65 die, while 4000 enter the age group, for a total increase in the aged population of nearly 400,000 per annum. And, if physical quarters appropriate for this group are in short supply, housing managers with necessary skills and knowledge are even scarcer.

We are going to need all the help we can get from many different sources in the social welfare network, particularly from psychologists and social workers.

We are going to have to learn to understand these specialists, even though they speak a jargon that seems designed to confuse the layman. For example, social workers never 'tell' each other anything; they 'share' even if it is the news that you have just been fired. They don't 'do' things, but have 'modalities of service.' In the professional literature one finds phrases like 'activity-propinquity' or 'cathectic flexibility'; real estate people must learn to understand the code. Picture, for example, the busy building superintendent who complains about a long-winded tenant and is told about the 'therapeutic value of reminiscence.'

The building manager must develop a sensitivity to the special needs of the elderly.

First of all, we must explore our own attitudes, our hopes and fears, denials and aversions, because in our actions we express our feelings in 101 different ways without meaning to; the elderly are all too aware that in this youth-worshipping, goal-oriented society they are considered "left-over" and "unnecessary."

Next, the housing industry must learn that the aged comprise several overlapping subgroups: the strong or feeble, alert or senile, poor or well-to-do, barely literate or well-educated. In competence, the aged range across a broad scale in their ability to function effectively on their own and to meet their own needs. The most dependent, of course, are the physically disabled and mentally impaired; those should really be referred to case-work agencies. The other extreme are those essentially able to perform well with complete independence. (The latter are known in social work jargon by the unfortunate phrase "intact aged.")

But all the aging tend to suffer some progressive loss of hearing, eyesight, or reflex speed. All, in varying degrees, can become momentarily confused or frightened or forgetful. So elevator doors must close more slowly for them; signs must have larger print, and directions should be expressed more simply and clearly and loudly and repeated often. Forms to be filled out should have larger blanks and boxes, because the elderly sometimes have trouble holding a pen or writing. Elevators need floor indicators so the passenger can get to the door before the car arrives; wind gusts which can knock down the frail or make a door difficult to open must be anticipated in building design. Extra handrails for bathtubs and showers, mailboxes and kitchen cabinets at convenient heights, gentle ramps and flush door-saddles designed with wheelchairs in mind – must become standard.

Just as the housing planner for the elderly must think in terms of easy access to adequate means of transportation, possible home-chore assistance, perhaps community living rooms and kitchens, and almost certainly, minor nursing care and round-the-clock emergency services, so the building manager must learn which social or psychological problems building staff should deal with and which are beyond their competence, and need specialists.

The National Jewish Welfare Board, of which I have been President for the past four years, has recently determined, for example, that while even regular social workers are not good predictors of which elderly are subject to bouts of psychological depression (about 30%), a brief, self-administered questionnaire called the Zung Self-Rating Depression Scale does the job accurately and can save everyone concerned much time and anguish.

Building staff need help in distinguishing between difficult or problem behavior that can be considered normal and that which is genuinely pathological.

The building management organization dealing with the elderly should learn to deal with calls for more handyman service, heavy cleaning help, housekeeping aid, and with personal services including some form of telephone reassurance; and (where economically feasible), it must learn to plan for concierge desks, security guards, and information and referral services.

Since even young and healthy bachelors sometimes have trouble with shopping, meal preparation, housecleaning, laundry, clothes-mending, and so forth, it is not surprising that the elderly do (and are grateful if they get it).

The other side of the coin, however, is that building staff need protection from "the clinger," who can't do anything unless you help him; or "the big boss," who must have the last word at all times on all subjects; or the "loner," who withdraws and can't be reached; or "the sitter," who just won't budge; or "the manipulator," who always has an angle, a counterproposal, or what he is sure is a "special situation"; "the Lothario" or "Great Lover," who needs to demonstrate audibly and sometimes visibly that he is still interested in sex; and, finally, from "the trouble-maker," who undoubtedly was a first-class pain-in-the-neck when young and has now become worse.

Everyone involved with the elderly in any capacity should be re-minded of the requirements that all human beings share throughout the life-cycle: the need to love and be loved, the need for a sense of identity and belonging.

Even with a tendency to fall into a role of dependency and pas-sivity and a reluctance to accept responsibility, the elderly have a le-gitimate and continuing need for advisors, consultants, and confidants. As individuals whose earning years are behind them, they are usually on tight budgets and need help in getting the greatest pos-sible value for their expenditures on housing, food, and medical care, and on transportation, without which an older person tends to feel isolated and depression-prone.

We must understand the elderly as individuals who, in retirement, leave not only the world of meaningful work, but also the social con-tacts that the workaday world represents; who feel themselves slipping out of the organized life of the community into a situation they often see as uselessness and dependence.

At the period in life when they are least able to cope, the elderly find themselves subject to psychological stresses (crushing at any age) such as the death of a spouse or close relative, severe illness or personal injury, dramatic change in financial status, or complete change of physical surroundings and neighborhood contacts.

Their problems are profound and it would be wrong to imply that the housing industry has the responsibility, let alone the means, skills or resources, to meet them adequately.

But as our society becomes increasingly aware of the problems and moves to deal with them, the housing industry should play its part.

True, we have our share of venal types for whom the dollars involved are not the chief consideration but the only consideration; we have our share of practitioners who think of real estate management in terms of supplying fuel oil and janitorial service, period; and we have our share of those who, having turned the subsidized building rehabilitation program into the expensive and wasteful farce it is becoming, are now eyeing with anticipation the governmental dollars beginning to flow for housing for the elderly.

But there are those, too, who are trying to convert the trade of building management into a profession; who set reasonable standards and try to meet them; who try to combine economic feasibility with social responsibility, integrity and compassion. These are the individuals who, in the words of the Bible, "with all their getting, get understanding."

If we can attract them to the field of housing for the elderly, if we can train them properly, equip them with the necessary legislative and economic tools, and compensate them appropriately, we will have discharged our responsibility to the aged who, for the moment, are "they" but who, before long, will be "we."

Cornell University
Cooperative Extension Program
May 15, 1978

GOTHAM APARTMENTS

AND SOVIET VEGETABLES

Rental housing in New York, like agriculture in the Soviet Union, can be counted on periodically for headlines, new initiatives, and disappointing results.

In each case, a major political figure 'discovers' the problem, demands action, and pledges fresh resources; in the Russian case, they usually promise "reforms" and new incentives. And with New York apartments and Russian crops, time passes, the quick fix doesn't work, and the attention of the public is diverted elsewhere.

In both situations, the problem is the same – failure to differentiate symptoms from causes and a reluctance to address the problem lurking beneath the surface.

The case of New York residential construction is the sadder of the two because it is so clearly solvable. The J-51 program created thousands of recycled residential units from unused industrial space, so we canceled it. The 421a program created thousands of units of new construction, so we effectively destroyed it. Saddest of all, the Mitchell-Lama program created vast numbers of units aimed at the middle-income population most in need, so we politicized and regulated the program out of existence. Would that the homeless of today had available 100,000 unbuilt, depoliticized Mitchell-Lama units that could have been developed in the 1960s and 1970s and were not.

That the New York housing mess (crisis is not the appropriate word for a situation that has existed since rent controls went into ef-

191

fect on March 15, 1943) is a "self-inflicted wound" is shown by the federal government's numbers. In recent years, U.S. housing production has averaged 1.7 million to 1.8 million units per year; and with 3% of the nation's population New York City should be producing 50,000 new units a year, right? Wrong! Roughly one-fifth of the nation's per capita rate is what New York figures show. Since our population has dropped by nearly a million people since 1970, we must have a high vacancy rate, right? Wrong, again; our rates of dilapidation and abandonment lead the country.

Why is the housing situation in New York so much worse than in the rest of the country? Why should the surging population in the Sun Belt be reflected in housing surplus, while our population is reflected in shortage? (Dallas, with one-third the population of New York City, had nearly ten times the new housing starts last year!) Why should the very mortgages so anxious to finance New York office buildings, hotels, and retail facilities avoid rental housing like the plague?

The answers, which our politicians don't want to hear and which our other civic leaders ignore, fall into three categories:

a) Our regulatory policies in the form of rent control and rent stabilization, discourage the inflow of private capital and provide "blind" subsidies to a constituency that is middle-aged, middle class and upper middle income at the expense of the poor, the young, and minorities;

b) Our land use policies rule out residential development in vast areas, such as the lower west side of Manhattan, in the hope that steel mills or auto assembly plants will choose to locate on the Hudson between Battery Park and West Forty-Second Street; and, finally,

c) Our construction policies and labor practices give us the highest construction costs south of Alaska.

Phase out rent controls, re-think city land uses, take steps to lower construction costs – and the mortgage money that found its way to Dallas will rediscover New York.

Until our leaders and civic spokesmen look realistically at these factors, we have little hope of doing more than applying Band-Aids to a terminal case. Albert Einstein liked the comment that, "In the physical world, there are neither rewards nor punishments, only consequences." The consequences of current policies, for New York apartments and Soviet carrots, are likely to be painful.

July 7, 1986

ALEXANDER POPE AND THE

CHALLENGE OF URBAN REGENERATION

It may seem odd to look at an 18th-century British poet for insights for a conference on urban regeneration, however, in his "Essay on Man" Alexander Pope got right to the heart of the matter when he wrote,

> *"O'er forms of governance let fools contest;*
> *What e'er is best administered is best."*

An analysis of the successes and failures in public/private regeneration efforts over the years reveals that what the successes have in common are the following:

a) An overriding vision or an imaginative concept;
b) A realistic financial plan that swims with rather than against the current of free market forces;
c) Tough-minded, detailed physical, social, and economic planning;
d) Astute local political sensitivity, resulting in effective local support; and
e) Competent, dispassionate implementation of the program.

Prudent flexibility, what in the U.S. space program is called "mid-course correction," adds to the chance of success; just as overloading a program with too many ambitious, often contradictory goals, diminishes those chances.

Experience shows that brick-and-mortar problems are the easiest to solve; social problems are the hardest; and economic problems fall somewhere in between.

On either side of the public/private negotiating table, one can find individuals of outstanding professional talent, character, imagination, and dedication. But one can also find intellectual frauds, self-serving cheats, and incompetents hopelessly out of their depth.

From the standpoint of urban impact, the important thing, as Pope realized, is to see that the right actions are taken at the right time in the right manner, regardless of the auspices under which they take place.

As a general rule, public entities should be expected to have a broader perspective than private, a longer range point of view, and a greater sensitivity to the needs of the entire community. Therefore, it is logical that public entities determine the broad outlines of large-scale urban regeneration programs, the goals, and nature of the public resources to be applied. I am not an admirer of the Houston, Texas, laissez-faire model.

The closer, however, that public entities get to specific instances and (if you will forgive the pun) concrete divisions, the more inept they become, the more doctrinaire, the more unresponsive to individual and immediate problems.

At some point, first-rate private entities usually far outperform them. Many of us have long known what Mr. Gorbachev seems first discovering.

Public entities suffer from a lack of understanding of the power of market forces in a free market. Even King Canute would have had greater success with his orders had he waited until the tide changed; and that applies to urban regeneration programs too.

In the case of my Boston activities, which began nearly 20 years ago at the suggestion of British real estate friends, we felt intuitively that the area had bottomed out economically and was poised for a long, continuing ascent. In speeches 17 or 18 years ago, I argued publicly that given the economic realities, Boston would be ill-advised to dissipate civic funds to retain inevitably declining blue-collar jobs, and that it should capitalize on its various educational and "quality-of-life" strengths to attract white-collar employment that provides better-paying jobs, higher tax revenues, and greater economic and social spin-offs. For our projects in Boston, which now involve nearly

6,000,000 square feet of commercial space, we required from the city government no financial help of any sort, merely zoning and land use cooperation.

However, such creative, seminal projects as Boston's Faneuil Hall/Quincy Market would not have been possible without the enthusiastic support of Boston Mayor Kevin White who ran Boston as his own personal fiefdom. He is architecturally knowledgeable, however, and had a vision of the downtown he wanted. It is no exaggeration to say that much of Boston's downtown bears his personal stamp. Our million-square-foot, 46-story office tower could not get its plans until he personally selected the color of the tinted window glass.

Today, each of our Boston projects is an unqualified success, for us and for the city; and there is credit enough for everyone.

In our major Washington, DC, project (Pentagon City) which will eventually comprise 6,000 housing units, 2,000 hotel rooms, a 1,000,000-square-foot retail mall, and 1,250,000 square feet of office space, we needed government support in zoning and land use controls. A local anti-growth group repeatedly challenged the master plan in the courts, but the local public officials successfully defended their approval of the plan all the way up to the U.S. Supreme Court. After that, we needed no financial or other involvement, since the site was obviously in the path of healthy and sustainable growth. Today, much of the office space is built, and construction on the retail mall and first housing unit is scheduled to get underway this autumn; and it looks as if they will be a rousing success.

Increasingly, in urban regeneration programs, Pope's advice seems apt: the well-administered public/private partnership approach, in which each side plays its constructive role for the general good.

"Partnerships in Urban Regeneration"
Queen Elizabeth II Conference Center, London
June 30 - July 1, 1987

LANDMARKS PRESERVATION AND THE LAW:

The 19th century American missionaries who set out to proselytize Hawaii were effective individuals; in time, when their families owned or controlled most of the islands, it was said that "they came to do good and did very well indeed."

In the same vein, a private developer involved with landmark preservation may have mixed motives and the wisest public policies reflected in law will be those that assure the maximum public good consistent with opportunities for competent and honorable private practitioners to "do well."

INTERPRETATIONS OF PUBLIC GOOD

These are loaded terms since each can mean what we wish them to mean; even the term 'landmarks preservation' represents different things to different people. To some it means restoration, putting a building of unusual history or aesthetic interest back into its original state; to others it means renovation, which implies physical upgrading; to others, it can mean adaptive use where older buildings are recycled to new uses.

Mount Vernon, a classic restoration, is presumably ready for George Washington to resume residence on a moment's notice and is fully equipped for him, down to a new set of his wooden false teeth. Ghirardelli Square in San Francisco and Boston's Old City Hall, on the other hand, are examples of adaptive use. They have been reincarnated in forms more imaginative and aesthetically pleasing than in their first lives. And many homes in Washington's Georgetown, Boston's Back

199

Bay, and Philadelphia's Society Hill have been superbly renovated, providing the same surroundings for new residents as for the original owners, but with steam heat, electricity, and running water.

The old French saying, "the Good is the enemy of the Best; the Best is the enemy of the Good," is applicable because if pure restoration is the goal, adaptive use can be destructive. On the other hand, if adaptive use or renovation is acceptable, all parties should agree on the degree of historic authenticity and continuity required because the economic feasibility (therefore the "do-ability") of an otherwise desirable project might be destroyed in the early planning stage.

Common sense would limit pure restoration to those philanthropic groups equipped, financially and technically, to undertake them. Private skills and guidance can be hired on a fee basis, but there is no place for private sector entrepreneurial involvement.

With pure restoration left to eleemosynary groups, renovation and adaptive use are areas for a fruitful cooperation between public and private entities.

Public Interest and Private Developers

Public interest in the recycling of older structures is increasing as it is an important factor in revitalizing key areas in decaying old center-cities. As properties are brought back to social and economic health, the effect on adjoining areas becomes evident. Property tax rolls increase, new jobs are created, fresh purchasing power is attracted back to declining areas, and more efficient use is made of an underutilized urban infrastructure.

The enterprise is a 'positive sum game' in which everyone comes out ahead. We preserve buildings, then neighborhoods, and finally the city itself. Given the public benefits that flow from such activity, it follows that legitimate public interest should focus on the problems a private developer faces and on steps to help overcome them.

The financial analysis a developer performs on a recycling project is the same he applies to any other development, and the basic equations are simple:

Gross Development Cost – Total Financing = "Equity Investment"
Gross Income – Real Estate Taxes, Operating Cost + Debt Services = "Net Cash Flow"
"Net Cash Flow" + Equity Investment = "Return on Equity"

Anything that lowers the gross development cost or increases available financing cuts down on the developer's cash required. Anything that increases income or cuts down on real estate taxes, debt service, or operating expenses increases a project's cash flow. It follows that the higher the return on equity, the more appealing the project becomes to the developer.

The legal problem is to devise mechanisms that:

a) Determine the appropriate public aims to be achieved.
b) Define the private role
c) Make optimum use of incentives available to the private sector that achieve public aims.

Stringent application of local building codes originally designed for new construction; superimposing on preservation projects of social goals (such as HUD's "targeting" rule with respect to low-income or minority populations) as a condition for an array of governmental subventions, grants, and aids; uncertainties and delays caused in one way or another by government added to the uncertainties and delays inherent in preservation work – all these add to the costs, and lessen the economic feasibility, of projects whose successful completion may be in the public interest.

Availability of capital (mortgage and equity) persistently plagues the preservation field (and "front-end" cash is difficult to come by). Contractors and architects are reluctant to provide firm bids and guaranteed completion dates where structural problems, initially hidden, come to light as work progresses and result in delays and cost overruns. The small size of many preservation projects prevents "economies of scale." All are risks the developer faces.

Risk-taking is part of the entrepreneur's role, but in the long run, society pays for undue risks, either in the form of worthwhile projects left undone or in rewards necessary to attract desirable developers.

On the positive side are the growing array of governmental aids for preservation work. The federal government's National Historic Preservation Act (1966), National Environmental Policy Act (1969), and National Historic Preservation Fund (1976) provide important preservation tools; a variety of HUD programs are aimed at preservation, and the Department of Commerce (through the Economic Development Administration and Small Business Administration) provides several sources of funds. The more accessible these are, the better for everyone.

The major federal benefit available to preservation developers is their allowable depreciation deduction against federal income taxes. Since Section 2124 of the Tax Reform Act of 1976 permits the developer of a historic structure to write off his capital expenditures over a five-year period and to sell off in advance his excess tax losses to high-bracket investors, a source of capital thus becomes available at a crucial early stage.

Local aids to the developer that make preservation appealing vary from locality to locality and often involve forms of property tax abatement such as New York City's J-51 program. TDRs (Transferable Development Rights) by which development densities may be transferred from one preservation location to another site, and 'façade easements' where a public body may assume the obligation to renovate and maintain a building's outer shell, are other tools whose use should be encouraged.

The problems of historic preservation law involve more effective use of current tools rather than the creation of new ones.
In 'the real world' the implementation of a law is as important as its formulation, the application and interpretation of preservation law must be seen as an area of importance. Clarity and internal consistency of regulations, speed and flexibility in administration, are of even greater importance in this field than in others. The credibility of local government, in living up to its obligations is significant in a field involving so many intangibles.

202

Imaginative use of existing tools should be encouraged at all levels of government because they are consistent with the underlying legislative intent.

Possible waivers of controls in preservation projects may be appropriate in building codes, zoning restrictions or social engineering.

CONCLUSION

Nothing I have said should be construed as limiting the legitimate controls, reviews, and inspections private developers should be subject to as it must be assumed that developers will do only what is in their financial self-interest. When relying on a developer's conscience, one would do well to remember H.L. Mencken's definition of conscience as "the small voice that tells you someone may be looking."

Properly harnessed, however, the private developer represents the best preservation resource we have; and for the public good his 'care and feeding' should be a matter of general public concern.

New York Landmarks Conservancy
Bar Association Conference
September 22-23, 1978

ULYSSES AND

MODERN BUSINESS ENTERPRISE

Public confidence in individuals, organizations, business and government today is at unprecedented low levels; and that affects attitudes toward how one sees the world. This loss of trust is neither parochial nor national; nor is it limited to any one social class, ethnic or religious group or geographic region.

Fidel Castro reports that over half of Cuba's state-controlled petroleum supplies are stolen by Cubans each year; international bankers estimate the billions of dollars donated to Nigeria by the world community are almost equal to the secret deposits in Swiss banks made by Nigerian government officials and their families; the oil-for-food scandals of the U.N. stimulate joking references to "Ali Baba and his 40 diplomats"; Russia's political system has been described as "kleptocracy"; the U.S President's credibility has rarely been so low; and in the United States and in Ireland, the Catholic Church is seen as more protective of its priests than of its young male acolytes; and on and on.

In the business world, the scandals of Enron, Tyco and World-Com were bad enough; even more heartbreaking (and unexpected) was the complicity of the world's leading public accounting firms, from whom the public expects standards higher than those of church or government.

High standards are important in all areas of life, but particularly in business, because large-scale business requires public trust for success. The stakeholders in large-scale modern business organizations—stock owners, employees, suppliers, customers, the government and the general public—will lower substantially the "transaction costs" of businesses they trust.

Google, Inc., for example, is better able to resist international controls because three quarters of the American public give Google in particular, but technology firms in general, high ratings for "innovative, reasonably-priced products that enhance their daily lives."

Companies like Johnson & Johnson, Coca Cola, 3M and Sony have real economic advantages because the public trusts them. Companies like UPS and FedEx are regarded as more reliable than government services; and although governments may still echo the comment of Herodotus ("Neither snow nor rain nor heat nor gloom of night stays these couriers from the swift completion of their appointed rounds"), the public increasingly puts its trust in, and its cash on, FedEx.

That is negotiation writ large; FedEx and UPS have made promises to the public; the public recognizes by its shift of package business to these firms that the firms keep their promises; and millions of transactions a day are the result. (Employees of those companies with "bad press," on the other hand, like Halliburton or Philip Morris, find themselves needing to prove why they are not to be distrusted.)

In the long run, "accountability" is the key concept of the modern business enterprise. This has been the stated position of business and economic thinkers since Adam Smith, in *Wealth of Nations* and *Theory of Moral Sentiments*. But this is not just a matter of theory or principle. It is demonstrably advantageous for business to operate in a climate of trust; even hard-nosed business schools increasingly emphasize that in their curricula.

Not all business functions in this way. Among private individuals, small firms, start-ups and others that feel they are below the radar screen of public awareness, some do anything they like to succeed; their unscrupulous, even illegal, behavior reflects Immanuel Kant's "crooked timber of humanity from which no straight thing can be

206

made." It is easy to overlook the principle that the larger, the more visible and more subject to public scrutiny an organization is, the more likely it is to strive for public approbation.

It is unfortunate that our culture's view of business was formulated before the evolution of the modern business enterprise, because moral dealings for most of these enterprises are dictated by real-world pressures. Employees want to feel proud of their companies; customer loyalty (acquired by perceptions of reliability and fairness) is "money in the bank"; and public condemnation is likely to be followed in time by legal regulation. In modern business, it pays to be and seen to be, on the side of the good guys.

Distrust of business has deep and ancient roots. The warrior class was traditionally ennobled; professionals such as doctors, lawyers, architects and the like were presumed to be motivated by more than self-interest; the clergy were guided by God; the farmer or small artisan earned his bread by the sweat of his brow. It was the money-changer, by contrast, who was driven from the Temple. Economic exchange was seen as a "zero sum game," in which one person's gain was someone else's loss; the modern concept of "value added" was unknown. It is easy to see why, in such a climate, the rich man's chance of Heaven and the camel's of passing through the needle's eye were similar.

Yet, even in the ancient world, there were those who thought and acted like modern business leaders. Ulysses demonstrated in the Odyssey an ability to think creatively with a long time horizon; to recognize opportunities not seen by others; to listen and to learn, to share knowledge with his team, and to lead by example. He knew that to be trusted he must be trustworthy. Commitment, passion, courage and the ability to negotiate successfully and credibly with an array of stakeholders were Fortune 500 CEO traits which Ulysses in Homer's epic demonstrated two and a half millennia ago. They still work today.

The best modern leaders try to function in a climate of tangible integrity, with "self-interest" seen as "enlightened self-interest." They know that when they fall short, the public is watching. Just as Sarbanes Oxley regulations—now a major nuisance and significant expense for all business—was the government reaction to public accounting failures, so future abuses will lead to additional regulation and possible prison terms.

Every business needs a profitable "bottom line" to justify its existence. Profit, though not sufficient, is necessary; and transparency and public spiritedness are meaningless for an enterprise in a free market economy that does not give its stockholders an appropriate return on their equity, provide employees with competitive salaries and benefits, and offer its leaders sufficient incentive. The optimizing of income and expenses is management's continuing challenge.

To achieve these goals, in some situations management will act like poker or chess players, following the rules but using any permissible strategy to overcome an opponent. In others, they will win by acting like team members with common goals. In some relationships, they perform like farmers fattening livestock for the butcher; in others, like farmers nurturing sheep for their wool. But in each case, accountability and enlightened self-interest are what you expect from the best firms.

Gamesmanship, Stephen Potter's classic, had as a subtitle, How to Win Without ACTUALLY Cheating. Winning by "gamesmanship" is okay; cheating is not.

Negotiators in business—like those in labor disputes, nuclear arms treaty discussions, international trade pacts and the like—think of themselves as adversaries, but also as colleagues. Their goal is to advance their own interests, of course, but to do so in a context of continuing relationships and an acknowledgment that one's opponent should come away with enough so he will continue to play the game.

Self-interest is not to be confused with selfishness, as Adam Smith reminds us in perhaps the most famous passage in economic literature, "It is not from the benevolence of the butcher, the brewer or the baker that we expect our dinner, but from their regard to their own self-interest." Their interest, yes, but our dinner; and each of us wins.

Good will and a favorable reputation may be intangibles not reflected on corporate ledgers, but their value is indisputable. Every business field has stories of individuals or companies whose actions went above and beyond the call of duty at short-term expense but long-term repayment.

In the New York real estate field, for example, the 9/11 catastrophe provided occasion for the demonstration of company values that were not reported in the press, not conducted with an eye to formal public relations, but that engendered trust and loyalty. In one high rise residential building a few hundred yards from the World Trade Center site, tenants were prevented by police from returning to their apartments for ten days, their dogs and cats and plantings unattended, with windows left open to the soot and fly ash from nearby fires. Senior building personnel never left the structure, used master keys to enter apartments to feed cats and canaries, walked dogs, watered plants, closed windows and in some cases vacuumed furniture and washed down soot-covered walls. Tenants in the building were notified by e-mail that no rent would be charged from 9/11 until ten days after re-occupancy and anyone wishing an immediate lease cancellation would be accommodated with the option open until the end of January.

The pride that the company's far-flung employees took in those actions, the goodwill and loyalty aroused among tenants, the warm feelings from mortgagees, bankers and professional colleagues (not to mention the profound satisfaction of the company's leaders) are remembered years after the profit and loss statements of 2001 were filed.

Question: Are these factors in "negotiations?"

Answer: Yes; they are intangible, but real.

At the other extreme of the negotiation spectrum is outright fraud, which in law has six characteristics:

a) Knowing
b) Misrepresentation (of)
c) Material
d) Facts

e) On which the victim reasonably relies

f) Resulting in damages

Threats, bribes, kickbacks and other forms of corruption are not unknown. Avoiding negotiations with such perpetrators is best. If that is not possible, one should try to enlist the services of experienced third parties, seek independent sources for facts and evaluations, use standardized contract procedures, and check applicable laws and regulations. Verify what you can; have claims stated precisely in writing; if possible, request bonds or warranties.

Bad adversaries appear from time to time; fortunately the majority of highly-regarded business practitioners "march to the beat of a different drummer"; and they set the tone and establish the standards of "what is done" and "what is not done."

Thank heaven for that, for those standards establish the level of trust that a modern society requires to function successfully.

In *The Moral Consequences of Economic Growth*, Harvard professor Benjamin Friedman points out that improving economic conditions in a society strengthens democracy and the prospects for freedom, and that the modern business enterprise is the key vehicle to achieve that growth and well-being.

Economically effective and socially responsible business organizations are fundamental parts of modern society. The values they espouse, the standards they set and the degree to which they implement them have profound ramifications. The aged Ulysses, as portrayed in Tennyson's poem, would have loved the challenge of running such a corporation.

Essay in The Negotiator's Fieldbook
American Bar Association Books
February 1, 2006

AGAIN

"**E**verything that should be said has been said," noted a philosopher; but added, "since they weren't listening the first time, it must be said again."

Your invitation to reflect on my half century involvement in real estate has proven thought-provoking; but rather than relay platitudes, I thought it would be more interesting if I posed questions that I have asked myself. My answers reflect my thinking and might stimulate yours.

- If business is part "art" and part "science," what steps are you taking to master the art and to keep up to date on the science?
- If business cycles and real estate cycles will always be with us, where are we now in the cycle and are you planning accordingly?
- Looking ahead five, ten or 15 years, where would you like to be and what plans do you have for getting there?
- Considering all the demands on your time—family, business, pro bono, personal development—are you satisfied with your present balance, and what changes do you contemplate?
- On a more fundamental level, are you the kind of person you respect and admire?
- Finally, how would you like to be remembered by family, friends and colleagues?

No one else can answer these questions for you, and each of us will have a different response; but the act of thinking them through can be helpful.

Take the first question, of "art" vs. "science" in business; we all know what we do, but we also know it can be done better, and even "art" skills can be polished.

In a world of technological change, the "science" part is more challenging. Many older people still do not use e-mail or the Internet; and younger people are often unaware of the mathematical tools and "business school techniques" that their competitors have mastered.

It is part of American folklore that Bill Gates, Michael Dell and Steve Jobs were college dropouts, but if they were asked today if they would recommend that route for their own children, or more significantly, for their professional "heirs apparent," is it likely they would do so?

Some things cannot be taught: the willingness to take risks when conventional wisdom is against you, a passionate commitment to an idea, the ability to rebound from failure and so forth.

But much can be taught;—learning to draft a good business plan, to read and understand financial statements, to structure a complex deal, to become familiar with techniques of personnel management, marketing, etc. All of these are valuable background for any aspect of the business world.

One recent graduate told me that the most important insights he gained from his MBA studies were a clear understanding of the time value of money, the power of compound interest and the concept of reversion to the mean.

Today young people are likely to have several different employers, to assume several different professional roles and to need several different skill sets. A knowledge of business fundamentals will help in all those situations.

The second question I pose relates to business cycles in general and real estate cycles in particular.

None of us has an unclouded crystal ball, each reads the same economic forecasts, and each makes personal judgments.

I confess, however, that I did not know what to say to a friend proud of his newly acquired condo in Naples, Florida, when a national study had just estimated that housing prices in Naples, Florida were overpriced by 84%!

We know that our country's "twin deficits," domestic and foreign, are unsustainable and that our rate of national savings is below zero. We know that by historic standards of price/earnings ratios, U.S. stocks are significantly overvalued; we know that, nationally and internationally, we are faced with important imponderables.

The consensus economic forecast is optimistic, and I desperately want to believe it; but I remember Tom Lehrer's comment about "being as nervous as a devout Christian Scientist with "appendicitis." You make your own call.

The third question I pose—looking ahead—is a personal one. Heraclitus noted that you cannot step into the same river twice because you are changing and the river is changing.

Since I entered the real estate field, its evolution has been staggering; there is no reason to believe that the rate or change will be any slower in the future.

Forty years ago, when I expanded Rose Associates' operations into Boston and Washington, the move was considered odd because at that time developers acted locally, architects worked locally, and banks essentially lent locally. Today, of course, real estate thinks and acts nationally; and tomorrow it will do so internationally. You are changing, the field is changing, and you should plan accordingly.

The fourth question deals with how we allocate time, energy and emotional involvement among family, business, pro bono and personal development. These are decisions each must determine for himself or herself. But the question should be asked again and again, because as we change, our priorities should change.

The fifth question I pose—are you the kind of person you respect, and even admire—is like a report card on life, but one we grade ourselves.

Our field has had some splendid role models—brokers and con-

213

sultants like Henry Hart Rice, James Felt and John White; developers like Lew Rudin and Fred Rose who were men leading full lives, a credit to themselves, to their firms and to our industry.

Psychologist Abraham Maslow drew up a famous hierarchy of values, beginning with one's basic material needs, then emotional and psychological satisfactions, first, in comparing our achievements to those of other people and then in how we are regarded by our community.

Finally, he noted, after your material needs have been met, after you have outperformed your next-door neighbor and your brother-in-law, and after you have received the honors you crave, what next? Then, he said, you should strive to become all you are capable of being.

Americans love to quantify intangibles—for example, Robert Parker's rating one wine a "95" as opposed to another "96." These days, social scientists have started to quantify "happiness," and statistics show that material possessions are of great importance only to those who do not have them.

Health and money are immensely important if you lack them. Health once regained tends to be taken for granted, and what economists call the "marginal utility" of money diminishes significantly as you get more of it, except for the purpose of display and one-upmanship.

All recent studies of "happiness" show it has three components—pleasure (some importance), engagement (more) and meaning (most).

Of all the pleasures you can buy, experience by far outranks material possessions; engagement with family, friends, work, romance, hobbies—is more important for happiness; and meaning—applying your personal strengths and resources to some larger end—is the most significant measure of happiness.

Last Spring, the Central Harlem junior high school chess team I work with won the New York State championship, and it cost an un-budgeted $20,000 to send them to the national finals, where they came in number two in the entire country. It is hard to think of another $20,000 expenditure that gave me more joy.

It is satisfying and it is fun to earn money; it can be even more satisfying to dispose of it appropriately.

So my final word is to wish you success in earning your fortune, success in enjoying it, and success in disposing of it.

Meet these goals and the likelihood is that you will be well-remembered.

National Realty Club
March 6, 2006

EVOLVING NEW YORK

New York City is seen today as the world's pre-eminent "global city." Its concentration of human and financial capital, its cultural attractions, and the energy and intellectual ferment of its populace are acknowledged throughout the world. Its advantages are formidable.

On the debit side, New York has become an increasingly difficult and expensive place in which to do business, raise families, and educate children. Middle-income workers and their families are moving to the suburbs, exurbs, and out of state—a continuing historic pattern—at a rate nearly equal to the inflow of newcomers. In addition, the city for some time has been losing market share in the industries in which it once led, lagging in business startups, and becoming unattractive to fast-growing smaller companies. These are not cyclical but structural problems that must be faced.

Other concerns are New York's dependence on a financial services industry under pressure to disperse geographically; and the fact that New York has the highest taxes in the nation, a scarcity of affordable housing, an inadequate public school system, and an undersized and outdated mass transit system that required the disaster of 9/11 to attract the major capital needed to expand.

In a broader context, New York shares the national challenge presented by the geographical and technological decentralization of the American workplace, and it wrestles with how to balance "lifestyle growth" with economic growth. Its local challenges include issues involving municipal, metropolitan, and regional coordination and governance; subsidies for current consumption versus investment for the future; and the complex ramifications of demographic change.

Retaining and capitalizing on the city's strength while adjusting to or modifying its weaknesses will be difficult in a climate in which federal and state governments mandate expensive services they do not fund, in which both the federal and state governments extract from the city vastly more in taxes than the revenues they return in grants, and in which city and state politicians lack the courage or strength to live efficiently within their means.

The New York City of the future will be a dynamic and exciting place; in what way and for whom will be determined by how it addresses issues such as the city's continuing role as the world's financial center; its ability to house, educate, and serve others as well as the rich and the poor; its constructive steps to diversify its economy, stimulate healthy expansion in the outer boroughs, and bring its immigrant and inner-city poor into the economic and social mainstream; and— most important— its determination to live within its means.

DEPENDING ON FINANCIAL SERVICES

The importance of the financial services industry to every sector of New York life is reflected by the fact that contributions from that industry make up one-quarter of the city's payroll taxes.

Technological innovation, high operating costs, even higher local taxes, and, most recently, post–9/11 concerns for physical safety have contributed to the fact that the overwhelming job growth in the financial services sector over the past decade has occurred outside of New York. This tendency toward geographic dispersion of financial services is likely to continue.

New York, must, of course, nurture its financial sector, but it also should learn from the examples of other cities that have overcome severe diminution of their major businesses (such as Houston and Los Angeles). It must develop a highly diversified, small business–oriented economic base that is spread throughout the city—not concentrated in midtown or downtown Manhattan.

218

Rigorous and imaginative efforts to encourage startups in high tech, new media, communication and entertainment—as well as in fashion, the arts, biotechnology, and life sciences—should be high on everyone's agenda, as should efforts to stimulate importing, wholesaling, and warehousing activities in the outer boroughs. Government, which should not try to pick winners, can coordinate industry efforts and information exchanges, can modify counterproductive regulations, and can provide appropriate infrastructure.

HOUSING

New York's housing problems—high costs and scarcity of affordable units—are to some extent self-inflicted wounds, but housing demand at the lowest economic levels is so great that it defies easy solution. To stimulate new affordable housing production, a recasting of the city's outdated 1961 zoning resolution—a 900-page document riddled with loopholes and gray areas needing interpretation—would be a major first step. The resolution's basis concept—strict segregation of uses—is no longer relevant, and some of its judgment calls, such as reserving a third of the city's waterfront for heavy industry, are misguided.

Long overdue are appropriate increases of permissible development densities in underdeveloped areas with access to mass transit, an overhaul of New York's byzantine regulatory practices and building codes, and a sensible revision of work rules for local construction trades.

Changing existing two-family zoning to three-family zoning would make available tens of thousands of inexpensive housing units for low-income immigrant groups, and proper code enforcement would make safer those units already converted illegally. In addition, small homebuilders in the outer boroughs, rather than high-rise developers in Manhattan, may provide an important answer to New York's housing scarcity.

Fresh approaches to developing single-room occupancy structures and congregate housing for the elderly are needed, as is continuing assistance for middle-income families through 80/20 and 421a programs, as well as similar efforts.

Blue Collar v. White Collar v. Sports Shirts

Fifty years ago, New York was home to 140 Fortune 500 companies; today, that number is down to 33. As the national economy continues its relentless shift from manufacturing to services, New York will never again boast the million industrial jobs it has in the 1950s. Since 1980, the city has lost 50 percent of its garment industry, 45 percent of its printing industry, and 15 percent of its wholesale trade.

As a high-cost area, New York cannot compete on the basis of price in the production of high-volume, standardized goods. But it can compete in design quality, customer service, and quick turnaround time, and those features should be encouraged and supported.

The talk of millions of square feet of new office construction in lower Manhattan ignores the millions of square feet of vacant office space available in New York today (at rents well below rents for new construction), and it assumes a degree of white-collar job growth that is unlikely to occur in the foreseeable future.

The far west side of Manhattan is rightly called the borough's "last frontier" for major commercial expansion, but the appropriate mix of uses would be best left to market forces, once improved mass transit is in place.

Shopping for Fun and Profit

Vibrant retail activity improves the quality of urban life, is an important source of municipal revenue, and is a factor in attracting the 40 million annual tourists that are so important to New York City's economic and cultural life.

The city is seriously under-retailed, with 265,000 retail jobs employing 33 out of every 1,000 residents; in Nassau-Suffolk, the ratio is 58 per 1,000; and in Bergen-Passaic, it is 56 per 1,000. Retailing in the outer boroughs deserves support because it makes those areas more livable and because it is a major source of entry- level employment for young people.

Additional municipal parking facilities would help small outer-borough retailers compete more effectively with suburban big box stores.

Educating the Populace

Traditionally, two of New York's glories were its police force and its public school system. By the 1980s, however, conditions had so deteriorated that the city's crime rate was a national scandal, and City College, which a few decades before had produced Nobel Prize winners, was granting degrees to some students described by one City College dean as "functionally illiterate."

Since then, the turnaround in the crime rate has become an internationally recognized triumph, with homicides down from 2,200 per annum in 1990 to fewer than 600 today. But the city's public school system still has a heartbreakingly high percentage of fourth graders who are unable to read and almost the same percentage of students who drop out of high school before graduation.

For the first time, New York's mayor has been granted effective control of the school system, and his energetic chancellor has pledged dramatic reforms. Mayor Michael Bloomberg and Chancellor Joel Klein have expressed their commitment to changing the culture of the school system from one of low expectations and defensiveness to one of accountability and high achievement, and their first steps have been promising.

Recent dramatic success at the undergraduate and graduate levels at New York's municipal colleges is a testament to what can be achieved by tough-minded administrators insisting on high standards for admission, retention, and graduation. Today, a degree from City College is, once again, a worthwhile credential; five years ago, it was not. If the same turnaround could be achieved at the elementary and high school levels, the impact on city life would be dramatic.

The Dollars and Cents of Culture and Entertainment

Culture and entertainment activities employ more than 150,000 workers in New York and add over $15 billion a year to local coffers. More important, such activities are significant factors in the quality of life that help the city attract the educated, sophisticated workforce that is its hallmark.

Government and philanthropies should encourage and support cultural groups to strengthen their viability. In today's real estate market, a shortage of space for rehearsal, performance, and arts exhibits, and for affordable office space for cultural nonprofit organizations, is a growing problem that merits attention.

FREE FLOW OF IDEAS, CAPITAL, AND GOODS— WHAT ABOUT PEOPLE?

Transportation access—once one of New York City's major competitive advantages— has today become an increasing disadvantage. The city's subways, commuter rail lines, and highway system are sadly out of date. In 1992, the John F. Kennedy International Airport was the country's busiest cargo airport and ranked seventh in passengers. In 2001, it ranked sixth in cargo and 14th in passenger traffic.

Change is on the way; the application of 9/11 federal aid to mass transit is triggering long overdue improvement of access to lower Manhattan, one-stop mass transit to the city's airports is now in sight, and Manhattan's first subway expansion in two generations will eventually open up the west side of midtown to overdue development.

The introduction of tolls on the East River bridges and the reintroduction of a commuter tax would each raise $500 million a year. Congestion-based road pricing for automobiles—already successful in London, Singapore and Oslo— would raise additional revenue, and if those sums were applied to debt service on mass transit capital expenditures, the impact on life in New York would be momentous. Better transportation into and within the city would not only improve the quality of life but also would help to reverse the decline of various business activities.

PEERING INTO THE CRYSTAL BALL

The remarkable resiliency of New York, demonstrated so clearly when the city came close to bankruptcy in 1975 and again when it faced the trauma of 9/11, shows that New Yorkers can do what they must.

And when their feet are held to the fire, politicians will acknowledge that wealth must be produced before it can be redistributed, that government services can be provided efficiently, and that overtaxed businesses will flee to lower-cost suburban or out-of-state locations.

The tax-borrow-spend policies of the administrations of New York City mayors Robert Wagner, John Lindsay, and Abraham Beame wrought havoc with New York business and with the stable, middle-class communities of the outer boroughs. What happened once can happen again.

Today, New York State's income taxes are five times the national average; sales taxes in New York City are double those of most states; the city's property taxes are more than one-third higher than the national average; and New York State has a higher ratio of public employees to residents than any other state. The state's semi-independent authorities and public benefit corporations, shielded from public scrutiny and saddled with over $105 billion of debt, are rife with inefficiency and cronyism. New York State's general obligation bonds have the dubious distinction of receiving the poorest rating of any state in the nation from Moody's Investors Services.

New York City's unionized municipal employees' salaries are among the highest in the nation, while the productivity of these employees is among the lowest. The privatization of many government services—from garbage collection and hospital and prison administration to the provision of children's services— which is so successful in other cities, would lower costs and improve service. Tying municipal salary raises to productivity increases would be another approach.

The city's advantages are extraordinary; its problems are manageable when it faces up to them; and, barring the unforeseen, the future should be bright. The application of vision, energy, and competence in the years leading up to World War II made New York City the world's first 20th century city. Today, it has within its power the ability to become the world's 21st century city.

Urban Land Magazine
September 2004

NEW YORK/LONDON
COMPARABLE, COMPLEMENTARY,
COMPETITIVE

C urrent discussions of New York and London focus on who can seduce from whom the lucrative fees from hedge funds, derivatives or Initial Public Offerings that enrich individuals and fill municipal coffers. The assumption is that the halcyon days of 2002-2007 will soon return, the financial services industry will once again be a "cash cow", and attention should focus on support for electronic trading or increasing the available electrical supply.

London's financial services sector is of great importance to the City itself and to the United Kingdom, employing over one million people and accounting for eleven per cent of the U.K.'s income tax and fifteen per cent of its corporate tax revenues. In the United States, financial services represent eight per cent of our GDP and more than five per cent of all U.S. jobs. Obviously it is in each nation's interest for its financial sector to thrive.

Our problems, however, are more complex than just those of the financial community. We face a slow and difficult economic recovery dominated by financial deleveraging and short-term deflationary risks, by massive public and private debt, high unemployment, frightened consumers and an aging labor force. Lack of trust— in government, financial institutions and civic leaders—is widespread.

The gross volume of financial transactions, the profits from the services provided and the numbers of those employed in the financial world will be lower in the future. The eastward shift of global wealth and the surge of competitive financial centers in Singapore and Shanghai, and those nearer home like Dublin, Luxembourg and non-EU regulated Geneva, Zurich and Monaco present growing challenges. Hong Kong, Bermuda, Paris and Dubai also seek larger pieces of the financial pie.

In such a climate, steps that strengthen the financial services industry and maintain leadership standing in a globalized world are called for.

New York and London, both high cost-of-living cities, share problems— public safety and education, effective mass transit, appropriate middle class housing, sustainable development, improved air quality, new "green" energy sources, etc.— and continuing joint examination and review would benefit both cities.

Like loving siblings who share values but eye each other competitively, we can agree to compete in some areas, cooperate in others and, above all learn from each other's experiences.

First we should face our joint challenge: to be world-leading global cities in the 21st century, centers that:

a) Attract, develop and nurture the human capital that generates economic value from ideas;
b) Have the physical and social infrastructure that supports a solid middle class that performs the work of society and an innovative, creative class that spawns new industries and modernizes old ones, that originates new products, new services and new ways of doing things;
c) Serve as both the repository and incubator of world class cultural achievement. Ideally, these cities should also be safe, healthful, fun to live in and have a low cost-of-living; but Utopia awaits another incarnation.

Attracting, nurturing and retaining the best and the brightest in all fields requires many things. For a rich society, the easiest component should be the physical, yet New York is the world's only major city without effective mass transit to its airports; and Heathrow (already at 99% of capacity) is considered one of the least efficient airports in Europe.

Education is another area in which New York and London should be pre-eminent, yet our public elementary school system is considered poor, and London does not take full advantage of the superb universities on its doorstep.

A rich nation should be able to keep its major city well-supplied with housing. In practice, the middle class is leaving New York because of the cost and shortage of middle income housing, and London is only marginally better.

Although the problems are similar, each city must address them in its own way. Greater London's newly-appointed Chief Economist, Bridget Rosewall, points out that, "London's taxes go straight to the National Exchequer (the U.K.'s treasury department) and less than 10% is raised directly by the mayor. Money comes back to subsidize transport, economic development and so on, but only by negotiation with central government departments."

New York's mayor must deal with a difficult City Council and a dysfunctional state legislature whose antics would be suitable for Gilbert and Sullivan comedy if the economic results were not so painful. A classic example is the repeal of New York City's lucrative and badly-needed commuter tax, which reimbursed the City for expenses related to urban workers living (and taxed) in the suburbs. That the repeal movement was led by a New York City-based State legislator to help the re-election campaign of upstaters defies logic. Londoners who recall Britain's ancient "rotten boroughs" understand what flows from the 98% re- election rate of New York State legislators.

London and New York are great international centers whose well-being is important to their inhabitants, their respective regions, their respective nations and the entire civilized world. Let us explore the ways in which they are comparable, complementary and competitive, and how they can learn from each other.

COMPARABLES

At this moment of economic trauma, London and New York are each blessed with a mayor fully conscious of the short term, intermediate and long term economic challenges. Economics, "the science of the allocation of scarce resources," is the key to how their respective administrations will be remembered. Each administration must consume less and invest more, think less "today" and more "tomorrow."

Mayor Boris Johnson's London Plan and Mayor Mike Bloomberg's PlaNYC are efforts to plan for emerging needs two decades ahead.

Each city has a population of eight million (London a bit less, New York a bit more) and each is expected to add one million in the next 20 years. The impact on housing, energy, water supply, waste disposal and infrastructure will be profound—difficult to implement and challenging to finance.

Each has over one third of its population foreign born. London, with 40%, thinks of itself as cosmopolitan; New York, with 36%, thinks of itself as an American city with many foreign born who are becoming American. Helping immigrants to enter the main-stream quickly and effectively is a challenge. (Half the students in New York's elite public high schools— Stuyvesant and Bronx High School of Science—are now Asians.)

Each has a theater district with over twelve million tickets sold annually. Broadway specializes in expensive, blockbuster musicals (which make their way to London), while the West End, in addition to imports, features smaller offerings often from a subsidized National Theatre. An increasing number of plays travel from London to New York, since a production costs four to five times as much to launch on Broadway as on the West End. A growing "off Broadway" reflects the need to cater to lower budget audiences.

Each has great museums of modern art. MOMA, with a fine permanent collection, attracts 2.7 million visitors annually, many of them tourists. London's Tate Modern, with imaginative shows, attracts 3.9 million, many of them locals.

228

In the three F's (film, fashion and food) each is a world leader. New York's film activity has been greater but London's is growing rapidly. The fashion palm goes to New York; but food is important in both. Star chefs are major celebrities on both sides of the Atlantic. In London, 'name' chefs charge high prices in smaller restaurants; New York stars charge less but make it up in volume. (In both cities, great chefs serve dazzling original creations, but, some of us miss the dowdy old Hotel Connaught, with its excellent traditional Grill, or New York's Carème-inspired Le Pavillon.)

Billionaires are attracted to both cities. Before 2008, New York had 71, largely American, while London had 36, largely foreign.

Each city boasts fine art galleries and auction houses. New York has been pre-eminent, but London has made great strides in the past decade.

Both cities have outstanding opera houses, concert halls, athletic stadiums, parks and libraries which attract the creative class, as well as tourists.

Climate change threatens to become a real-world problem for both cities, which Londoners recognize but most New Yorkers do not. For older New Yorkers, the term "ecology" refers to vanishing Bengal tigers and snow leopards, and the term "flood plain" refers to New Orleans. Younger New Yorkers are more alive to the problem.

London seeks to reduce its carbon emissions by 60 per cent by 2025. Many New Yorkers are not sure what carbon emissions are.

The world's leading financial institutions have offices in both cities. London's top income tax rate is now 50%, as is Manhattan's total of federal, state and local charges; Switzerland, Singapore and Hong Kong have rates half as much, and in Dubai (where few want to live) the rate is zero.

London has twice the percentage of its population engaged in manufacturing as New York does, but both are low compared to other cities. New York's energy costs (60% higher than the national average) are a factor. Manufacturing wages are higher than wages in health care and personal services, which are growing in both cities.

As a general rule, provision of infrastructure should precede economic demand, while provision of office space and quality housing should follow economic demand. Vacant offices and unsold condominiums help no one.

Economic diversification is crucial; its implementation merits highest priority for both cities. History has many stories of "one company towns" or "one industry cities" that came to grief, and the reliance that both London and New York place on financial services is unhealthy.

What Each Can Learn From the Other

New York prides itself on its fierce energy and openness to all possibilities; London, on its appreciation of "high culture" and history and its openness to foreign influence. London is its nation's capital, while New York is not even capital of its State.

Some of my older British friends believe the introduction of American breakfast meetings in London was an act of barbarism. Some of my younger American friends cannot understand why their London counterparts consider vacations sacrosanct when business emergencies arise. New York audiences regard "standing ovations" as mandatory; Londoners feel most are undeserved. Broadway audiences are usually sober at curtain time; West End theaters have bars.

London and New York can both learn from Singapore's public toilets, which are the world's best, and from the bicycle provisions in many world-class cities.

New York crime-fighting strategies under Mayors Rudy Giuliani and Mike Bloomberg, implemented by their Police Commissioners Bill Bratton and Ray Kelly, have proved their validity. Murders are down from 2,200 in 1990 to some 500 this year and even graffiti has disappeared. These tactics, if introduced in London, could dampen that city's soaring crime rate.

An American equivalent of the Financial Services Authority, England's sole regulator of financial services, should be considered.

London's Forensic Audit Panel to review municipal expenses and operational efficiency, is an excellent step New York can take, too.

London has exorbitant taxi fares and an Underground system that stops at midnight. New York has a litigious business climate and onerous post 9/11 restrictions on talented immigrants. London's "congestion pricing" has stimulated debate in New York; and London's competitive bidding for municipal bus services would work well in New York.

Effective private, non-profit entities such as the Central Park Conservancy ($70 million annual budget), the Prospect Park Alliance and Friends of the High Line have been a boon to New York and could be replicated. The time has come for Britain to realize the importance of a philanthropic, non-profit sector, especially when the government is broke. This will require a change in public consciousness, but is long overdue. Boris Johnson's new Mayor's Fund for London is a promising start.

Government-subsidized operations like the National Theatre run against the American grain (as our naïve discussions of national health care reveal), but merit consideration. Much of off-Broadway's best work is supported by non-profit groups.

"Jane Jacobs thinking" and "Robert Moses thinking"— maintaining the fabric and character of a city on the one hand while providing necessary infrastructure on the other— are necessary. In New York the excessive power of "community" and "single issue" groups working against the public interest often stymie important university, hospital and other expansion. The defeat of the important Westway underground highway rankles still.

London, Warsaw, Dresden and other cities rebuilt wonderfully after WWII. After 9/11, New York's model could have been Pericles' rebuilding of the Acropolis, instead of our current plan.

PlaNYC, the Bloomberg administration's vision of New York in 2030, is imaginative. What the city needs, however, is a comprehensive reconsideration of out-dated zoning concepts (floor area ratios, air rights transfers, etc.) to stimulate the kind of development New York needs.

The failure of the U.S. Embassy in London to pay its large and overdue congestion charges is a national embarrassment.

Terrorist threats are always with us. The New York Police Department's intelligence and counter-terrorism unit, called "the gold standard" by other U.S. police departments, should be emulated. Britain's ubiquitous closed-circuit television cameras seem destined to be applied here as well.

JOINT CHALLENGES

Each city should focus on its regional, as well as its metropolitan, problems. New or improved subway, bus, commuter rail, light rail and ferry projects are needed, especially for dense areas with inadequate mass transit, high poverty levels and low auto ownership.

New York's population density is twice London's, and 55% of New Yorkers use public transportation vs. 37% of Londoners. London's Tube costs three times what New York's subway does. New York's air conditioned subway cars are cooler in summer than London's, but air conditioning is scheduled for the Tube in 2010.

Each city must demand greater efficiency from its public sector to assure better services and lower—not higher— taxes. "Doing more with less" should be the motto.

Each city must press its national government for appropriate taxation and financial regulation practices that achieve legitimate public goals but do not strangle the financial sector for the benefit of foreign markets.

New York's powerful public sector unions must be brought back-into the real world, and their off-the-scale pension and health benefits and overtime payments should reflect the practices of the federal government and other states (which also have 40-hour work weeks rather than New York's 35-hour week).

Defined Contribution pension plans should replace Defined Benefit pension plans for all new government employees, and 401(k)'s should be encouraged.

Offshore tax avoidance by rich Britons and Americans should be faced frankly.

Both cities face governance issues, but New York State's chaotic conditions are of mythic proportions. Calls for a constitutional convention to reform New York State government have come from former governors Mario Cuomo and George Pataki and former mayor Rudy Giuliani, among others.

Substantial cuts in State spending, wage freezes for all public employees, caps on local property taxes, term limits for elected State officials, non-partisan political redistricting, major legal tor reform and re-thinking of the operations of the state's autonomous public authorities like the M.T.A. call for open discussion and review.

Governor Paterson should be encouraged to submit without delay legislation for an early convention.

FINANCIAL SERVICES

Recent studies by McKinsey and others detail the steps London and New York must take to improve their competitive positions in regard to each other and to the rest of the world.

Commissioned by Mayors Boris Johnson and Mike Bloomberg, these studies spell out the micro and macro steps needed; and involved citizens of each city should support their suggestions.

Lowering New York's strangling taxes (per capita, roughly double those of America's other large cities) is mandatory if the city is to thrive. The cutting of public expenditures which must accompany such tax cuts requires a degree of political courage not normally apparent in New York.

CONCLUSION

Neither London nor New York can rest on its laurels or assume that the past will be reflected in the future. Each must capitalize on its strengths and address its weaknesses. Each must restore public trust in the character and competence of public leadership.

Difficult trade-offs (Heathrow's third runway vs. environmental impacts, New York's public services vs. the need to cut expenditures, etc.) must be presented to the public clearly to gain support for

233

painful but necessary choices. Everyone loves Santa Claus (Father Christmas) but we shouldn't lose Scrooge's email address.

The encouragement of small and medium-size business enterprises and the creation of "start-ups" are crucial. Financial services are important, but they are but one of many components of a diverse economy and vibrant society in a globalized world.

That London and New York will retain an international role seems certain; but, as Oliver Wendell Holmes, Jr., one of America's wisest jurists noted, "The mode by which the inevitable comes to pass is called effort."

Global Mayors Forum
Columbia University
September 15, 2009

YOU DIDN'T BUILD THAT ALONE!

The suggestion that I reflect on lessons learned from my six decades' love affair with real estate has been thought-provoking. My first thought was of Isaac Newton's comment about seeing further by standing on the shoulders of giants.

It has been my good fortune to have learned from a number of giants of our time. Their message about the importance of character and competence—doing the right thing and doing it with professionalism— has been proven time and again. Learning not the "tricks of the trade" but "the trade itself," and earning a reputation for reliability and for operational expertise have always been a winning combination.

Another lesson is the importance of understanding the conventional wisdom but knowing when it is crucial to think 'outside the box.' Our tendency is to assume that all trends continue, but in the real world fluctuating economic cycles and demographic changes, changes in public taste or values, and "black swan" (unforeseeable) events do occur. Charles Mackay's 1841 classic *Extraordinary Popular Delusions and the Madness of Crowds*—which should be on every student's required reading list but never is—tells of the "bubbles," manias and witch-hunts of the past and those that inevitably will take place in the future. "Bernie Madoff," "sub-prime mortgages," "Lehman Brothers"—these are stories with old plots but new names.

In America today, we are at economic and social inflection points whose timing and impact are unclear, unlike the decades after World War II when my career began.

From the mid 1970's, when I first saw 116 acres of nearly empty fields across I-95 from the Pentagon, to the moment in 1991 when Pentagon City received the Urban Land Institute award as the nation's best mixed use development, what I was doing seemed obvious. Similarly, developing office towers in Boston's burgeoning financial district in the 1970's—when good sites, enthusiastic public officials, many prospective tenants and abundant mortgage money were all available— seemed like shooting fish in a barrel, as was my brother Fred's development of residential towers in Manhattan. No one would claim that today's path is as clear.

At this moment—Autumn 2012—the problems of our national economy are so formidable that they overshadow everything. American resilience, flexibility and common sense ultimately will prevail. But it may require a crisis and an aroused citizenry demanding that our short- sighted legislators retreat from destructive partisanship and resulting gridlock that make it impossible for government to function effectively. Our excessive government expenditures and inadequate tax revenue produce deficits that are not sustainable.

To make matters worse, public confidence in our national institutions is at an all-time low. America is suffering from a profound crisis of authority; we have little trust in the integrity or competence of our political leaders, our bankers, our corporate chieftains, our educators, our news media, our law courts, even our religious leaders. When polls show a 10% public approval rating of the job Congress is doing, one wonders on what planet that 10% is living.

Fears of a 'fiscal cliff'--$600 billion in automatic tax increases and governmental spending cuts set for the end of this year—are already dampening private spending, postponing business investment and coloring short term economic decisions. Uncertainty about tax rates, the continuity of government programs and the threat of another governmental shutdown over a debt ceiling increase encourage caution which further weakens an already feeble recovery. Add negative external factors—a worsening Eurozone crisis, slower growth in China and in emerging-market economies, turmoil in the Middle East which

236

may lead to higher oil prices—and it is difficult to be optimistic in the short term. With interest rates historically low, government options are few. After the 2012 elections, Congress will be under pressure to face the entitlement reform and revenue increases we need to balance our budgets over time.

The pendulum swings back eventually, however. 2015 is the year auto industry forecasters predict the first 16 million car sales since the financial crisis began; just as current pessimism can be a "self-fulfilling prophecy," so can auto industry optimism. Volkswagen is opening a new plant in Chattanooga, planning to double its U.S. sales. Honda is expanding production facilities in Greensburg, Indiana; Kia is expanding in Georgia, and Hyundai in Alabama—all these facilities will be ready before 2015.

Goldman Sachs expects housing starts to reach 1.4 million in 2015, up from 700,000 this year. The durable goods sector of the economy— which produces products that last more than three years—also is preparing for an upsurge in demand in 2015. The multiplier effect will be impressive. By 2015, personal debt is likely to be reduced, home equity values increased and, most important, some expect America to achieve energy independence from Middle East oil by then, with a corresponding lowering of oil prices.

Although Europe may face an economic and social 'lost decade'—as Japan did in the 1990's—our economy can rebound if legislators make the short term, intermediate and long term compromises and trade-offs indicated in "Simpson-Bowles" thinking ($3 trillion in budget cuts and $1 trillion in added revenues over the coming decade). Reduced military budgets will require informed discussion about our engagement in "wars of necessity vs. wars of choice" (Richard Haas) and about fighting our battles by "hard vs. soft power" (Joseph Nye).

When Americans spend less on consumer goods and invest more on education, scientific research and public infrastructure (and infostructure); when we borrow less and save more; when an appropriate balance between public goods and private goods is restored; when equality of opportunity again becomes an accepted American goal, and when our politicians are no longer for sale to the highest bidder, we will regain our momentum toward a constructive future.

No crystal ball is unclouded and there are no easy answers, but we must make prudent 'guesstimates' and assess reasonable probabilities. In the world of real estate, Joel Kotkin believes that the suburbanization of America will continue; but Alan Ehrenhalt points to trends showing exurbia shrinking, suburban middle classes re-attracted to the city and some inner city poor moving to older suburbs. If the tax-deductibility of home mortgage interest is lessened or mortgage lending standards are tightened, the negative impact on suburbs will be significant. Richard Florida feels that future workers will change jobs more frequently and will prefer the flexibility that renting homes rather than owning them permits. Edward Glaeser praises high density center city development for its face-to-face interaction, stimulus to creativity, competition, social and economic diversity and social mobility. Everyone predicts continuing gentrification (Harlem is now 10% middle income non-black and Jane Jacobs would be dismayed to see her economically-diverse West Village commanding the highest rents in New York). That future development will be ecologically sound and environmentally sensitive is a given.

My own belief is that high density rental housing—with smaller apartments, smaller rooms and lower rents—built near suburban mass transit stations (with retail and recreational facilities adjoining) will be an increasingly popular model. The appeal of housing, retail, recreational and cultural facilities in downtown office and industrial centers will continue to increase; Rose Associates' current high quality residential conversion of the 66-story, one million sq. ft. Art Deco office tower at 70 Pine Street near Wall Street is an example. The conversion of unused rail facilities into Lower Manhattan's wildly successful "High Line" is another.

Over the long term, the mutually reinforcing factors of automation and globalization will transform American society. The automation story is told eloquently in the recent N.Y. Times headline "Skilled

Work Without the Worker"; and globalization's impact on sending jobs overseas is universally recognized. The prospect of well- paying high tech and managerial employment for the well-educated few and low-paying 'service' employment for the less-educated is a challenge our society must face constructively.

Educating our youth appropriately in light of socio-economic patterns requires dramatic new educational thinking.

Stimulating economic growth and increasing national income while apportioning the proceeds fairly require new economic thinking.

Balancing the needs of the young, old and underprivileged while providing necessary incentives and rewards for those producing our income require new social thinking.

EDUCATION

In 1870, when British factory owners found that their illiterate workers could not compete against literate German factory workers, and British politicians realized that the Reform Bills of 1832 and 1867 had given the vote to illiterate farmers who could vote against them, Britain passed its first compulsory education law not to benefit the workers and farmers but to help the nation (i.e. the rich and powerful). In 21st century America, the 1% must realize that an educated, motivated and productive 99% is in their best interest in an internationally competitive world.

Universal pre-school education—which instills in a child the self-discipline, self-confidence, curiosity and future-mindedness that are necessary pre-conditions for educational success—is an important first step. And the message must continue through elementary school to avoid "Head Start fade-out." The rest of the world—especially China and India—is increasingly providing good pre-schooling. Europe already does—98% of Finland's children receive excellent pre-schooling while fewer than half of American children do.

High quality teachers (drawn from the top 10% of the academic pool, as in Finland, rather than the bottom 25% of the academic pool, as in the U.S.) are key ingredients in the educational process at all levels. Pay, perquisites and prestige should be high enough to attract and keep the best teachers.

Teachers should be held to high entry standards, given opportunity and encouragement to continue their professional development, and recognition for outstanding performance. When teachers are determined by fair methods to be inadequate, they should be removed. (In Europe, teachers are considered professionals; in America they are viewed as union members, and treated accordingly.)

All children should be encouraged to advance to their highest potential.

At the high school level, German- and Swiss-style vocational and apprenticeship options should be offered to those desiring them, and we must rethink the question of "life-preparation" for those for whom conventional schooling has not been successful.

At the college level, we should expand and improve community colleges and junior colleges, which can be either "final" or "transitional" to four year colleges.

A "bigger bang for the educational buck" should be a national priority, with higher quality and lower costs achieved by longer school days and school years; we need an end to "lifetime tenure" for senior professors and more efficient use of faculty, including on-line education and "live" teaching available for face-to-face interaction when discussion, questioning and personal intellectual involvement are indicated.

Higher education in the sciences (four year college, graduate and postgraduate) should be available without cost—as a national investment—for those who qualify.

Expanded intramural athletics and an end to inter-collegiate athletics would lower college costs by as much as 10%, and produce healthier college students and fewer who later become "couch potatoes."

Producing an educated public with the knowledge and skills required in the 21st century should be a national priority, and the expenditure to achieve that must be considered our most important investment in our future.

Our Economy

How to stimulate economic growth and how to apportion the proceeds appropriately are questions our politicians should be debating, not "big government" vs. "small government" but how to achieve smart government—transparent, efficient, respected for its fairness and wisdom. We should consider revenue producers like the V.A.T. (Value Added Tax), universal in Europe, a tax on consumption rather than production without lessening incentives for high earners (with proceeds dedicated to scientific research programs, an infrastructure bank, etc.).

Since we cannot indefinitely distribute (or redistribute) wealth we have not created, we must allow and encourage our free market economy to 'make the pie bigger.' This requires: a) national savings guided by our financial sector to productive use by our innovators and entrepreneurs; b) incentives and rewards for wealth producers and c) investment in human, industrial, mineral and social capital.

The proceeds (the U.S. $16 trillion GDP) of our 'farm' should then be allocated by market forces or by government dictate:
to reward the "farmers"; b) to replenish the "seed corn," and c) to distribute to "others."

In the past, our economy grew because we reinvested much of our proceeds in the future. Today we live for the present and consume not only all we produce, but all we can borrow from others or steal from the next generation by increasing the national debt and incurring multi-trillion dollar unfunded pension liabilities.

The economist Arthur Okun wished to be remembered for Okun's Law which states "That which is not sustainable will not be sustained."

Social Thinking

Although our cyclical economic problems can be dealt with by short term stimulus and long term rebalancing, our social problems are more complex.

One important problem is the growing stratification in American life— not by color, religion or ethnicity but by education. The less-educated have fewer "life chances" in employment, health, family stability and life satisfaction. One quarter of U.S. students do not finish high school, and some 40% have no post-high school training. How will they fare in an increasingly competitive world?

In that world, America faces a "new normal" of inadequate job creation for our growing population. The resulting levels of unemployment and underemployment will have profound social effects.

When Work Disappears by William Julius Wilson and *Citizens Without Work*, the 1930's classic by E. Wight Bakke, describe the destructive psychological impact of long term unemployment, and Nobel Laureate Edmund Phelps' *Rewarding Work* discusses the degree to which our employment—or lack of it—defines us. Providing employment, no matter how uneconomic, is less destructive than creating a culture of dependency, which demoralizes and immobilizes its victims.

CONCLUSION:

Future historians may describe the period from 1945 to 2000 as "America's Golden Age." During that time, "American" was the thing to be, New York was the place to be, real estate development was one of the things to do; and I was fortunate to have it all.

Born the week of the 1929 Great Crash, I celebrated my 70th birthday shortly before the World Trade Center terrorist attack.

The "we're all in this together" mindset of the Great Depression; the cocky determination of WWII; the G.I. Bill and Levittown optimism of the decades following the war; the sense of relentless progress in the Civil Rights advances; the social turmoil of the hippy, Beatnik late '60's; the smug complacency of our economic advances in the '80's and '90's; the troubled soul-searching after the George W. Bush years; the anxiety of the Great Recession – I experienced them all, but the fundamental characteristics of American society remained constant.

The widespread pessimism and loss of self-confidence America is experiencing now will pass; but it will require some upheaval or the emergence of a charismatic new leader to galvanize us into action.

The self-absorption and focus on narrow material self-interest that pervades all aspects of American life today are, I hope, temporary. A more communal-minded, future-minded ethos, with less emphasis on material possessions and more on life experience and satisfaction will prevail in time. Our young may focus less on the verb "to have" and more on "to do" and "to be." With such values, our rich won't deny proper free school breakfasts to our poor school children; a Da Vinci, a Mme. Curie or an Einstein born to poor parents will have the opportunity to develop his/her God-given talents. The vitality of our cities, the dynamism of our cultural life and our justifiable pride in the fairness of our society will again be the envy of the world.

Printed on every U.S. dollar bill (above the pyramid) is the motto Annuit Coeptis—"God has favored our undertaking." Our Founding Fathers believed that, and so do I —now and for the future.

Narrow material self-interest may reign today, but as Shelley said, "If winter comes can spring be far behind?"

NYU Schack Institute of Real Estate
November 2, 2012

POWER

"Power" is usually defined as the ability to influence the behavior of others, with "force" and "persuasion" the two conventional methods.

Nicolo Machiavelli (whose chief lesson from the Bible, he noted in *The Prince*, was that "all armed prophets have been victorious and all unarmed prophets have been destroyed") is the protagonist of the first, known as "hard power." "The end justifies the means" and "It is better to be feared than loved" are other Machiavelli messages.

Dale Carnegie, the author of *How to Win Friends and Influence People*, is the spokesman for "soft power." "Talk in terms of the other person's interests." "Show respect for the other person's opinions." "Be a good listener." "Let the other person feel the idea was his."— are some of Carnegie's rules.

Variations on power are common. Robert Moses used his form of "hard power" to create a staggering array of New York's bridges, parks, highways and beaches, while Jane Jacobs used her "soft power" to prevent him from extending Fifth Avenue through Washington Square Park and from putting an east-west expressway through lower Manhattan.

Today life is more complex; modern thinking focuses not on hard or soft but on "smart power"—the application of the range of tools available to achieve goals with wisdom in considering strategy and shrewdness in selecting tactics. Foreign affairs in a multi-polar world, for example, require diplomatic, military and economic resources and astute use of alliances, partnerships and institutions. In military acad-

245

emies, along with Clausewitz's classic *On War*, Sun Tzu's 2000 year old *The Art of War*— with its balance of psychology and armament, deception and threat, short term tactics and long term strategy—is on every reading list. Generals Colin Powell and George C. Marshall felt that the thoughtful, balanced insights of Thucydides, the ancient Athenian general, were as applicable now as when they were written 2,500 years ago. (If George W. Bush knew of the Athenian experience in Sicily he might have thought twice about a land war in Iraq and Afghanistan.)

In our current partisan political climate—with the 'legalized bribery' of political campaign contributions, with massive expenditures on television commercials and newsprint advertising, with 'public relations' the art form in which we excel today, the ability to influence the behavior of others is more difficult than ever, but results vary, depending on the cards you are dealt and the skill with which you play them.

Lyndon Johnson passed a Civil Rights bill that John Kennedy could not, an interesting lesson; the differing approaches to gun control legislation of Barack Obama and Bill Clinton provide a rerun of a similar script.

President Obama, an eloquent idealist, has proposed sweeping measures that Republicans have pledged to defeat. The National Rifle Association, with vast lobbying sums at its disposal, is marshaling powerful forces in opposition. Public opinion polls show that the public is now ready for appropriate measures.

Bill Clinton, an astute political operative, points out that passing the 1994 federal assault weapons ban "devastated" more than a dozen Democratic lawmakers in the 1994 mid-term elections, including then Speaker of the House Tom Foley, who lost his job and his seat in Congress. Speaking to Obama's National Finance Committee during the second inaugural weekend, Clinton advised fighting the gun control battle by "using the combination of technology, social media and personal contact the way the Obama campaign won Florida, won Ohio. Really touch people and talk to them about it." Taking a page

246

from Dale Carnegie, Clinton said, "Do not patronize the passionate supporters of your opponents by looking down your noses at them. Don't underestimate the emotional response gun controls evoke from people in rural states," Clinton warned; "I know because I come from this world." Lyndon Johnson came from the anti-civil rights south, and the story of how he passed the landmark Civil Rights Act of 1964 is brilliantly told in Robert Caro's book *The Passage of Power*.

How he kept Judge Howard Smith, Chair of the House Rules Committee, from keeping the legislation bottled up indefinitely in committee (the south's traditional strategy); how he played on Senator Harry Byrd's weaknesses (taxes) and used his strengths, while coopting Senator Richard Russell; how he gave Martin Luther King, Jr. a list of specific Republican congressmen to be worked on; how he brazenly used Brown and Root's deep-ocean drilling project called "Mohole" as a hostage; how the Steelworkers Union's 33 lobbyists worked at his behest with those of the Electrical Workers and the Auto Workers; how Roy Wilkins was asked to repeat openly "the NAACP's intention of purging congressmen who voted against it"; how he pleaded, bullied, threatened—until on December 24th, 1964 at 7:00 AM (so congressmen could get home for Christmas) Lyndon Johnson got the crucial vote he needed.

Will effective gun control legislation be passed soon? It depends on how the "mechanics" are handled, and if President Obama's team follows the suggestions of Bill Clinton and the approach of Lyndon Johnson.

California's anti-gun Democratic Senator Dianne Feinstein has submitted to the Senate a stringent 'winner take all' bill, while Senate Majority Leader Harry Reid said last week that an assault-weapons ban could not pass the Senate. Senator Max Baucus of Montana, the only Democrat with an A plus rating from the NRA, suggests strengthening existing gun laws effectively before tackling more stringent ones.

Given public sentiment, it seems clear that a deal can be made— if it is handled with political deftness. This is not always the case. Early in Bill Clinton's first presidential term, I had lunch with an apoplectic Senator Daniel Patrick Moynihan, who had just received from Ira Magaziner a report from Hillary Clinton's secretly-conducted Task Force to Reform Health Care. "This must be passed," said Magaziner to Moynihan, "without changing the dotting of an "i" or the crossing of a "t." Moynihan (in favor of a health bill) nearly wept when he said "Not a chance; not a chance." Pat had just agreed with Republican Bob Dole on a major, but more modest, measure that would have been widely acceptable. As a result of Magaziner's (and Hillary's) intransigence, it was two decades before a major health care bill again was presented.

New York's effective Mayor Michael Bloomberg has achieved many things for the city he loves, but 'congestion pricing was not among them. Had the new revenues from cars coming into Manhattan been specifically designated and promoted to improving mass transit in the outer boroughs (extended subway lines, better bus service), a constituency in support of the bill would have been created. As presented, the proceeds flowed to the Metropolitan Transit Authority, which refused to reveal how the new funds would be used. The public reaction: "Just another tax and the Hell with it." So much desired congestion pricing was never passed.

In the cases of Hillary Clinton's health care bill, Mike Bloomberg's congestion pricing proposal and current gun control legislation, it would be worthwhile to contemplate what Clausewitz, Sun Tzu and Thucydides would have advised.

What should ordinary folks who want to influence public policy do?

The answer is: be active rather than passive, join groups of kindred spirits, write, speak, communicate with public officials. As a centrist appalled by the extreme views of Tea Party types on the right and Occupy Wall Streeters on the left, I recognize their impact and hope that the moderate groups I espouse—"No Labels," "Common Cause" and others—will be heard over extremist din.

Effective activities must have messages and messengers—specific agenda items and vehicles to promulgate them.

Whether on macro issues such as immigration, health care or climate change, or on micro issues affecting your town or borough, your local school or local zoning, your trade or professional concerns, the basics are the same:

a) Become well-informed on the issues—not just the headline generalities but the specific details;
b) Think through carefully your long term, intermediate and short term goals;
c) Know, relate to and cultivate your allies—actual or potential;
d) Understand the goals, strategies and 'levers of power' of your adversaries, especially their strengths and weaknesses;
e) Confer, consult, seek advice and support from kindred spirits, being prepared to modify your views when necessary to strengthen the general case;
f) Prepare concrete plans of action subject to revision as unfolding events dictate. (Clausewitz worried about "the fog of war.")
g) Persist, persist, persist;
h) Invite me to your victory celebration.

The "Big Idea" Workshop
January 27, 2013

GERTRUDE STEIN AND THE
REAL ESTATE MARKET

On her deathbed, the redoubtable Gertrude Stein supposedly asked her companion, Alice B. Toklas, "Alice, what is the answer?" Hearing no reply, she asked, "In that case, Alice, what is the question?"

In the same way, the experienced banker becoming involved in real estate must learn at the onset what questions to ask, and then he must learn how to interpret and apply the response.

All of us to a certain extent "know" things that are not true or, more likely, that are irrelevant or misleading half-truths; and in no field is this truer than in real estate. The generation-long, post-World War II inflation obscured harsh realities that became painfully apparent in periods of slack demand and stable or declining values.

The banker of today can no longer lend on the "great fool theory" that some other lender will necessarily come by to bail him out, nor can he automatically count on having his load made good by the relentless increase in paper values reflected in the comment that "the rising tide lifts all the boats."

In the real world, some buildings depreciate physically or economically and not merely in the eyes of the tax lawyer; not all mortgage 'balloons' meet anticipations. Self-serving projections can turn out to represent hopes rather than expectations, and carefully documented forecasts often appear in the cold light of day to be mere extrapolations of the rising segment of a curve.

David Rose, our senior partner has proposed Rose's Rule – "In a free market economy, shortage tends to create surplus and surplus, shortage."

The lender is often confused by hearing unfamiliar appraisal terms such as the Ellwood Formula, the Hoskold Method, the Inwood Factor, or the authoritative-sounding Internal Rate of Return. When he asks for hard numbers, he sometimes gets impressive computer printouts (accurate to the nearest feather) of how many angels can dance on the head of a pin.

"What," the banker asks, "should I do?"

There is no easy answer, for we are dealing with an art rather than a science. Real estate values are based on anticipations of the future; and the future implies unknowns. In real estate, unlike archeology, the past is of interest only to the degree that it throws light on the future.

The goal of the lender is to improve the odds by sound judgment about the future.

NEW CONSTRUCTION

With new construction, understanding the role of the developer, his nature, and, above all, his aims, is a fundamental importance.

The usual aim of the developer is to achieve the twin goals of controlling as much brick, mortar, and land as he can with as little of his own cash as possible, while at the same time achieving the highest possible cash-on-cash return on what he does have in the job.

In the purchase of existing income-producing real estate, the unknowns involve future income and expense, and one can usually project accurate extensions of current items.

In new construction, however, the gross figures are unknown, and the numbers can be a leap in the dark.

Gross Cost, for example, can be broken down into:

    a) initial land cost,

    b) tenant relocation, possession, and demolition,

    c) "field cost" of brick and mortar.

252

d) fees for a wide variety of professional services,

e) real estate taxes and building loan interest during construction,

f) interim operating losses from Certificate of Occupancy to rent-up.

The possibility of unforeseen cost increases in each of the last five items is real, and the cumulative impact of substantial errors in each can be severe.

Gross Financing can involve funds from combinations of straight fee, leasehold-and-fee, construction and permanent loans, proceeds from the sale of tax losses, cash contributions of a Limited Partner, etc.

Unless one is dealing with a standard product, Total Income figures for a job yet to be built are more difficult to estimate than those for an existing, occupied (and therefore "market-tested") project; and the same is true for expenses.

The conclusion a reasonable person must reach is that new development is anything but 'shooting fish in a barrel'; it is a high risk game with anguish for the losers, but with rewards proportionate to the risks for the winners.

For a banker, the moral of the story is not that one should not lend on new construction, but rather that such lending should be done knowledgeably and prudently.

The skills of the successful developer consist in making important decisions, key trade-offs that suit the nature of the project. Partly by experience, partly by intuition, and sometimes (when the size, complexity, novelty or uniqueness of the job requires it), by formal feasibility studies, market analyses, and the like, the developer tries to make "sufficient decisions on the basis of insufficient information." What the construction lender is lending on is:

a) the ability of the developer to make such judgments accurately;

b) the "margin for error" represented by such conditions as the percentage of fullness of the loan; and

c) where there are personal guarantees, the developer's net worth available to back any shortfall.

To a wise lender, the competence, track-record, and integrity of the construction borrower are of great importance, since experience has shown that even the best-conceived project may not be able to withstand a well-intentioned incompetent or an able fellow who cockily and without sufficient preparation tackles a job unlike anything he has done before or an experienced character with larceny in his heart. If I were a lender, I would require substantial collateral from a borrower whose competence I questioned, and the assistance of highly skilled professionals to aid an able, but newly arrived entrant into the field. I would not lend money at all to a borrower whose professional integrity was in question, and I would go out of my way to encourage loans to highly regarded development teams with projects of prime feasibility. It is important to emphasize the phrase "prime feasibility," because even the best in the field can be seduced into jobs because "the money is there." The wise lender should not only have confidence in his own negative judgment, but for projects of size and complexity, should seek independent analysis of feasibility.

Our brief aside on interest rate: It never seemed to me that real risk on the part of a lender was adequately compensated by another point or two of interest. Like Groucho Marks, who wouldn't join a club that would take someone like him, I would not feel comfortable lending money to a borrower willing to pay exorbitant rates.

Assuming an able, experienced, and honorable developer whose project appears to make economic sense, the lender is faced with the question of what terms and conditions to impose. Unless he is prepared to be the lender of last resort, the construction lender should require a permanent financing take-out of an amount greater than the construction loan (ten percent is the usual difference), with loan conditions dove-tailing with those of the construction loan. Stringent inspection during construction should be understood by all parties to be an absolute must, and the disgraceful experience of the recent past (when loan advances far exceeded the value of construction in place) need never be repeated.

The question of loan guarantees is sticky even when the borrower's commitment is "to complete" rather than "to repay." One cannot ignore the recent sad examples when personal guarantees against outside collateral proved worthless because other liens had been placed against the collateral. Reasonable control over the borrower's other loss exposures is not out of order. Several of the nation's largest developers who came to grief in the recent shake-out might not have done so if their lenders had insisted on the right to monitor the cumulative total exposure assumed by the borrower.

WHEN LOANS GO BAD

The story of the American banking industry and the real estate debacle of the 1974-75 is probably destined in time to stimulate as much research and professional discussion as the Dutch Tulip Craze or the South Sea Bubble.

Developments that should never have been planned in the artificially financed "super-boom" of 1971-73 emerged from the ground to be greeted by soaring construction costs, unforeseen shortages in key materials, and unheard-of construction loan rates.

Irritation turned to despair when final demand proved inadequate to absorb the avalanche of prematurely produced product; it takes no savant to predict that the resulting headaches will be around for some time to come.

Bankers becoming involved with real estate today should be required to become familiar with the case histories of the great fiascos – not because of morbid interest, but for the same reason that a prominent New York structural engineer has made the study of engineering disasters a lifelong hobby – the better to understand sound projects.

The banker who doesn't ask himself what lessons are to be learned from the blood-letting is cheating himself needlessly.

Conventional wisdom may hold that one is better off with small participations in a number of large loans rather than in total financing of fewer big ones; but actual experience shows that some of the worst headaches were those in which the lending participants fought destructively among themselves. In *Poor Richard's Almanac*, Benjamin Franklin said that there is nothing wrong with putting all your eggs in one basket, so long as you watch the basket.

Bankruptcy, or rather the threat of bankruptcy, is being used as a form of blackmail against lenders by some defaulting owners; creative thought must be given to strategies of defense.

A number of observers feel that at the first sign of real trouble, when the developer looks to the lender for the concession, revision of terms, etc., the lender should insist on re-casting the arrangement to make it more "Chapter XII-proof." For example, in return for additional cash advances, a property can be conveyed to the lender, with the original developer having an option to re-purchase it if he meets prescribed conditions.

Obviously, each job must be dealt with in terms of its unique factors; but in general, early defensive action is advisable in dealing with a sick job or a stumbling developer.

Another important point involves the individuals (developer and lending officer) best equipped to deal with a sick job; those who were in on the launching of a project are not necessarily the best ones to be involved in the turnaround.

Individuals can get psychologically "locked in" to a view either disapproval or outdated by subsequent events; and whether for reasons of pride, rigidity or mental block, they often tenaciously hold on and "go down with the ship."

"Percussive Sublimation" (being kicked upstairs) and "Lateral Arabesque" (moved elsewhere out of harm's way) are two frequently employed management techniques in such cases in the corporate world, but in the real estate field, many people feel that the developer who got himself (and the lender) into the fix should be entrusted to get them both out (even if there is no necessary common interest).

A third generality is the tendency to forget the importance of nuts-and-bolts real estate management competence.

Politics is often defined as "the art of the impossible," but the tag applies equally well to the field of real estate management.

256

It seems unglamorous and lacking in entrepreneurial razzle-dazzle to point it out, but the turkeys laid by wheeler-dealers can often be turned into something fit for the banker's Thanksgiving table by such prosaic steps as careful, professional attention to personnel selection and supervision, preparation of realistic operating budgets, imaginative but cost-effective advertising and promotion campaigns, institution of honest and efficient purchasing and control procedures, and so forth.

In real estate as in anything else, poorly-conceived or sloppily re-inforced controls may provide such great temptation to dishonesty that they render the supervisor responsible, almost an "accomplice-in-fact."

A banker cannot be expected to determine capital and operating costs of fluorescent vs. incandescent lighting; carpet vs. resilient floor tile; #6 oil vs. electric heat vs. New York Steam, or the hundred and one other details that constitute the day-to-day concerns of the management professional. It is important for him, however, to realize how significant to the numbers on a sick job these mundane questions can be.

There is an adage in the field to the effect that "good management doesn't cost; it pays"; and that is one real estate generality that admits no exceptions!

RULES OF THUMB
One danger to the new entrant to the real estate world is the natural but sometimes harmful tendency to rely on unsupported generalizations that may be irrelevant or misleading

My favorite example of this thinking is the statement that "the average American has one mammary and one testicle." I also like the fellow who refused to let his wife have more than four children, on the grounds that every fifth child born today is Chinese; and his friend who drowned crossing a lake whose average depth was only one foot!

Kidding aside, when one speaks of dollars-per-room do we mean large rooms or small, in efficiency apartments or in four-bedroom du-plexes?

A popular rule says that for a large residential subdivision, one should allocate 20 percent of the gross land area to streets. Depending on shape, topography, governmental requirements, perimeter facilities, etc., actual requirements can run from below 15 percent to over 30 percent.

Everyone used to 'know' that in a suburban shopping center 5.5 parking spaces were required for every 1,000 square feet of gross store area. Experience has since proved that availability of mass transit can be an important factor, and (less obviously) that adding office space by as much as 20 percent of the total area may not require one extra parking space.

Percentage of income people spend on housing is another rule of thumb frequently applied, yet in practice the poor spend a much higher and the rich a much lower percentage of their income than we used to think.

The conversion factor between the rental value and the condominium sales price of a given apartment unit is another "rule of thumb" that can be misleading, as is the corollary of what a condominium converter can afford to pay for a rental building he plans to flip. In each case, the specifics of the project must be examined carefully, in terms of the structure, the neighborhood, the current market, the financing available, and so forth.

It must be strongly impressed on an individual becoming involved with real estate that each plot of ground, and usually each structure, should be considered unique in its specifics even if it can be grouped as a class in one way or another.

Use of Outside Professionals

Woodrow Wilson used to say that in tackling a serious problem, he tried to use all the brains he had and the best he could borrow.

The wise banker, too, should avail himself of the best talent available. His problem is to determine who should perform what service when and at what-cost. The often misunderstood fact of life is that it takes skill to be a good client.

258

What the property is worth (appraisal), what the property is worth to a given user (investment analysis), and how much can safely be lent on the security of the property (underwriting analysis) are separate questions.

Project X is not able to meet its objectives. Is it a bad loan, is it bad real estate, or is it a fundamentally sound parcel badly handled or hit by short-term negative factors (marketing, financing, etc.) that in time will right themselves?

In school examinations, a student who gives a brilliant answer to the wrong question gets little sympathy, and the same is true in real estate. The statistical material prepared for one purpose (the development process) may not relate to another problem (the lending process).

Academic types are not always equipped to deal with renting and management problems, whereas they may be ideal for hotel or shopping center market analysis; the reverse would be true of operating people.

Be sure that
   a) the right question is being asked; and
   b) the person being asked is trained to deal with that problem.

CONCLUSIONS

The effective lender must develop in-house competence; he should make good use of properly qualified outside professional assistance of proven soundness; he should be aware of events and trends in the field and, he must seek that happy balance between deep-seated mistrust and enthusiastic optimism that all of us aim for but few achieve.

In the Rubaiyat, Omar Khayyam wrote:

> *"Myself when young did early frequent*
> *Doctor and Saint, and heard great argument*
> *About it and about: but ever more*
> *Came out by the same door wherein I went."*

Those things worth knowing must be learned without being taught; The chief value of one's own experience and that of others is to ripen judgment: Common sense and imagination must be applied to all situations; finally, a gentle, good-natured skepticism may be the best frame of mind with which to approach real estate as well as life.

Chase Manhattan Bank, N.A.
In-House Seminar
January 7, 1977

AMERICA'S UNFINISHED AGENDA

The problem of the severely disadvantaged, inner-city minority child is heartbreaking and our national failure to remedy it is eating at the heart of our society. Black spokesmen and white liberals are certain that "white racism' is the overriding factor; conservatives are certain that 'black culture' is the cause; others cite the 'culture of poverty,' unequal educational opportunity, social class bias, economic deprivation, social isolation, or a changing economic climate that provides few blue-collar jobs by which unskilled workers can rise.

In 1965, Daniel Patrick Moynihan issued a study citing the debilitating influence of the single-parent family as a factor. Attacks on him as a 'racist' for "blaming the victim" ended for decades efforts by academics and social scientists to discuss their views.

Even today, in our climate of 'political correctness,' it is difficult to conduct a dispassionate discussion of similar topics crying out for rigorous analysis of what has worked, what has not worked, and what has been counterproductive, without becoming involved in mudslinging.

The answer, it seemed to me, was to stay out of debates and to put into practice programs that by their success would prove the soundness of their premises. That was the genesis of HEAF, the Harlem Educational Activities Fund.

Beginning in the late 1980s and incorporated by my wife and me in 1990, HEAF was designated a 'public charity' by the IRS in 1995. Today, it has a distinguished 'outside' board, a full-time staff of 12 educators and social workers, 40 part-time assistants, over 40 volunteers, and a budget of a million and a half dollars a year, supporting programs that take students from middle school to high school and then through college, and often to graduate school.

By September 1999, HEAF will have 78 Central Harlem students enrolled in colleges such as Harvard and Haverford, Bryn Mawr and Barnard, Columbia and Cornell. Many of these students are the first members of their families to finish high school. Over 100 students in the HEAF pipeline are enrolled in the city's competitive public high schools such as Bronx Science, Stuyvesant, and Brooklyn Tech. The HEAF-sponsored elementary school chess team, The Dark Knights, from Harlem's Mott Hall School, ranked Number One in the United States in the national chess competitions this spring, and the HEAF-sponsored junior high school chess team again ranked Number One in the United States this year, as it has for several years. The Director of HEAF's chess program, Maurice Ashley, with encouragement, leaves of absence, and financial support from HEAF, has become the first African-American player in the history of chess to be designated an International Grand Master.

Not one of HEAF's college or high school students has ever dropped out of school. Of HEAF's first three college graduates, one (a Yale alumnus) is now attending medical school, one is in ROTC, and one plans to return to graduate school after appropriate work experience.

Although HEAF gives no sex education lectures and distributes no contraceptives, only one female student has had a baby and only one of HEAF's male students has fathered a child. (Each of these students is pursuing college and determined to proceed to graduation.) The results speak for themselves.

While conventional wisdom focuses on 'teaching,' which is what takes place at the blackboard, or on the 'mechanics' of education, such as computers, curriculum, class size, etc., HEAF focuses on 'learning,' which is what takes place in the head of the student.

If a child does not want to learn, or thinks he or she cannot learn; if a child does not understand the importance of learning, or the joy

262

and satisfaction of learning; if a child is tired or angry or hungry; or cannot see or hear properly, HEAF believes that you could have Albert Einstein at the blackboard and Bill Gates at the computer without success. So HEAF creates an atmosphere in which a child is convinced that he or she can learn and feels proud of learning, an atmosphere of high aspiration and positive peer pressure; above all, an atmosphere in which a child focuses on long-term goals and rewards that more than repay short-term effort and sacrifice.

HEAF creates an atmosphere of personal responsibility in which parent, school, and HEAF work together to be supportive, but in which the child accepts responsibility for doing homework, taking the test, writing the book reviews or lab report, etc.

HEAF operates in an atmosphere in which excuses are irrelevant and performance is judged by high standards because our youngsters are being prepared to compete in a meritocratic world, one in which their competitors may have started to prepare earlier and may be working harder than they, or have had advantages they have not.

Our students know that we understand that everyone has defeats and failures, and that success depends on how one reacts to setbacks. Winners respond with intensified effort and determination, while losers lose self-confidence long before they lose the game.

Our students understand that we respect them, that HEAF is with them for the long haul, and that we pledge continuing attention and involvement throughout their careers.

Our students agree, as an important part of their relationship with HEAF, that HEAF will get copies of their report cards so that we can monitor their academic and social progress. They know that HEAF is on their team, but that in order to do our job, we have to be fully informed of their activities.

Our students know that, as they advance from high school to college and into the larger world, their identification with groups should be life-enhancing, not limiting; their choice of friends, roommates, dining companions, professional colleagues, and so forth will be best for them if they choose those who bring out the best in them, who challenge them to keep growing, who encourage them to become all they are capable of being.

Our students understand that high achievement should be a source of pride, not embarrassment, and that their success will make it easier for those around them and those following them to succeed, too.

They understand HEAF's philosophy: that we want to engage them not only in 'schooling' but in 'learning' (reading, travel, music, art, the theater, and other things which bring knowledge and delight); learning which will help them not only in "getting a job" but in "pursuing a career," learning which will help them not only in making a living, but also in leading a life that is satisfying, productive and fulfilling.

Finally, our students understand that HEAF's goal is to increase their life chances, providing them with a broad choice of careers.

That is the story of the Harlem Educational Activities Fund.

When making presentations to foundations for financial support, I sometimes repeat a Talmudic parable I love.

In biblical times, a traveler wandering along a mountain ridge came upon three exhausted laborers sprawled by the roadside. When he asked what they were doing, the first replied that they were carrying a heavy load on a hot day and he wished he were home. The second laborer looked at the first and said, "These are the famous Cedars of Lebanon; we are carrying down this mountain the world's finest building materials." The third laborer looked at the second and replied, "We are helping King Solomon to build his Temple." The Talmud notes that all three were carrying the same log.

At one remove, HEAF is involved in tutoring, test preparation, and other mechanics of education. At a second remove, HEAF is changing lives and demonstrating that lives can be changed. At a third remove, analogous to helping King Solomon to build his Temple, HEAF is moving the disadvantaged, inner-city minority child into the mainstream of American life, and I feel that is the most important unfinished job America faces.

Spring, 1999

264

SERVICING THE GLOBAL CITY – PART ONE

"**N**ecessary but not sufficient" is how the relationship between oxygen and fire is often described, and the characteristics of great global cities fall into the same category.

Those cities are centers favorable for the international exchange of capital, ideas, goods and people, and for the generation of economic value out of ideas. They nurture the communication and information technology that financial networks rely on; they reward high risk investments with even higher returns; and they attract the people that make the system work.

In an age of electronic communication, easy national and international travel, and professional mobility, middle and upper middle class populations that bring dynamism to a city and relate well to the world economy can live wherever they choose to live. And where those bright, educated, creative and dynamic types choose to live and work affects what takes place there, global networking included.

Experience has demonstrated that those who can, shun threats to their physical safety and avoid political jurisdictions with high local taxes and poor services. On the other hand, they are attracted to cities with good transportation facilities, with welcoming public spaces, social peace and, above all, with recreational and cultural activities that come under the heading of "quality of life."

With appropriate infrastructure, an educated population for support and an encouraging political climate, a critical mass of talented people will assemble. The stage is then set for an agglomeration of highly specialized legal, accounting, high tech communication, consulting, advertising, forecasting, engineering and other services which international financial centers require.

Rudolph Giuliani's dramatic success in lowering crime rates and business taxes did not create the New York business boom of the nineties, but it permitted it to land there rather than somewhere else.

Those cities which followed his lead have benefited accordingly. Taking seriously small crimes ("the broken window" syndrome) and carefully analyzing current crime data (the Compstat program) pay off, and we now know that lowering taxes can indeed increase revenues.

Good retail outlets, good health care facilities and a wide choice of housing are desirable; but in a free market economy, well-to-do populations can outbid others for choice housing; they can afford private doctors for what ails them; and they can purchase whatever goods they wish.

Good education should ideally be a universal free good; but sadly it isn't. The widespread failure of public education is the greatest tragedy in American life today, not only for global city types but for all those who cannot afford private schooling.

The success of parochial schools with the same inner-city students failing in public schools (and at a fraction of the per capita cost, too!) indicates that the solution lies in a reversal of educational and social policies that our public refuses to recognize.

Perhaps the day will return when New York's public schools again produce literate and numerate graduates and when our public colleges again produce Nobel Prize winners, as they did between the two world wars.

For now, education is our greatest governmental failure; and New York's global workforce will tend to attract single or childless individuals and those who live in the suburbs or who can afford private schooling.

In other matters, Adam Smith's "invisible hand" will soon fill (for those who can afford it) whatever needs government does not. And free market entrepreneurial types are the fingers of that "invisible hand.""

To perform successfully, we must understand, anticipate and meet the needs of sophisticated clients with complex requirements.

If Tokyo is an exporter of capital, and London a processor of capital, and New York an importer and provider of services for capital, their agents must be in efficient contact. If Kuala Lumpur is an important market for financial futures and Singapore for currency trading (and they are), their agents must be in contact with colleagues in New York and London, Tokyo and Paris, Frankfurt and Boston.

In many types of financial activity, cooperation rather than competition is the order of the day and linkage rather than isolation is the goal. Cities may compete, but today individual firms often cooperate.

And we, the entrepreneurs, must help global city participants meet their needs at a charge greater than our cost. While they are involved in market-making, underwriting, mergers and acquisitions, risk management and so forth, we supply the platform on which they operate.

We must provide them with physical premises, the varied services on which they rely and a context within which they can operate successfully- for their benefit, for ours, and for the cities in which they operate. We must make our respective cities more receptive to those business and professional activities.

For the urban generation of the 1960's to the 1990's, business was seen as a "cash cow" whose taxes paid for government-supplied social services for the urban poor; today, business is seen more often as the provider of jobs that permit people to earn incomes which enable them to take care of themselves.

In the previous generation, demagogic or misguided politicians applied municipal revenues to subsidize short-term consumption rather than long-term investment: the clearest examples are New York's decision to save the five cent fare at the expense of building the Second Avenue subway or trading the benefits of the remarkable underground highway and river front park system called Westway for subway operating subsidies. Today, at long last, capital investment in infrastructure is back on the agenda.

Healthy cities today are seen not so much as vehicles for wealth transfer as for wealth creation, not so much as donors to those on the bottom as catalysts of upward mobility for immigrants and others, not so much as the home of static business activities as the incubators of new business enterprises, new ideas, new cultural forms that flourish in this new world of privatization, deregulation and digitalization.

Although the first stage of the high tech revolution took place in the shadow of universities, the next, explosive stage (designing software content and so forth), is taking place in the creative sections of dynamic cities, often in the recycled manufacturing premises of a previous economic cycle. It is not surprising to find that in New York, for example, the massive old Lehigh-Starrett freight warehouse is today the address of choice for cutting edge new-media companies.

Cities like Detroit or Philadelphia (before Mayor Ed Rendell), which imposed punitive taxes to support swollen public payrolls or which regarded their police departments as part of the safety problem, not as a solution, witnessed painful economic and demographic decline in the same time frame in which cities like New York have flourished.

Today; the beleaguered city of Cincinnati looks with wonder at nearby Indianapolis; sophisticates in Detroit are painfully aware of the positive developments in Cleveland, and the word is spreading. In Europe, everyone is aware of the exciting resurgence of Spain's Barcelona and of the fierce problems of Manchester, England. Copenhagen's triumph of the pedestrian over the automobile is well known, and Bilbao, whose Frank Gehry museum brought the city over $500 million in economic activity in its first three years (which recouped its cost) and over $100 million in new taxes.

In New York, the quintessential global city, the combined impact of the World Trade Center disaster and (God willing) the 2012 Olympics* could lead to changes making New York the world's first truly 21st century metropolis. Once we dismiss the equally ill-advised ideas of restoring exactly what was destroyed or creating a 16-acre cemetery, something wonderful can emerge.

Thoughtful observers understand that Lower Manhattan has always had a relatively poor transportation network compared to that of midtown. We now have an opportunity to make the area a mass transit dream come true. Federally-funded improvement in mass transit will be the catalyst for the entire redevelopment effort, which can turn a former white collar ghetto into a 24-hour, seven- day mixed use paradise with office, housing, retail, hospitality, recreational and cultural facilities in proper balance.

An appropriate memorial for the World Trade Center site is a sensitive subject because wounds are still raw and an unemotional exchange of views is not yet possible. Newly-bereaved families have little interest in the long-term aspects of urban design or regional planning, and significant time must pass before important irrevocable judgments are made.

The memorial models most often suggested are Oklahoma City, Pearl Harbor, Hiroshima and the Vietnam Memorial in Washington, DC, the first conveying a deep sense of sadness, the second one of serenity, the third of the need for education, and the last of remembrance.

I believe the ideal model is Pericles brilliant rebuilding of the Athenian Acropolis after its destruction by the Persian King Xerxes in 480 BC, since the Greek goal was both to remember and to create, to memorialize and to move forward. But even the Greeks let the idea simmer for a number of years.

Even the biblical books of Noah, Daniel and Job all end on an upbeat note, and it would be wonderful if the World Trade Center story could, too.

The global city of tomorrow will have the gravitational pull to attract those with the skills and talents, education and mindset, that the cutting edge activities of our time demand; and human capital is acknowledged today as important as financial capital.

Local and regional populations will benefit, too, from having access to the urban strengths that create a global city.

Obviously, not all benefit equally, and in global cities worldwide we are witnessing increasing polarization of income and of wealth; and the ramifications of these disparities are complex.

Precise calculation of costs and benefits is difficult in a setting in which manufacturing jobs evaporate, in which heavy foreign immigration clouds the statistical picture, and in which the benefits of formal education and appropriate credentials are crucial, and where their absence puts the uneducated and uncredentialed at a severe handicap.

Someday we will understand that the crucial question is not why some are poor but rather why some are not; and we should reflect on the role of education in the difference.

But make no mistake-the poor in a global city do not benefit if stockbrokers lose their jobs or if tax accountants or corporate lawyers move away. And we should ask if a Third World country isn't better off if a First World country locates a manufacturing plant there.

This week's headlines proclaimed that fully one-third of the youngsters in the State of Washington will drop out before completing high school. Perhaps the protesters against globalization in Seattle last year should have focused their attention on public education instead. Improved education for women in the Third World is the single most important immediate goal well-intentioned groups should fight for.

The wealth creation of a global society is a positive, not a negative sum game; and everyone benefits.

Our challenge is to stimulate such wealth creation and to spread its benefits widely.

Global Cities in an Era of Change
Harvard University
September 4-6, 2002

---

* God was not willing.

SERVICING THE GLOBAL CITY – PART TWO

Many thought-provoking comments have been made in these three days, and I believe that they can be summarized by five images:

The first image, a message to the entrepreneurs present, is of the Marquis de Lafayette in the early days of the French Revolution, having a drink in a Parisian café. Someone dashed in, shouting, "Where is that mob going?" Lafayette replied, "I don't know; but I must get there first because I am their leader."

Following From the Front, Lafayette's goal, is what successful entrepreneurs do. The entrepreneur must understand and anticipate and fill the needs of his demanding and sophisticated clientele; if he does so effectively, he will be handsomely rewarded.

The second image is for local government planners who wish to attract and retain global city activities, with the jobs, tax revenues, purchasing power, etc., they bring. They must remember the picture of the 82-year-old multi-millionaire, questioning his 22- year-old chorus girl bride, 'Honey, if I lost my money, would you still love me?" She replied, "Of course I would still love you. *I would miss you but I would still love you!"*

Capital flows to where it is rewarded, global city types to where they are encouraged. When they do not feel nurtured, they will move elsewhere.

The third image is for those anti-city social scientists who are out of touch with the real world. That image is of a large *Mound of Horse Manure*. One hundred years ago, it was widely believed that great cities could not function without horses, that horses deposit manure, and that the key factor limiting the size of great cities would be their ability to dispose of horse manure.

More recently, some of the world's most important social scientists met in 1968 in a group called The Club of Rome; they predicted the precise year in which the world would run out of each major non-renewable resource. Today, tungsten, molybdenum, etc., are still here but the Club of Rome is not. A similar group predicted that Calcutta, with an expected population of between fifty to sixty million people before the end of the 20th century, would be the first human settlement to collapse and stop functioning. Calcutta was not listening, and is still in business.

Finally, consider the social scientist who reasoned that because roses are prettier, roses would make a better soup than cabbages. That kind of thinking posits that, for ostensibly rational reasons, the world's great cities will fade.

The role of cities will change with time; yes, but bigger is not necessarily better. London and Paris will exist as long as social scientists on government grants seek the world's best theater or the world's best dinners.

A fourth image, relating to public education in our large cities, is of the event held in Stockholm each year when the *King of Sweden presents Nobel Prizes*. Picture 1937 when New York City's free public university, City College, won three Nobel Prizes, a feat never equalled by Oxford or Cambridge, by Harvard or Yale. That over-crowded, under-resourced free college educated the children of poverty-stricken, often non-English speaking foreign immigrants.

Fifty years later, City College was granting degrees to students even the college deans described as "functionally illiterate."

What had changed? Only the social and educational policies. In those days, public school served two functions: to inculcate the values of a civilized society and to teach children to write with precision and read with understanding.

A decade ago, conventional wisdom held that crime in large cities was insoluble. Today, thanks to Rudolph Giuliani and others, we know that it can be solved. Perhaps when our social and educational policies revert to what they were, we may again produce literate and numerate students from the inner city (and Nobel laureates!). When that happens, the middle class families that have been fleeing our failing public schools may again choose to live in our cities.

The fifth image I suggest is that of *Aristotle and his Friends at a Party*.

Last night, one speaker had forebodings about the future of cities, citing the impact of modern electronic communication, terrorism, the failure of inner-city education, and so forth. He ended his talk by flashing on the screen a citation from Herodotus, who said, "Human prosperity does not long abide in the same place."

I treasure Herodotus for his imagination and his curiosity, but I prefer Aristotle for his wisdom and his accuracy. It was Aristotle who said, "Men first come to the city for safety; they stay on to earn a living; and they remain to pursue the good life."

Some may choose to retreat to a mountain top with their computers; others may choose to retire to places like Florida. But there will always be some of us who remain attached to the dynamism, the vibrancy, the excitement and the stimulus of great cities.

In *The Communist Manifesto*, Karl Marx praised the bourgeoisie for creating cities that saved the world from "the idiocy of rural life," in which even a computer is of limited help.

Let us hope that those attending this conference on Global Cities share Aristotle's view; and that we all work toward the common goal of making global cities wonderful international centers where civilized people can pursue the good life.

Global Cities in an Era of Change
Harvard University
September 4-6, 2002

273

WORKING TOGETHER
FOR THE BENEFIT OF ALL

Sharing a podium with Mayor Kevin White is a rare opportunity, and I want to express the great respect the development community has for his positive impact on Boston of today and tomorrow. The mayor gives tone and guidance to the city.

England's great architect, Christopher Wren, is buried under one of his structures with the inscription "Si Monumentum Requiris Circumspice." (If you seek his monument, look around you.) Someday visitors to downtown Boston may say the same of Kevin White.

In considering the relationship between public and private factors in developing the built environment there are two points to keep in mind: The first is the assumption that all involved wish the city well. The second is that good intentions are not enough.

While we share a vision of the city in which we would like to live, work, shop and play, honorable individuals can have different opinions about how to achieve that vision. On the other hand, meaning well is not enough; errors are errors, regardless of intent. The Robert McNamara team that designed the Edsel automobile did not wish ill to the Ford Motor Company. The people who designed the Maginot Line were decent; they did not wish ill to France. The Argentinian generals who programmed a quick war for the Falkland Islands did not mean to harm Argentina. The people who designed the Pruitt Igoe complex in St. Louis won a prize for the best large-scale public development in the country that year. A decade later the buildings were were blown up.

What are the specifics of our desired city, given the constraints we have and the real-world trade-offs and how do we get from here to there?

Getting from here to there involves the physical and the social environment. "Should we have parks and playgrounds?" "Will the parks be occupied by mothers wheeling baby carriages or occupied by muggers and derelicts?"

Today I will deal with the built environment and how we get from here to there.

Historically there are four models of the planning process in America. The first is a city shaped by free market forces (the Houston model). The second (the 1916 zoning type) is a city planned for density and use, with the developer retaining rights so long as he builds a building for an appropriate use within the density requirements. The third model is the one that has been prevalent here in Boston in recent years: active government participation in the planning process, with private implementation. I call that the old Boston model. The fourth model is emerging in more and more cities. It is characterized by active community participation, often at the local neighborhood level.

Any system can work well if properly administered, properly structured and implemented. I remember the lines from Pope's Essay on Man, "O'er forms of governance let fools contest, what e'er is best administered is best." However, of these four types of program I think prudence will direct us toward the old Boston model.

It requires first that honorable, competent and efficient public administrators find and train men and women who will bring professional judgment and discipline to their work. Secondly, it requires private sector development types who will play the game with 52 cards and deal from the top of the deck. Thirdly, all relevant public voices must be heard. One of the roles of government is to serve as a buffer, a conduit, and a mediator between conflicting pressures. Fourth, such a program requires political leadership of a high order.

Government should be willing to lead, and to take the political flack that short-term decisions may involve, if they will create long-term benefits. It is important to have a leader who says, "This is going through; have faith in me; I believe it's going to work in the long run."

We have outgrown the economic Darwinism of the Houston model. Oscar Wilde referred once to cultural Darwinism leading to survival of the vulgarest. Something comparable might be the result if only the developer's taste and judgment determined the nature of the project.

There have to be constraints, legal and moral, unless you define conscience as, in H. L. Mencken's words, "that still quiet voice that tells you someone may be looking." You can rely on a developer's conscience if someone is looking, and the person looking has some degree of control. We should not forget the free market, but it cannot be left to function totally alone. The 1916 zoning concept is inadequate. Our society has gone beyond the point where we require buildings to be freestanding and individual. Now we think of their context. We think of neighborhoods—of buildings in relation to one another.

If each building rivals another, if every building is made to be, above all, distinctive, planning based on context is impossible. That has been one of the weaknesses, I think, of modern architecture. Buildings in the recent past tend to say, "Look at me, I'm different, I'm significant."

We are entering a period in which developers, city officials, and individual architects will think more in terms of the context, environment, and setting. When you think of an Utrillo picture of Paris, you think of buildings. They are each sort of faceless but they hang together well. When you think of memorable cities, the general impression is pleasing. You might not remember the individual structures, but you remember the ambience. I think that is the direction in which we are heading.

The fourth model of planning, local neighborhood involvement, presents problems that a Center such as this one at MIT can solve through leadership and organized discussion. First of all, not all of the participants in neighborhood, community, or special interest groups, whether they are interested in landmarking, the environment, or any other concerns, will necessarily have the same level of professional training. Not all of them come with clean hands. Some will come with hidden agendas, including issues such as political careers. Some of them are thinking entirely of what might be best for their little neighborhood and not necessarily what might be best for the greater urban context. Airports and community centers have to be somewhere.

For all of us, a certain amount of modesty is realistic. For example, Jane Jacobs was correct in her vigorous (and successful) effort to keep Robert Moses from building a highway through Washington Square Park and Greenwich Village; she was wrong (and unsuccessful) in her effort to prevent the creation of Lincoln Center for the Performing Arts.

What form of administration is most conducive to good administration? Ideally, it should involve a city planning department (in Boston, it's the BRA) of technically trained and competent planners, with the tenure in office associated with senior civil service people. Planners in this kind of department would think in terms of the city's best interests and could run interference between the neighborhood and the development entity. They could play a part in the planning and also reflect legitimate community concerns. In such a planning context, the question of trade-offs is increasingly important. Trade-offs must be made between immediate and long-term benefit, cost and affordability; what's best for the neighbors vs. best for the city. Decisions about older buildings require subtle distinctions in terms of historic preservation.

On the issue of historic preservation, it's wise to remember the French expression, "The good is the enemy of the best, the best is the enemy of the good." When dealing with a cultural gem like Mt. Vernon, it's important that the substance be kept; it should not be turned into a motel or a fast food chain store. Mt. Vernon should be preserved exactly as it was—with George Washington's false teeth and his spectacles on the table. If, on the other hand, you're speaking of the recycling of an old mill, one might want to keep the handsome physical exterior, but the time may have come for such a building to take on a new life. One hopes that the new life will be as integral to today's society as its old life was in a previous milieu. Another set of problems occurs in dealing with a situation in which it is desirable to preserve the fabric and texture of a street by retaining the façade of an old building, but it is necessary to put in plumbing and so forth to make it usable.

How does one deal with these subtle distinctions? We have to come up with ways, and then enforce the decisions we have made.

On issues involving not only the local community but the general public, our goal should be on the one hand how to have maximum input from all interested parties, but on the other hand, how to de-politicize them. It's almost impossible in any political jurisdiction with residential rent control to find an office holder who is opposed to it or who will speak out against it. Everyone understands that the long-term side effects of residential rent control (like unbalanced budgets) are counter-productive, but politicians choose to leave those problems for their successors.

Private developers should not consider each other adversaries; our relationship can be cooperative rather than confrontational. We have to ask ourselves what is the social and physical fabric of the society in which we want to live. What are the constraints? Economics is the science of the allocation of scarce resources. How are we to balance the physical setting and the social setting? How do we bring the various voices to bear on these decisions? Our goal should be to design a society in which rational, civilized people in settings of grace and charm and human scale, can lead productive and satisfying lives.

The public good should be the guiding principle.

M.I.T. Center for Real Estate Development
Conference—Public and Private Development Roles
1984

URBAN CHALLENGES TODAY

The near-paralysis of our federal government, because of political partisanship poses problems for our cities, states and regions. Faced with unsustainable deficits, our national government will be unable to maintain its contributions for local benefit; and those burdens will have to be borne locally. Courageous city and state leaders must extract higher revenues while getting a 'bigger bang for the buck' on expenditures and retrenching where necessary. Future-minded, pro-active mayors and governors will determine what urbanist Richard Florida calls "the boom towns and the ghost towns of the new economy."

Those areas blessed by oil and gas reserves or critical masses of high tech innovators have advantages that declining industrial areas of the Rust Belt do not, but flexibility and resilience will be crucial for all.

Informed observers see the flashing yellow lights. Martin Wolf, of the *Financial Times*, sums them up in the question, "Will Americans pay for the government they have legislated?"

Our decaying infrastructure, unfunded government pensions, housing shortages for the poor and the young occur in a context of slow economic growth, sluggish employment, worsening socioeconomic inequality, poor student achievement levels by world standards, growing numbers of retirees and a diminishing number of tax-paying workers.

The 'new normal' with low economic demand resulting in low production and fewer jobs, raises fears of short term deflation and long term inflation.

How to live within our means yet maintain the quality of life Americans have come to expect is a challenge that must be met creatively. A 'sharing economy' in which fewer own cars but more use Uber, Zipcar and bike shares; micro-housing units with common facilities; high density, cheaper housing at suburban transit centers – all are becoming more common. 'Invest more for the future' and 'consume less in the present' must be the response.

What urban vision should we have for the future? In cities like New York and Washington it is a choice between 'growing the pie' and 'redistributing shares of the pie.' In cities with a dramatic loss of jobs and population, like Baltimore or Cleveland, it will be planned shrinkage or astute programs for abandoned housing and vacant lots, and energetic efforts to reduce crime and blight.

In all cities, our defective criminal justice system should be rethought. Incarcerating first offenders beside hardened criminals merely indoctrinates them. First offenders who cannot read, write or count should spend their prison time in classes. Those with high school equivalency should be given vocational training to help them earn a living to keep from becoming recidivists.

In facing the future, each locality must deal with the challenges of: economic sustainability; physical infrastructure; the built environment; employment; social services; education; cultural life; and quality of life.

ECONOMIC SUSTAINABILITY

Balancing long term income and outgo- to pay for municipal services and to cover debt service for future capital investment – should be our highest priority. Politicians can no longer be permitted to promise the undeliverable, to saddle our children with our expenses or to pander to special interest groups, whether municipal unions or protected businesses.

Political leaders and public intellectuals must be honest in explaining the economic facts of life to their constituents. Stimulating private sector job creation, encouraging business diversity and increasing 'human capital' are keys to the value-creation that helps everyone. The macro-economics of a city can change. Cities must adapt to new conditions, and those that are resilient will thrive.

Michael Bloomberg's high tech programs for New York – first with upstate Cornell and Israel's Technion on Roosevelt Island, next with Columbia and New York Universities on their campuses, then with Carnegie Mellon in Brooklyn - show pro-active leadership at its best.

PHYSICAL INFRASTRUCTURE

New York's achievement in completing Water Tunnel No. 3 (the largest capital construction project ever undertaken in the five boroughs) went unnoticed, but such major projects call for long term statesmanship rather than short-term politics as usual. Improved utilities, improved public spaces, improved mass transit – local and regional – are imperatives for future municipal administrations, as are protection from rising sea levels and hurricane damage.

THE BUILT ENVIRONMENT

High densities provide the adrenalin that makes great cities special; effective internal transportation makes them "job friendly", and a pedestrian-friendly atmosphere makes them fun. Congestion and sprawl are counter-productive.

EMPLOYMENT

Jobs – meaningful employment at appropriate compensation – should be the focus of our economic policy in an age when globalization, automation and exponential high tech growth diminish employment for our unskilled, semi-skilled and even some skilled workers. And almost all job growth comes from new business 'start-ups.'

All strategies should focus on creative, innovative ventures. Widespread unemployment undermines civic life and must be fought with all tools, including wage supplements for the working poor where necessary.

SOCIAL SERVICES

Social services should help recipients develop the skills and values for productive lives. Poor children, the handicapped, etc. must, of course, be helped appropriately, while means testing should guarantee that public aid goes where it is most needed. Transparency and accountability would assure the public that its funds are well spent. We can no longer assume that government can do everything for everybody at all stages of life.

EDUCATION

Effective public education is a key civil rights issue and the best investment a society can make. What's best for students, not teachers or parents, is the mark of a successful school.

We need higher standards for entering teachers; a longer time frame before granting tenure; greater opportunities for teacher training and professional growth; merit pay for excellence or for service in difficult areas; reasonable procedures for eliminating the worst teachers.

Effective pre-schooling (not the glorified baby-sitting now prevalent) should be available for everyone. Reading preparation, vocabulary building, socialization and inculcation of self-discipline are crucial preliminary steps in early education. Although ideally taught at home, first-rate pre-schooling can be a worthwhile substitute and is cost effective.

Vocational training and apprenticeship are programs whose time has come again. They should be optional for all high school students and mandatory for first offenders in prisons.

The high cost of a college education is a national scandal. More effective use of on-line teaching; the elimination of inter-collegiate athletics and mandatory retirement ages for regular faculty would lower costs and make college more widely accessible. More resources and higher standards for community colleges and greater availability of adult education programs are also overdue.

Financial aid for college should focus on poor but qualified students whose college enrollment percentages have been plummeting.

284

The lowest feasible interest rates for student loans and longest repayment terms are in the national interest.

CULTURAL LIFE

Intellectual, artistic and musical stimuli provide the satisfactions a civilized public needs; and should be readily available. New York shows the way in its role as the nation's leading showcase for culture as well as its key incubator of culture.

Broadway and off-Broadway theater, Lincoln Center and B.A.M. concerts and our world class museums and libraries delight residents, transients and tourists alike. The 50 million tourists who visit New York each year pay us handsomely for the privilege. Government aid and encouragement of philanthropic cultural assistance have been successful. Over six million tourists visited the Metropolitan Museum of Art this year, and over 40 million cited Central Park as a prime destination.

Thirty years ago, Central Park was an unsafe, garbage-strewn mess, with Belvedere Castle graffiti-covered and the Great Lawn a dust bowl. Today, the private non-profit Central Park Conservancy spends $60 million a year keeping Central Park the city's crown jewel. Incoming Mayor de Blasio's plan to tax the Conservancy to help other parks may prove a disaster. More, rather than less, effective private philanthropy should be encouraged in all areas of public life, not to replicate government services but to stimulate innovation and creativity.

QUALITY OF LIFE

Personal safety is a key aspect of this. New York's murder rate, lowest in half a century and the lowest of any major city in the nation was not achieved by accident. Use of modern technology to analyze, anticipate and prevent crime was responsible. Good policing can be fair and effective, and is even more important in trouble neighborhoods than elsewhere.

Ease of movement is another goal. Density without congestion and first-rate mass transit and innovation like "light rail lines" and "congestion pricing" which have worked well in London, Singapore, Copenhagen and elsewhere are acknowledged techniques for achieving it.

Place creation, such as New York's High Line, DUMBO, revitalized waterfronts, cultural and high tech enclaves, etc. give a city character and individuality. In troubled Detroit, the TechTown District plan is leading the way toward municipal rejuvenation.

Competent public service supervised by talented, well-selected officials, is often a forlorn hope. The Bloomberg administration set a high standard for personnel that should be followed.

CONCLUSION:

Safe, beautiful, livable cities – where the public has access to appropriate employment, housing, medical care, safety, recreation and, above all, good education – are what we all want. Such cities are achievable, if we will it and are willing to pay for it.

Twenty-five hundred years ago, Aristotle wrote, "We come to cities to live; we stay to lead the good life."

No one has said it better.

M.I.T.
November 16, 2013

NEW YORK—TODAY AND TOMORROW

"If you want to give God a good laugh, tell him your plans" is an old folk saying that could refer to activities in New York in the days ahead.

The economic unknowns facing the city are so many and so varied that forecasts are apt to reflect hopes and fears rather than careful analysis.

What future office space the financial services industry will need, for example, or the print publishing industry and its affiliate, the advertising industry, are beyond knowing. How the macro-economic challenges of our national economy will work out; how New York City will deal with deficits of $6.6 billion in fiscal 2010, predicted to grow to $9.6 billion by fiscal 2013; or even how our banks will deal with toxic loans on their books that have not yet been written down, no one can say.

What we can say is that New York City has immense resources: a critical mass of talented human capital and a history of flexibility in times of crisis.

We have a Mayor whose shrewdness and practical experience are well-suited to the short term, intermediate and long term challenges.

For New York to thrive, and maintain its leadership as the world's foremost global city, it must capitalize on its strengths, move resolutely against its weaknesses, and no longer indulge in wishful thinking that we can live beyond our means indefinitely.

Wealth must be created before it can be distributed, and we must do the first imaginatively and the second wisely. Creating and sustaining high-paying jobs and appropriate tax ratables while maintaining a high quality of life is our challenge.

Just as President Obama is trying to do nationally, New Yorkers must deal effectively with our immediate short term crisis without creating worse problems a few years ahead. At the same time, we must not "eat our seed corn" but must invest wisely in infrastructure and capital projects (human and physical) that will bear fruit in the future. Crises reshape economies, and we must not let this crisis "go to waste."

Mayor Bloomberg understands the five major challenges that 21st century New York must meet:

a) To think 'five boroughs' rather than Manhattan alone, for the outer boroughs are not mere bedrooms for Wall Street; urban sub-centers are the pattern for the future.
b) To think occupational and professional diversity, with a 'small business' orientation, without heavy and unhealthy reliance on the financial services industry for employment opportunities and municipal revenue;
c) To think 'middle class' as well as 'rich' and 'poor,' since, in the 21st century, a well-educated, hard-working and productive middle class is the backbone of a healthy society; and New York's middle class is declining;
d) To think 'creative class' as an engine for economic growth. New York must continue to attract, nurture and, yes, produce, a critical mass of innovative, dynamic individuals whose human capital represents the 21st century equivalent of the agricultural, mineral, industrial and financial capital of the past;
e) To think "quality of life."

New York must maintain and strengthen public safety, high quality public education, appropriate physical infrastructure and other 'quality of life' characteristics that are the sine qua non, the "that without which" of all great cities. Appropriate housing is high on the list.

To achieve these goals Mayor Bloomberg needs the vocal support of an informed and involved public that understands the problems and endorses difficult choices and painful trade-offs that must be made if New York is to have the future we all wish for. We can do it, but, as Oliver Wendell Holmes said, "The mode by which the inevitable comes to pass is called effort."

THE FIRST CHALLENGE: THINK "FIVE BOROUGHS"

Manhattan's share of New York City's non- governmental jobs has declined steadily from 67.6% in 1958 to 61.6% in 2008 due primarily to an explosion of new enterprises by immigrant entrepreneurs in the outer boroughs whose growth represents one of the city's great economic hopes.

Immigrants create more "start up" businesses than native born (more than half of Silicon Valley's start-ups were founded by immigrants), and while foreign- born individuals comprise a third of the city's population, they account for half of the self-employed. For example, some 90% of New York's taxi drivers are immigrants, and over a third own their own vehicles.

Immigrants put in longer work hours and save a higher percentage of income than do the native born, and immigrant children in our public schools out- perform native-born children.

The Bloomberg administration has encouraged outer-borough growth, but this exercise is a work in progress that justifies continuing attention and support. Better coordination, integration, promotion and funding of city efforts would be highly cost- effective.

Micro-lending, provision of professional advice and a continuing review of onerous regulations about which small entrepreneurs complain, are areas to be expanded.

Provision of standard municipal services to the outer boroughs, such as sanitation and transportation, are also important. Not so long ago, comedians joked that Mayor Robert F. Wagner had a secret weapon for snow removal in Queens. It was called 'spring.' Even today, the city's transportation authorities seem preoccupied with world class train stations and developments in Lower Manhattan, but ignore the crowded and inadequate subway and bus services to the outer boroughs. We can do better.

THE SECOND CHALLENGE: A DIVERSIFIED ECONOMIC BASE

The perplexing question for New York is not how much of its finance industry will move to other places (not much) but how much will evaporate. Nationally, the share of GDP from finance reached a peak of 8.3%, and observers believe that will decline to 7% or lower. It was 5% a generation ago. Much of that loss will come from Wall Street, which at the height of the boom supplied 9% of the city's jobs, but one-third of local wages.

Where will the warm bodies come from to fill the millions of square feet of proposed new office buildings in lower Manhattan and the West Side? In the film Field of Dreams, the theory was "if you build it, they will come," but experience in Las Vegas and Miami reveals otherwise (at least not right away). Current office rents in Manhattan are far below those necessary to support new construction.

Fortunately, New York already has a diverse and innovative economy reflecting a range of creative industries, including high tech, media and communication, design, arts, entertainment, tourism, fashion, music, film and TV, international trade, health care and medical research, specialty manufacturing and so forth, with bio-tech and 'green' activities expanding. These provide high paying employment, tax revenues and the excitement that makes New York the stimulating place it is, with its elevated "urban metabolism."

Manufacturing accounts for 3.2 % of private sector jobs in New York City, vs. 12.7% in Los Angeles, 11.3% in Chicago, 10.6% in Houston and 7.1% in Boston. Since manufacturing wages tend to be higher than those of our growing service industries, we should focus on what manufacturing activities might be encouraged here, given our seaports, airports and rail access.

THE THIRD CHALLENGE: THINK 'MIDDLE CLASS'

New York cannot function with only the rich, the nomadic young (who depart when they start families), foreign immigrants, and the local poor; yet that is the direction in which our demographics are heading.

More people with B.A. degrees left New York last year than entered.

We need the book editors, web designers, lab technicians, architects, nurses, paralegals, actors, university professors and other skilled and educated people who make modern society work.

A Brookings Institution study found that New York City has the smallest proportion of middle-income families of any metropolitan area in the nation and that the number of middle-income neighborhoods is shrinking.

The high cost of living is the most cited reason that so many middle-class New Yorkers leave when they start families. Studies show that a similar standard of living that costs $50,000 a year in Houston, $51,430 in Charlotte, $53,630 in Atlanta, $63,421 in Chicago, $69,196 in Philadelphia, $72,387 in Boston and $95,489 in San Francisco costs $123,322 a year in Manhattan.

New Yorkers pay the highest cost in the nation for housing (three times the national average) and dramatically higher costs for virtually all other services or purchases. And NYC's taxes are roughly 50% higher than those in our other large cities.

One important factor in the successful evolution of New York University from a 'commuter' college to a world-class university was its provision of cheap housing for professors and students; Columbia University, too, keeps its great professors by providing inexpensive housing.

Our universities, institutes and research centers are more important to the life of the city than most New Yorkers realize, and appropriate housing strengthens that significantly.

There are, of course, many factors involved in the City's costs and difficult trade-offs to be considered; but, at the end of the day, we must try to keep our middle class in New York. They are the ones who are "voting with their feet" at the high pension costs of New York

City employees compared to the rest of the nation or the federal government. They are the ones aware that New York's teachers unions make it virtually impossible to fire an incompetent or dysfunctional teacher or to hire high school teachers of physics, math, chemistry or biology who have majored in those subjects in college.

Second only to high housing costs, better educational opportunities elsewhere for their children are cited by many of those who leave.

Albert Einstein noted that, in the real world, there are neither rewards nor punishments, only consequences. And we live with the consequences of the conditions we create.

THE FOURTH CHALLENGE: NURTURE THE CREATIVE SECTOR

Plato was the first to say that "Buildings do not make a city. People do." He could have been speaking of the imaginative, educated individuals who give character to world class cities in the 21st century and who drive the new economic paradigm where knowledge, innovation and creativity are key.

These individuals reflect the creative sector of the economy; their ideas spawn new industries and modernize old ones, originate new products, new services and new ways of doing things in science and technology, art and design, culture and entertainment, and the many knowledge-based professions. They staff the idea-driven industries that range from software, communications devices and biotechnology to culture and entertainment.

Every job created in the "innovation sector" leads to 3.5 jobs created overall.

Until recently, New York had little to fear from competition elsewhere in attracting the world's best and brightest. That is no longer the case.

Every major city in the world is striving to increase its share of creative workers; in China and India especially, massive resources are being applied, not only to develop their own, but to re-attract to their shores their brain power that has come here. In Europe, cities like London are making major efforts that we can study.

292

THE FIFTH CHALLENGE: QUALITY OF LIFE

Physical safety, the top requirement for the good life, gets high marks in New York City, a tribute to Mayors Giuliani and Bloomberg, and to their lieutenants, Bill Bratton and Ray Kelly. We must never revert to the "bad old days."

Our public education gets high marks at the university level, fair marks at the high school level, but poor marks at the elementary level. Although conditions are improving, public perception is that our schools have a long way to go to equal those elsewhere, but continuing mayoral control of our public schools holds out hope for the future.

A shortage of affordable housing, especially for the middle class, is widely seen as New York's "Achilles heel."

The time has come for large scale rental housing development in the outer boroughs in a new version of the 1955 Mitchell Lama rental housing program which gives middle class renters real estate tax exemption, low financing costs and limited profits for developers.

Huge savings, resulting in lower rents, could be achieved if these housing units were built "non union" rather than "union" since union work rules and regulations stifle productivity and add some 20% to construction costs.

We must get the maximum amount of housing out of the dollars available. Higher densities at existing transit hubs in the outer boroughs are indicated.

The subject of rental housing vs. ownership is complex, but rental is preferable for young people who are mobile, for families whose needs change, and for those who are better off with the flexibility renting permits.

The union/non-union question goes against New York traditions and customs, but the dollars-and-cents impact on middle class rent charges is substantial.

This is one example of the painful trade-offs we must face.

'Short termism' has become the prevailing weakness of our time encouraged, sadly, by empowered leaders. A thoughtful public can demand better.

CONCLUSION:

We face a difficult time, but past experience shows that New York can rebound stronger and more vital than ever. Not by inertia, but by "taking arms against that sea of troubles and by opposing, end them." The rebound will be faster and easier if an informed public supports its leadership.

Two other examples would be to support Mayor Bloomberg in initiatives he espouses: 'congestion pricing' and reintroduction of the city's commuter tax. Both programs would gain public acceptance if marketed appropriately.

Congestion pricing, which works effectively in London, Oslo, Singapore and wherever else it has been tried, was unfortunately presented to New Yorkers as an environmental effort to reduce gasoline consumption and to improve air quality. Had it been made clear that every penny would be applied to improved subway and bus service to the outer boroughs, a powerful constituency would have been created.

The reinstitution of a successful commuter tax, which helps the city defray the substantial costs commuters impose on the city, is another "no brainer."

First introduced in 1966 by Mayor John Lindsay, this source of revenue brought billions of sorely needed dollars until it was revoked in 1999 by our dysfunctional State legislature, prodded by New York City Democrat Sheldon Silver who wished to help an embattled political crony in Rockland County. The commuter tax can and should be reinstated.

Another area in which Mayor Bloomberg needs public support is to rein in our municipal unions and bring their off-the-scale pension benefits, unproductive work rules (such as stopping at 4 PM), and excessive overtime payments in line with practices elsewhere.

One possible outcome of the present crisis is a restructuring of union arrangements, with some relationship between benefits and increases in productivity.

New York can transcend its present difficulties.

We need only the leadership (which we have) and the political will (which we can muster), to focus on the long term general good (meaning investment) rather than on our short term benefits (meaning consumption).

In ancient Greece, young men assuming leadership positions took a vow to transmit their city to future generations "enhanced if possible, but in no case diminished." That is not a bad guide for us today.

Urban Land Institute
June 24, 2009

SECRETS OF REAL ESTATE DEVELOPMENT

Good afternoon, graduates; and welcome to the ancient and honorable calling of real estate development!

The individuals who planned and built the Acropolis in classical Athens, who created the Forbidden City of Beijing in ancient China and the mountain complex at Machu Pichu, are in a sense your forebears; and when, as entrepreneurs, you scurry about for financing, think of Christopher Columbus coaxing Ferdinand and Isabella into underwriting his voyages of discovery or of Sir Francis Drake cajoling Queen Elizabeth the First into financing his privateering ventures.

Queen Elizabeth's cash-on-cash return was approximately 50 to one, as I recall; although real estate syndications do not deliver quite so much, the nature of the promoters' pitch was probably similar.

It is a matter of historical record that the majority of opinions given by the Delphic Oracle in ancient Greece were similar to those presented to a potential mortgagee or investor.

Seriously, when a new Greek colony was being projected by its promoters, handsome gifts (now called fees) were presented to the priests at Delphi, and, in due course, the Pythia delivered the desired opinion that the colony was sure to succeed and that smart participants could make a killing by getting in on the ground floor (today, the first equity position).

"Plus ça change, plus c'est la même chose," say the French; and they are essentially right.

Today is your Commencement, literally, your "beginning," and it seems appropriate at this auspicious moment to let you in on some secrets that you will soon share with your professional colleagues, secrets of which the "uninitiated" are unaware.

The first is that our field (although we try to deny it) is really a lot of fun.

The range of people you will meet, the variety of problems you will deal with, the rhythms of a project—its planning, its implementation and its completion—are exhilarating to a degree that few outside the real estate field can fully appreciate.

Perhaps actuaries really do enjoy toting up columns of numbers or dentists, pulling teeth, and, for all I know, morticians may actually look forward to visits to the morgue; but there is absolutely no doubt that developers approach their activities with zest and enthusiasm.

The Bible was probably referring to us when it said, "Man is conceived in ecstasy but born in labor," "By the sweat of thy brow thou shalt earn thy bread" and so forth; but you would be hard pressed to prove it by seeing in action the exuberant developers I know.

When you try to explain to your family and friends exactly what it is that a developer does, perhaps the closest analogy to your role that you can use is that of the producer of a play, with the architect like the playwright, the tenants like the audience, the mortgagee like the angels, the construction people like the actors and stagehands, the general contractor like the director, and so on.

Theatricals close, however, whereas, for better or worse, buildings last. Some are a source of pride, some of embarrassment (or they should be!) but they are there.

The poet Paul Valéry observed that most buildings are silent, others speak, but some rare buildings sing. We all hope that at some point in our lives we will be involved with those rare "singing" ones of which we and our whole society can be proud.

The Seagram Building, Lever House, Rockefeller Center and projects of similar quality represent our field at its best—where major capital values were created for the owners, where the occupants enjoy their space, and where the general public takes delight in the addition to the cityscape.

298

All three are legitimate and simultaneous goals for the developer. I will always remember my father's comment when he saw the civic award our company received for developing the Bankers Trust Company Building on Park Avenue. He was pleased to note, he said, that the ink on the award was as black as the ink on our corporate ledger!

Of course you want your project to be economically successful; but the pride, the satisfaction, the pleasure one gets from the successful exercise of one's professional skills are also important forms of recompense; and in the course of your careers I wish you all much of them.

A second secret that developers share is an awareness of the hard work, the professional skills, and the knowledge of current financial and market conditions that go into successful ventures.

Today, in many fields, it is the custom to try to make accomplishment look easy or due to luck; I think that is a dangerous hoax being played on the young.

Olympic champions make light of the formidable amount of hard work that precedes their success; great musicians and opera stars act as if they were born playing or singing the way they do; and the public, especially the less perceptive part, never learns the true price paid for consistent success.

When the great pianist Paderewski was once introduced as a "genius," he replied, "Yes, I am a genius; but before I was a genius I, was a drudge."

The truth is that in the real world short cuts are few and far between, and you will be wise to learn, not the "tricks of the trade," but the trade itself.

A third and final secret deals with the personal character that most successful developers share, since a thick skin, formidable perseverance and polished negotiating skills are more crucially important than they may appear. Everyone knows that imagination and an appetite for risk are required, just as they know that there does not exist in nature a timid, pessimistic or lazy individual whom other developers would accept as one of their own. But in today's climate of increasing hostility toward development everywhere, that does not begin to tell the story.

In working his way through the obstacle course that invariably confronts him, a successful developer needs the determination of a salmon swimming upstream to spawn. In putting up with inevitable delays, he must feel in his gut Ambrose Bierce's classic definition of "patience" as a "low grade form of desperation masquerading as a virtue."

As for negotiating skills and the ability to present his case effectively to the public, he knows that he cannot survive without them. Before the concept of zoning was introduced in 1916, the developer could paint as he wished on a blank canvas. After that date, government in one form or another set the ground rules.

Today, however, a new wind is blowing; and it is interesting to note that in the recent controversies of, for example, Westway, the proposed highway restructuring along the Hudson, or the major re-development at Columbus Circle, it is not government officials, but the general public which played the decisive role.

From today on through the rest of your careers, it is likely that community planning boards, public interest groups, even next door neighbors will have an increasingly important influence on what you are permitted to do on your property.

In a climate of public opinion increasingly hostile to development of any sort, environmental impact reviews, so-called "linkage" requirements, and exactions of various sorts will be continuing facts of life. The sophistication required to deal successfully with such issues will be, for most developers, a major stock in trade.

The widespread hostility today toward development and developers calls to mind Lenin's comment about the Russian mob—"They cry bread, bread; and to accentuate their demands they burn the bakeries!"

As the problems faced by our field become increasingly complex the skills required by you and your fellow practitioners will multiply. It is interesting that the very program for real estate development from which you are being graduated today at Columbia is only four years old, and that similar programs at MIT, Penn and other universities were created only in the last four or five years.

A Jain Buddhist expression says that "When the student is ready, the guru appears." Just as your studies in real estate development represent the newest of the new, so, in a sense, they also represent the oldest of the old.

The oldest known manual for the formal training of builders and architects was written by the Roman architect Vitruvius in the first century B.C. In his opening chapter he described eloquently the background that a practitioner should bring to our field, and your professors today would not disagree.

Of course, Vitruvius was not aware of phrases such as "time value of money," "internal rate of return" and the like, but his attitude was as current as tomorrow's headlines.

Vitruvius states in his opening paragraphs his belief that theory must go hand in hand with practice, that those who trust only to theory "follow a shadow and not reality." He goes on to plead for a broad general education for builders and architects, saying that the student should, in addition to his technical training, be knowledgeable and well-rounded, in order to fulfill properly his important responsibilities.

Specialists think that the world is divided into specialties, but, says Vitruvius, wise men know that, "All studies are related to one another and have points of contact" and that "A general education is put together like one body from its members." He noted that "those who from tender years are trained in various studies recognize the same characters in all the arts and see the intercommunication of all disciplines, and by that circumstance more easily acquire general information."

Graduates, today we are called "the information society," but wise men realized we were that all along.

In addition to Vitruvius, a second influence should be Adam Smith, the apostle of the marketplace, who felt that serving the community and serving oneself are not necessarily in conflict if the ground rules are wisely thought out and clearly stated.

It is not up to the marketplace to make the ground rules; its contribution, as even Mr. Gorbachev now seems to understand, is to function efficiently and effectively under them.

Adam Smith understood the limitations of the marketplace and the corresponding roles of other entities.

Determining and meeting unmet needs, legally and profitably, is the role of the entrepreneur in our society; and rewards, both material and psychological, flow to those who are successful.

In practice, whether they realize it or not, successful entrepreneurs in all fields follow the Lafayette approach. The story is told that during the French Revolution, the Marquis de Lafayette was having a glass of wine in a Parisian café when someone burst in shouting, "Where is the mob going?" Lafayette gulped his remaining wine, pulled on his jacket and said "I don't know; but I have to get there first, because I am their leader!"

Like Lafayette, the successful entrepreneur "follows from the front," anticipating as best he can what his clientele wants so that they will pay him something over his cost in supplying it.

Perceptions of what constitute needs are always changing, and one interesting instance is worth exploring.

In the 'teens and 1920's throughout the United States, the centers of public excitement and celebration were grandiose railroad stations; and monuments like Grand Central Terminal or the old Penn Station, modeled on the Roman baths of Caracalla, were replicated in every major city.

In the 1930's they gave way to dazzling motion picture theaters like the Roxy, the Paramount and Radio City Music Hall. In the 1940's the center of excitement shifted to major airports, where people delighted in watching the arrival and departure of airplanes with exotic destinations. In the 1950's and '60's excitement shifted to regional shopping malls which were really new "town centers." In the 1970's vast hotel atriums several hundred feet high were the focus of public excitement, just as today glitzy gambling casinos seem ready to fill that role.

If you, as a group, seek an appropriate challenge, here it is:

With gambling casinos the structures that seem to represent our time, with affordable housing for a sizable fraction of our citizens our greatest failure, surely those entering real estate development today have their work cut out for them in finding new and better solutions. Solve those problems and you will receive cheers from your society—and what is more, you will deserve them!

And now one last comment from the classical world:

The Roman theologian Tertullian could have been thinking of you when he wrote that, "Any calling is noble if nobly pursued."

Columbia is sending you out into the world with your Masters Degree in Real Estate Development. As you end your formal training
and embark on your professional careers, may you pursue your activities in a way that reflects well on yourselves, your teachers, your families and your society.

If you do, all of us will benefit, and all of us will bless you!

Commencement Address
Graduate School of Architecture, Planning and Preservation
Columbia University
1988

ON HAPPINESS

Good morning, friends.
To the faculty, to the parents, and most of all, to you, the students of this remarkable institution on this joyous day –WOW!

What you have accomplished, what you are accomplishing and what you give promise of accomplishing in the years ahead are wonderful!

All those whose hopes and prayers, whose devotion of time, effort and concern have led to today can take pride in a job well done.

In the Bible, when God contemplates creation he doesn't say he found it "fabulous." He says he found it "good."

In the same sense, the Mott Hall enterprise is "good!"

As a sign of how the rest of the world is beginning to understand what is happening here on 131st Street and Convent Avenue, I am happy to present to the Mott Hall School on behalf of United States Senator Daniel Patrick Moynihan his gift of an American flag that has flown over the Capitol in Washington, DC.

While this gift is in specific recognition of the achievement of Mott Hall's nationally acclaimed chess team, Senator Moynihan, an admirer of all that Mott Hall stands for, hopes that this national emblem will serve as a continuing reminder of the best of the American experience.

More than any other nation in history, our country has encouraged and cheered the growth of the individual; it has praised the person who overcomes handicaps and a modest beginning; it has lavished rewards on those whose determination, persistence and will-to-succeed overcome all obstacles. But more than success, we wish you happiness, as in "life, liberty and the pursuit of happiness."

The wisest people in all ages and societies understood the difference between happiness and pleasure. They knew you can say, "Tomorrow afternoon, I am going to have fun," but you cannot say "Tomorrow afternoon, I am going to be happy."

For happiness is a by-product that comes, not from an activity you engage in, but from the life you lead. Happiness reflects values, attitudes, and the sense of being at peace with oneself.

Material things can relieve pain and bring immediate pleasure, but they have little relationship to happiness. The rock star who said sadly that "There must be more to life than having everything" hit upon a profound truth.

Happiness flows from producing more than you consume, from seeing the shine in the eyes of those you have helped, from expending your energies in a struggle, whether won or lost, that you know was worth the effort.

The happiest people have family and friends; they belong to a community; they have more than jobs, they have careers; they identify with causes bigger than themselves; and, most important, their lives have meaning and purpose.

We wish you full, productive and satisfying lives in which you achieve the potential you have already revealed, lives which will be a source of joy to all who love you and who watch as you grow to your full height.

Let me add a final wish for your parents.

I love the story of the artist Bernini, who presented his genius son and the boy's drawings to Pope Paul V; the Pope looked at the boy's work and said to the father, "You had better watch out or your son will outstrip you."

The proud father replied, "Sire, that is a competition in which he who loses, wins!"

306

As a parent speaking to fellow parents, I pray that we each find ourselves in such a competition, in which by losing, we win.

To the graduates, I say, "May the future shine bright for you fine young people of whom we are so proud!

The larger world you will soon enter has good people and bad. The bad will try to corrupt you, tempt you, thwart you.

The good can serve as role models and encourage the best in you to flower.

I wish you the wisdom and strength to choose your friends and models wisely.

Good luck and God bless you!

Mott Hall Public School
June 14, 1994

RESTORING TRUST, CONFIDENCE AND HOPE

America is approaching a state of political paralysis because militant ideologues of Right and Left have taken control of the national dialogue. Extremists on the Right demand "small government"; those on the Left call for "big government." Few voices call for "smart government," with cost-effective, pragmatic solutions to short term, intermediate and long term challenges.

In discussions of spending, no distinctions are drawn between consuming for today and investing for tomorrow; and we watch in silence as the underpinnings of American society weaken while competitive nations strengthen. The 'quick fix' has become our national obsession, with no concern for the unsustainability of current trends. A society once proud of building canals and railroads and sacrificing the present for the future now sacrifices the future for the present. We will pay a price for our "present- mindedness," and it may be painful.

Some observers like Singapore's Lee Kuan Yew or Harvard's Larry Summers believe that after some "mid-course corrections" we will right ourselves, but we should recall Oliver Wendell Holmes' observation that "the mode by which the inevitable comes to pass is called 'effort.'" And that effort must be ours.

We, the sensible middle—the moderates, centrists and pragmatists— must enter the game before a crisis strikes, not after. For the common good, we must work to help our society regain its forward momentum.

Today, a polarized American public contemplates its social

progress with satisfaction but its political and economic problems with foreboding. Dramatic changes—both for better and for worse—have not yet been fully digested and have left us off balance.

A black Democratic second-term president giving a rousing State of the Union speech responded to by the official Republican spokesman, a Latino senator; gay marriage legalized in many states; women permitted in combat; the United States approaching energy independence from Middle Eastern oil—none were seen as likely a decade ago.

On the other hand, America ranking below all European countries in social mobility, with a degree of financial inequality greater than all other developed nations; U.S. high school students scoring poorly in international academic rankings; U.S. births to unmarried mothers skyrocketing; America's physical infrastructure deteriorating seriously before our eyes—those, too, were previously unthinkable.

Most disturbing, however, is our loss of trust in the competence and integrity of our national leaders; the loss of confidence that our national institutions are working fairly for the public benefit; and the increasing loss of hope that the future will deal kindly with our children and grandchildren. Public opinion polls in these areas make grim reading.

Public approval of U.S. banks and public schools are at or near all-time lows. Congressmen are widely seen as "for sale" to large campaign donors. Over half the public has lost confidence in the politicized Supreme Court, and even organized religion is losing support. Only the military, small business and the police are still admired and respected. Revival of public trust, confidence and hope is our most pressing national challenge; and we—as citizens and as real estate professionals—must play a part in that restoration.

As concerned citizens in what has become a combative rather than cooperative culture, we must address the process by which our legislators are nominated and elected and how political decisions are made. How our legislation is written, passed, implemented, reviewed and reconsidered—all deserve our critical thought.

Some challenges, like those of our deteriorating physical infrastructure, are relatively easy for an aroused citizenry to change. Others, such as technical improvements to the operations of our dysfunctional Congress, are possible only if voters demand them. Crucial issues such as the destructive role of money in the political process must be faced frankly. Still others—like the painful "present-mindedness" of a society that refuses to face the future of an aging and needy population along with poorly-educated young people—must be discussed and resolved 'before the fact' rather than after.

Some observers feel that only a crisis will force us to implement the necessary changes. The Triangle Shirtwaist Fire of 1916 was a necessary precursor to the industrial safety and health measures that followed; the 1929 stock market crash and Depression that followed were required before a New Deal was possible; Russia's Sputnik was a necessary goad before America headed to the moon.

An aroused public should demand action beforehand in four areas: A) Physical Infrastructure, B) Banking and Finance, C) Public Education and D) National Government Administration.

Physical Infrastructure

If New York's outdated and deteriorating Tappan Zee Bridge (now scheduled for repair) were to collapse as did Minnesota's I-35W Mississippi bridge (killing 13 people and injuring 145), the nation might finally read this month's report of the American Society of Civil Engineers, which gave us a grade of D+ on infrastructure. With 70,000 U.S. bridges rated "structurally deficient" by the Federal Highway Administration, someone should take notice. Our water and sewage systems, dams and levees are in equally bad shape; our airports, public transportation systems and hazardous waste disposal facilities are only marginally better; our electrical grids are inadequate for the 21st century; and some authorities insist that our 104 aging nuclear reactors should be replaced with newer, safer technologies.

The A.S.C.E. estimates that we should spend $2.2 trillion on national infrastructure repairs and upgrades over the next five years.

They point out that every billion dollars spent on infrastructure creates 18,000 jobs, almost 30% more than if the same amount were used to cut personal income taxes. Bond interest rates are low today, as is construction industry employment. The time is ripe.

What should you, as real estate professionals, hoping to keep New York competitive in a global economy fight for, with your Op-Ed pieces, political contributions, etc.? A good start would be to support the No. 7 subway line extension from Citi Field in Flushing to Grand Central Terminal to the proposed Hudson Yards development and on to the Lautenberg commuter rail station in Secaucus. Another would be to support Amtrak's Gateway project connecting the northeast corridor lines in New Jersey to Penn Station in Manhattan. A third would be support for a revival of the now-forgotten Bloomberg congestion pricing program, which has worked so well in London, Singapore and Stockholm in reducing traffic congestion, shortening commutation time and reducing air pollution. (This time the proposal should specifically declare that all revenues raised go to improve mass transit in the outer boroughs.) The proposal would have passed last time, but for opposition by the N.Y. State Legislature, led by Sheldon Silver. Silver, although supposedly representing New York City, also killed N.Y.C.'s commuter tax, which raised $350 million annually to cover costs the city spends to help suburbanites.

A redesigned and substantially improved Penn Station and a relocated Madison Square Garden are important and timely steps we should encourage. We can't move the tracks, but we can move the arena, and we should do it NOW!

A worthwhile negative step would be to oppose the current proposal to landmark—to save unchanged for all time—the uninspired 1.5 million square foot tower at 270 Park Avenue. No rational person would confuse that 1958 office structure with Chartres Cathedral or the Parthenon, but the Landmark Commission must keep busy, so they must landmark something. Whatever your feelings, speak up!

BANKING AND FINANCE

The major market failures of recent years—Japan's economic crash of 1989, the dot.com bubble of 2000, the world financial explosion of 2009—took most observers by surprise. Charles Mackay, the author of the 1851 classic *Extraordinary Popular Delusions and the Madness of Crowds* would not have been among them. He recognized Bernie Madoff under another name, and his study of the Dutch Tulip Craze, the South Sea Bubble, etc. would have prepared him for the recent credit default swaps, unregulated derivatives, sub-prime mortgage fiasco, etc. But even he might have been surprised that after the collapse of Barings Bank in 1995, Long Term Capital Management in 1998 and Enron in 2000, we had to wait for Lehman Brothers and A.I.G. to implode in 2008 before asking who in the financial world was doing what to whom.

Albert Einstein defined insanity as doing the same thing over and over, expecting different results. Those who expect unregulated financial free markets not to soar in booms and to crash in busts are in that category, as are those who believe that an unregulated 'wild west' banking sector will not eventually come to grief.

A complex commercial and financial world requires a complex and sophisticated banking system; effective government regulation must prevent the bad lending practices, bad risk management and outright fraud and deception prevalent in the banking world. The public deserves a "fire wall" between an insured depository institution and a non-insured investment bank. Elimination of absurdities such as favorable tax treatment for hedge funders' "carried interest" would increase public confidence in the fairness of the system.

One obvious answer to the problem is to require higher equity-to-loan ratios for banks; more of their own "skin in the game" would encourage more prudent risk-taking. Greater transparency—to bank regulators, to shareholders and to the public—would bring constructive scrutiny that could rein in untoward activities.

Most important would be prison sentences for criminal financial activities rather than "wrist-slapping" civil fines. After HSBC admitted to laundering $881 million for Colombian and Mexican drug cartels and admitted to violating our sanctions against Iran, Libya, Cuba, Burma and Sudan, they merely paid a fine. True, at $1.9 billion, it was the largest fine ever imposed on any financial institution, but HSBC shares rose .5% on the news, showing that stockholders expected "business as usual." No one will go to jail, because the toothless S.E.C. can only levy fines and other government agencies involved that could bring criminal charges choose to let the statute of limitations do its magic. The message to our 'crony capitalism' bankers is clear—you have a free pass to commit crimes without going to jail.

The topic of inept rating agencies and sleeping government regulators is complex. The ancient Romans asked "Who will guard the guardians?" and we might ponder the same question.

A sustainable banking system is in everyone's interest. Speak up!

PUBLIC EDUCATION

If our physical infrastructure is a cause for alarm, our national pre-college educational systems are in equally poor shape. The shocking 1983 federal education report A Nation at Risk began with the comment, "A rising tide of mediocrity threatens our very future as a Nation and a people." Thirty years later, that warning is more relevant than ever. The dismal ratings of U.S. high school students in comparative international ratings should be a cause of national outrage and cries from employers that they cannot find qualified employees must be heard.

There are several causes of our K-12 educational failure; but foremost is our casual acceptance of the deficiencies of bad K-12 teachers. The best (and there are many good ones) should be rewarded; the worst should be dismissed.

In Finland, with the world's highest high school test results, teachers come from the top 10% of the nation's academic pool. In the U.S., public school teachers come from the bottom quartile of all students. In the rest of the world, bad teachers are fired. In the U.S. they get life-time tenure.

Students in advanced nations, who substantially surpass ours, are

314

instructed by teachers who consider themselves members of a prestigious and well-paid profession, like doctors, lawyers or engineers.
With high educational entrance standards, continuing encouragement
for growth and development, rewards for the best performers and removal of the worst, they are the pride of the nation. Internationally,
America's public school teachers are protected union members with a
civil service mentality. Entrance standards are the lowest in the developed world, performance is not evaluated and virtually no teachers
are ever fired.

Some day we will require our public school teachers to pass the
educational equivalent of a Bar examination or medical Boards, and
some day we will remove bad teachers at the same rate we disbar bad
lawyers or decertify bad doctors.

NATIONAL GOVERNMENTAL ADMINISTRATION

One argument supporting claims of "American Exceptionalism"
has been the fairness, wisdom and sound judgment displayed by our
Founding Fathers in writing our Constitution.

These thoughtful men, however, never considered the possibility
that angry, capricious and continuing use of filibusters could bring
effective government to a halt; that delayed approval of qualified Presidential appointments could be used to blackmail a President; that
legislators would routinely leave government service much richer than
they entered to become highly-paid K-Street lobbyists on leaving government; or that the "legalized bribery" of campaign contributions
would become the most significant factor influencing our legislation.

Our Founding Fathers believed their separation-of-powers system
avoided the adversarial politics of a parliamentary system. They never
anticipated a Tea Party "No Tax Pledge" or that in the 110th Congress (2007-2008) filibusters would be employed 52 times vs. one-
per-Congress in the 1950's. Nor did they anticipate that a 60 vote
Senatorial supermajority could be required to pass any significant legislation.

Many believe that when the Founding Fathers wrote of free speech they never equated it with money and when they wrote of the rights of individuals they never thought of those rights applying to artificial legal creations called corporations. They took for granted the bipartisan legitimacy of the Supreme Court, not anticipating endless 5-4 votes based on politics rather than on law.

They did give us the rights of impeachment and of Constitutional amendment; and if a Constitutional amendment is required to overturn the monstrosity of "Citizens United" (the worst Supreme Court decision since Dred Scott), so be it.

The Code of Hammurabi (1700 B.C.) states in Law #5 that a judge in obvious error "shall be publicly removed from the judge's bench, never to sit there again to render judgment." Ham, where are you when we really need you?

CONCLUSION:

As thoughtful people like Lee Kuan Yew and Larry Summers point out, America is fundamentally strong—economically, politically and socially; but we are going through difficult times.

Economically, we must reform our tax system to make it simpler, fairer, growth-oriented and ecologically sensitive. Some exemptions, such as home mortgage interest, must be rethought; some impositions such as a carbon tax, should be considered. A Value Added Tax which every other developed nation has, taxing consumption rather than income, must be on our agenda. With exemptions for food, clothing and housing, a V.A.T. can be progressive, and give us the revenue we need.

Politically, we must return to a climate of reasoned discussion based on facts, with greater mutual respect and civility and more openness to consensus and compromise—a climate in which each party wins by sacrificing something to the other, but by which the national status quo has been improved. Vehement election campaigning is one thing, governing competently and fairly thereafter is another, the latter is what we need.

Socially, we must aim at effective measures to increase equality of opportunity and social mobility, the hallmarks of an effective society. In the 21st century, we realize that education doesn't cost, it pays. If a potential Isaac Newton, Marie Curie or Leonardo Da Vinci goes unrecognized and undeveloped in an inner city slum or an Appalachian backwater, we all lose.

Friends, we have our work cut out for us. If a slogan is required, let it be Hamlet's, "The time is out of joint. Oh, cursed spite that I was born to set it right."

Positive change can only occur when good (and smart) people act. Let's start now.

NYU Schack Institute of Real Estate
Princeton Club
April 23, 2013

BLACK AND WHITE IN THE NEW CENTURY

Many of us remember being told that politics, religion and sex were not appropriate topics for a social gathering. Today, those are often the first topics the young wish to discuss, unless it is sports or entertainments, which really interest them.

Today, "race" and "social class" are the taboo subjects, so sensitive and controversial that a veil of discreet silence has been drawn over them.

We find little open discussion, no frank exchange of views on topics of immense importance. As a result, there is no forthright dispassionate examination of social policies that have succeeded (and why), that have failed (and why) or that have been counterproductive (and why).

Tonight I would like to present some observations that may prove thought provoking and which, like a bright flame, give maximum light with minimum heat.

I believe that there are three keys to understanding race relations in America today.

First is the realization that, historically, revolutions take place not when conditions are worsening but when they are improving, although not quickly enough.

Second, just as W.E.B. Du Bois noted that the problem of the 20th century was "the color line," he might note today that the problem of the 21st century is "self-identity."

The third key is an awareness that the philosophical and psychological differences across the racial divide are deeper and more emotional than most of us imagine.

At the start of this new century, white Americans look complacently, even smugly, at how far we've come; many black Americans look resentfully, even hostilely, at how far we have to go. Optimistic whites extrapolate into the future the progress that has been made; apprehensive blacks fear a backlash that will deprive them of what they have. Thoughtful observers understand the power of a self-fulfilling prophecy and pray that all parties will think and act constructively.

For the short run, at least, the prospects for a color neutral society-to which non-blacks look forward with hope, but which growing numbers of blacks believe is impossible-appear to be receding.

A visitor from outer space, considering our present social turmoil, might report home on insensitivity and even obtuseness on the white side and cynicism and even paranoia among blacks, compounded by a condition called "political correctness" which substitutes polite non-communication for meaningful discourse which could mitigate problems, if not solve them.

Let's start with the first premise-that of progress for those middle class blacks able to avail themselves of current opportunities.

- Between 1970 and today, the number of black college professors more than doubled, the number of black physicians tripled, the number of black engineers almost quadrupled and the number of black attorneys is up more than six fold.
- The U.S. Department of Education reports that in 1997 (the latest figures available) there were 1,551,044 blacks enrolled in the nation's colleges, comprising 10.7% of all students. Of these, 131,000 were in graduate schools.
- The number of doctoral degrees earned by black Americans increased from 787 in 1987 to 1,467 in 1998.
- The percentage of blacks on college faculties nationally stands at 4.9%, with Columbia University at 7.2% and Emory

University at 7.1%.

- Black students make up 13.2% of law school enrollment at the University of North Carolina at Chapel Hill and over 11% at the law schools of the University of Illinois, Columbia University, University of Southern California, Vanderbilt, George Washington and Duke.

- Black law faculty are 12.5% at Duke, 12.5% at the University of Illinois, 10% at Columbia and 10% at Stanford.

- Nearly 58% of all black American college students are enrolled full time, almost identical to the rate for white students.

- In World War 11, blacks served in segregated military units. Today, not only has the Chairman of the Joint Chiefs been black, but so are 11% of all U.S. Army officers with 58 black generals on active duty, comprising 8.5% of all Army generals. Throughout the military, blacks routinely supervise whites without comment or incident.

- Black students compose 8% of the cadets at the U.S. Military Academy, 6% at the U.S. Naval Academy and 4.9% at the U.S. Air Force Academy.

- In 1940, 60% of employed black women worked as domestic servants. In 1999, that number was 2.2%; and 60% of employed black women today hold white-collar jobs.

- In 1963, 50% of whites told the Gallup Poll that they would relocate if a black family moved next door; today slightly more than 1% tell that to the pollsters.

- In government today, the Congressional Black Caucus has 40 members (out of 435 Representatives) and President Clinton's administration has an all-time high of nearly 400 black Americans in senior positions. In 1998, 445 blacks served as U.S. mayors, several in the nation's largest cities; and the black political figure, Douglas Wilder, served as Governor of Virginia, whose capitol, Richmond, was the seat of the old Confederacy.

- Marriages between blacks and whites have more than tripled in the last 30 years, and in 1990 some 6% of black households had non-black spouses.

- The proportion of black families earning more than $75,000 annually (adjusted for inflation) has tripled since 1970, reaching 9%.
- The number of blacks with a net worth of $10 million or more has skyrocketed; some, like Oprah Winfrey, Michael Jordan and Bill Cosby, have net worth in nine figures.
- While only a twinkling of an eye ago no blacks were seen in the higher reaches of the business world, today black Americans serve as President or Chairman of mega- corporations such as American Express, Time-Warner, Maxwell House Coffee, Avis Rent-a-Car, Godfathers Pizza and Maytag, among others.
- Between 1982 and 1992, the number of black police officers nationwide more than doubled, to reach 60,000. The nation's 50 largest police departments increased the number of black officers by nearly 500%, and black police chiefs or commissioners have been appointed in New York, Los Angeles, Chicago, Houston, Philadelphia, Washington, D.C., and Detroit, among others.
- The unemployment-rate today of college-educated black men is just over 3%.

While black two-parent families have lower incomes than comparable white families, the income differential is now 13%, a figure that is significant, but not earth-shattering.

These statistics reflect the condition of those black Americans able to take advantage of what our society now offers. They have completed their education through college, have married and have embarked on fruitful careers.

I believe that if the black leadership of half a century ago (A. Philip Randolph, Whitney Young, Walter White, Roy Wilkins, Bayard Rustin, Martin Luther King, Jr.) heard these numbers -and only these numbers - they would exult, and say, "We did it! We ushered in a Golden Age for our people!"

But, of course, we all know that these are not the only statistics we have about black Americans. The other set of numbers relates to those who have not been able to take advantage of what society has to offer. Those numbers are horrendous.

No one in this room can paint a clearer picture than can I of the heartbreaking educational failures, criminal justice encounters, health disparities and social pathologies of those who have been "left behind."

If those numbers only were to be shown to the black leaders of half a century ago, they would be appalled. And when they learned that over ONE TRILLION DOLLARS had been spent by our government on well-intentioned social programs over the last decades, they would ask with bewilderment, "What went wrong?"

What would we tell them? Concerned people should ponder that question, ask what lessons have been learned and where we should go from here.

Now we turn to the second key to understanding our present social scene, the question of personal identity.

As individuals, we each must struggle with the question of "Who am I?" We have multiple, complex identities; and the ethnic factor is one of many.

Erik Erikson, who coined the term "identity crisis," knew that we all need a positive sense of self, that we all can be open to feelings of alienation or self-doubt or self-hate, and that we all struggle with the concept of authenticity. This is a universal problem of our time and no one group has a patent on it.

The problem of creating a positive sense of self was hard enough for the immigrant Irish, the Italians and Jews. When marginal social status is compounded for blacks by skin color discrimination, the challenge to overcome a lessened sense of self is compounded, but as a society, we must learn to overcome it.

Few whites can understand fully the destructive psychological effect of racial disparagement or harassment, or the inadvertent racist signals our society routinely sends out.

Facing the problem of racial prejudice squarely, analyzing it, discussing it and acting on it are things that we all must do. And helping each individual to understand himself and live comfortably with himself is a continuing and long-term challenge.

As for "group identity," we have three distinct American models, the first being the Amish (or Pennsylvania Dutch) who reject and turn their backs on mainstream society; the second is the German, who have been totally assimilated into the mainstream, with no remaining distinctive identity; and the third is those groups who make appropriate accommodation with mainstream mores, but retain a distinctive identity.

The Amish want nothing from the rest of the world and ask only to be left in peace.

The German Americans (who, according to U.S. census figures, constitute the largest single ancestral group in the United States) have blended so completely that no one today thinks of President Dwight Eisenhower or of General Norman Schwarzkopf as German. The only German cultural impact left is in words like "kindergarten" or "delicatessen"; today in all of New York City one is hard-pressed to find a decent sauerbraten or a genuine apple pancake. So far as German Americans are concerned, they are no longer German.

The rest of us, who don't want to isolate ourselves like the Amish or disappear like the Germans, just muddle through.

Black commentators often see the world in black/white terms; white Americans see a nation in which Latinos and Asians combined will soon outnumber all other groups. Furthermore, while black commentators usually see the white world as a homogeneous and hostile whole, white Americans know their world consists of John Cardinal O'Connor and the Lubovitcher Rebbe, Boston brahmins and Mississippi rednecks, the Marlboro Man and Woody Allen, the KKK and the ACLU.

Heavy immigration and steadily increasing rates of intermarriage among ethnic groups are creating a society in which Tiger Woods will soon be a more common model than Jackie Mason or Archie Bunker. Will the child of a Kennedy/Cuomo marriage think of him/herself as

324

Irish, Italian, both or neither?

Today, law professor Lani Guinier publicly identifies solely with her black father; how much more interesting and socially productive might it have been had she identified strongly with her Eastern European Jewish mother as well? It would serve to highlight today's social complexity.

Self-identity will be the problem of the 21st century, for us as individuals and as members of groups, and our answers over time will be many and varied. Perhaps the focus will turn from what divides us to what unites us. It seems likely that public sentiment, interpretations of law, and government interventions will over time acknowledge economic rather than ethnic difference; and that may weaken minority group cohesiveness. But we will still have to ask, "Who am I?"

The third key to understanding today's social situation is awareness of the profound philosophical and psychological differences across the racial divide and the depth and intensity of feelings about them; on that, I can only nod sadly and silently.

The unasked questions, the unexamined premises, the painful misunderstandings and confusion on all sides, are the fearful penalty we pay for our inability to communicate.

To advance the discussion along non-controversial lines, I would like to point out two situations from which valuable lessons can be learned.

The first is the condition of destitute whites in the Appalachian coal fields and hollows of West Virginia and in the Yazoo Delta of Mississippi; the second is the remarkable, but generally unanalyzed and undiscussed record of success of recent arrivals in New York City from African countries such as Gambia and Ghana, Senegal and Sierra Leone.

In Appalachia and in the Mississippi Delta, submerged white populations have been studied by Ken Auletta and described in his book *The Underclass*. Cynthia Duncan's recent book, *Worlds Apart-Why Poverty Persists in Rural America*, confirms Auletta's observations and conclusions.

The same lack of exposure to the world of work, the same violence in the home, the same absence of positive role models, the same dependency and rage at a degrading welfare system, the same lack of self-confidence, the same sense of hopelessness and despair, the same weakened family structure and prevalence of female-led families, the same hostility or passivity, the same poor work habits and low self-esteem, the same alcoholism and drug addiction prevail in those rural settings as in many urban areas.

Both Auletta and Duncan note that those submerged whites who somehow make it to college join mainstream America, while those who do not enter college tend to stay mired in poverty. If we can solve the problems of Appalachia, the lessons can be applied elsewhere.

The other case worthy of study is that of recent arrivals from Central or Western Africa who come to New York City seeking better lives for themselves and, more significantly, for their children. Like other immigrants, these recent arrivals take any jobs offered, no matter how arduous or low paid. They save their money, pool their savings, and invest them in the purchase of taxi medallions, the opening of small restaurants and clothing stores or the starting of small service businesses. Their housing conditions are terribly over-crowded with newly arrived friends or family members, but in due course they move up to improved accommodations. Most important, they know that education is the key to their children's success. They not only encourage their children to perform well, but they themselves try to learn along with the children. As a result, the children of recent arrivals from Africa frequently outperform in school the children of longtime U.S. residents.

The sharp contrast between the upward mobility of recent African immigrants and the stagnation of Appalachian whites should give pause to those who still confuse attributes of "social class" with those of "race."

Economist Gary Becker, who won the Nobel Prize for his groundbreaking work on "human capital," writes, "Schooling raises earnings and productivity mainly by providing knowledge, skills and a way of analyzing problems; ... [for potential employers] degrees and education convey information about the underlying abilities, persistence and other valuable traits of people." The highly regarded Journal of Blacks In Higher Education says bluntly, "Completion of higher education accomplishes more than any other force in our society to close the personal success gap between blacks and whites."

Twenty-first century American society will be multi-ethnic, highly technical and highly credentialed; the painful economic and social gap between the less-skilled and more-skilled will increase. Those members of any group with college degrees and appropriate social capital are destined to prosper in the mainstream and those without them will struggle at the margins of society.

Machiavelli observed that in the Bible the armed prophets succeed, but the unarmed ones fail. Today, he could say the same about a college education and he would be correct.

And helping inner-city children to and through college is the mission of the Harlem Educational Activities Fund. (www.heaf.org)

Pierson College Fellows Forum
Yale University
April 5, 2000

CAPITALISM TODAY:

TRIUMPHS AND CHALLENGES

Maurice Chevalier, the French entertainer, was asked on his 75th birthday his thoughts on reaching that advanced age. He replied, "I think it's great, considering the alternative." Capitalism, too—the most productive economic system known—is preferable to the alternatives. And unlike death, its excesses can be mitigated.

Ever since Adam Smith pointed out that the butcher and baker provide us with dinner, not from benevolence but from self- interest, it has been clear that, creativity and productivity are galvanized by incentives which harness the producers' interests in a competitive society.

When the savings of prudent lenders were transformed into the investment capital of innovative entrepreneurs, Modern Capitalism was born, creating what Smith called *The Wealth of Nations*; prodigious growth in productivity followed.

The two sides of uncontrolled free markets were soon revealed, as baronial splendor accompanied Dickensian poverty, Rothschild's chamber pot was admired while children worked 14-hour days in coal mines. Soaring economic booms and devastating busts occurred periodically, along with staggering differentials in wealth and income between those at the top and those at the bottom; monopolistic practices crushed the small business that Smith praised.

Eventually graduated income taxes and inheritance duties were imposed; government regulation modified the worst excesses of the free market; and the creation of trade unions gave labor effective bargaining power. Public services in health and education became available, with housing and income benefits for the poor and disabled.

Thanks to its open frontier, its political institutions, communal practices and philosophy of Calvinist self-reliance, America never developed an angry protesting proletariat like Europe. The 'animal spirits' of its entrepreneurs were seen as serving the public good.

Until recently, American public sentiment viewed the ground rules as fair and efficient, reflecting the goals of our Founding Fathers— liberty, equality, democracy.

Today, however, the public feels less free, less equal, and less in control than in the past. Opinion polls proclaim that respect for Congress, the Supreme Court, bankers and public school leaders is at an all-time low. As Robert Putnam, author of *Bowling Alone*, puts it, "a sense is abroad in the land that our national experiment in self-government is faltering." When the full negative impact is felt on unskilled and semi-skilled employment because of automation, globalization and high-tech developments like robotics, three-dimensional printing and microtechnology, the strain on our ecosystem will be serious.

The realization that social mobility in America today lags behind that of other developed nations, the poor academic performance of our students compared to those of other countries and the decaying state of our national physical infrastructure are facts of life, as are the disparities in well-being between the 1% and the 99%. Worst of all may be our growing fear that life will not deal kindly with our children and grandchildren.

Belief in the legitimacy of the 'ground rules' is fundamental to the functioning of a stable society, and if we do not take steps now to restore that diminishing sense of legitimacy, we will pay a painful price in the future. The time has come to rethink our Social Contract, to reconsider the rights and responsibilities, privileges and obligations, of who owes what to whom.

What Hobbes, Rousseau and Mill wrestled with must be reformulated to deal with the complexities of life today—to give incentives for creation and production without destructive imbalances.

Conflicting visions on that question abound. Tea Party types lacking compassion cite 2 Thessalonians 3:10 ("If any will not work, neither let him eat.") while Occupy Wall Street types cite Keynes' Economic Possibilities of our Grandchildren, which in turn quotes Matthew 6 on "the lilies of the field; they neither toil nor spin." Machiavelli perpetually debates Dr. Pangloss.

In the real world, practical thinkers such as Arthur Okun produce volumes like *Equality and Efficiency—The Big Tradeoff*, which wrestle with commonsense compromises in society's long term interest. What is the appropriate relationship between public goods and private, between present consumption and investment for future benefits? What are the rights and responsibilities of the old vs. the young, the present vs. generations to come?

As we await mature discussion on these issues from our political leaders and public intellectuals, the clock is ticking. If we do not resolve these issues, some charismatic demagogue, a latter-day Huey Long, may arrive first.

To forestall the possibility of social upheaval if public perception is that the ground rules no longer work, several topics must be addressed: A) Tax Reform; B) Entitlement Reform; C) Social Ineffectiveness and D) The Monetizing of Politics.

TAX REFORM

"Taxes are the price we pay for civilized society," said Oliver Wendell Holmes, Jr. "Legalized robbery" is what the Tea Party's platform calls any government revenue "more than is absolutely necessary." A confused public votes for a dysfunctional Washington that is making ours a dysfunctional nation.

Full and frank discussion must be held about the appropriate level of graduated income taxes and graduated inheritance taxes; about what constitutes a capital gain and how it should be taxed; about the rationale behind property tax exemption; about what should be "tax deductible," and about what "loopholes" should be closed.

Important for discussion, on our national agenda should be the V.A.T. (Value Added Tax) that every other developed nation imposes—one that taxes "consumption," not salaries or wages, returns on savings or investments, incentives for production, etc. With limited exemptions for food, clothing and rent, the V.A.T. is the most rational source of government revenue devised, and in America today it is rarely discussed. If the proceeds were designated for scientific research, an infrastructure bank and higher education, a V.A.T. would help the U.S. regain its leadership in the world. (The timing for the introduction of such a tax must await our economic recovery.)

Another form of taxation—called Pigovian after Arthur Pigou—is my second favorite; it decreases "negative externalities." Examples are taxes on polluting fuels, alcoholic beverages, smoking tobacco, congestion pricing on traffic, 'recreational drugs,' if they are ever legalized, etc. As Pat Moynihan suggested, it could be reflected in severe taxes on hand guns, bullets, on ammunition of all sorts.

ENTITLEMENT REFORM

That no one in America today should starve, go naked, be homeless or walk around with infectious disease is universally accepted. That no one should be illiterate is open to debate, but most would agree. Beyond that, opinions vary.

If a Leonardo da Vinci, Isaac Newton or Marie Curie were born in an isolated Ozark or Appalachian Mountain hollow to an unmarried, semi-literate teenage mother, many would say that it is in society's best interest to see that child's talent blossom, at public cost if necessary. Others, contemplating the problems of Greece in 2013, might not.

Orlando Shaw of Nashville, Tennessee, has fathered 22 children by 14 different mothers; Desmond Hatchett of Knoxville, Tennessee, has fathered 30 children by 11 different mothers. Some Orthodox

Jews and Mormon groups produce more children than they can support. Society's obligations to the father, to the various mothers and to each of the children merit discussion.

There are those (and I am one) who believe it is in society's interest for education to be a "free good," available to all from pre-K to graduate school. "Equality of opportunity for all" and first-rate "public goods" (parks, museums, etc.)—are essential; after that—let's talk. If the aggregate benefits available to an unemployed worker are greater than those to the employed, disincentives are obvious.

SOCIAL INEFFECTIVENESS

A free market economy requires regulation to avoid chaos. Proper regulation can guide and encourage the good and impede and discourage the bad.

Government regulations today reflect the power of trade union influence or corporate arm-twisting, the legalized bribery of campaign contributions or the impact of K-Street lobbyists.

Transparency in proposing legislation; transparency in its drafting and its appearance in regulations; transparency in the interpretation and imposition of regulations; and transparency in debate over when outdated regulations should expire—merit discussion.

Regulations to protect the family farm when there are no family farms distort U.S. agriculture; regulations to protect the worst public school teachers from being fired harm our school children; regulations that permit government workers' overtime payments to distort lifetime pensions will bankrupt U.S. cities. Let the sun shine on our strangling regulations and clear up the sickness!

THE MONETIZING OF POLITICS

At the root of much of what ails the U.S. today is legalized corruption of politicians, stemming from the cost of election. Congressmen are widely seen as for sale
—at one time to trade unions, then to large corporations, today to rich private individuals.

John McCain describes the American political system as "an elaborate influence-peddling scheme in which both parties conspire to stay in office by selling the country to the highest bidder." Lobbying by oil, pharmaceutical, insurance, television, banking and other industries generates billions of dollars of questionable federal subsidies, along with other advantages that should not be "for sale." Pandering to government employee unions has saddled us with unfunded liabilities that will haunt our children.

Other democratic societies have avoided the 'monetizing of politics' and we should study their electoral practices.

Providing free television time to political candidates; limiting the length of campaigns; revoking the corrosive impact of "Citizens United" (the worst U.S. Supreme Court decision since Dred Scott) which equates free speech with money and personal civil rights with corporate rights are important first steps. Another, of course, is focusing attention on the pernicious practice of gerrymandering. Some 400 of the 435 seats in the House of Representatives are all but impossible for an opposing party to contest.

The public disdains Congress but takes no steps to improve it, and shows its level of interest in politics by appallingly low voter turnouts.

CONCLUSION:

Has capitalism failed? No, but our political will to control it has. Is democracy failing? No, but its success requires the continuous attention of honorable and public- spirited citizens who think long term as well as short term, for "we, us, our" as well as "I, me, mine."

Our society's strengths represent the best of the democratic process, of free market capitalism, of the right of each "to do his own thing" so long as it harms no one else. I, for one, accept the concept of "American exceptionalism." But our weaknesses are apparent, as obstructionist political leaders increasingly apply parliamentarian practices in a constitutional system not designed for them.

Where are our "public intellectuals" demanding leadership that puts the long term public good over short term partisan advantage, that consider the moral as well as the expedient?

Which economists today remember that Adam Smith also wrote *The Theory of Moral Sentiments*? Which political scientists recall that when de Tocqueville coined the phrase "individualism" to describe American society he also praised our community spirit of cooperation and civic involvement?

How many of our political leaders have demonstrated the character and competence to merit our respect? Where is today's "trust-busting" Teddy Roosevelt to rein in the "malefactors of great wealth?" Where is today's FDR, to propose a fresh "New Deal" to provide for all our citizens, while rewarding the creators, the risk-takers, the hard-working, the productive?

If we do not find them soon, we will have demagogues instead.

Finance Seminar
September 18, 2013

PHILANTHROPY VS. CHARITY
AMERICA'S THIRD SECTOR

International House in New York is an example of American philanthropy at its best. It provides an important service that the free market cannot provide as inexpensively and that government cannot or will not. And it provides that service competently and imaginatively for over 700 scholars from 100 countries who could not find it elsewhere.

The free market is efficient, Americans feel, but lacks a sense of public responsibility. Government is well-intentioned, they believe, but inefficient at best and inept at worst. The third sector—nonprofit, voluntary, philanthropic, public interest, NGO's—aspires to market-like efficiency and pro-bono values.

Of all that foreign scholars will absorb during their time in America, an understanding of the potential of a third sector may be the most important. When governments are under pressure to cut all expenditures, the arguments for philanthropic entities (national and international) to underwrite cultural and educational activities are compelling. Today, the world's 300 richest individuals have a collective net worth of $3.7 trillion. Why should they not be encouraged to support the arts and sciences—in addition to, not instead of—whatever government provides from tax revenues or the market does for profit.

The track record of America's third sector over the last century is awe-inspiring. Sponsorship of the post WWII Green Revolution's new varieties of wheat, corn and rice dramatically increased crop yields and prevented starvation for hundreds of millions in Asia, Africa and Latin America. Ending the scourge of yellow fever in the developing world and of hookworm in the American South were life-changing, as was the early and crucial sponsorship of Mohammad Yunus' Grameen Bank, the brilliantly successful and widely-replicated micro-financing project in Bangladesh. George Soros' role in encouraging democracy in post-Soviet Eastern Europe and Bill and Melinda Gates' role in Third World medical aid are becoming legendary, as are the impact of CARE, the International Rescue Committee and Save the Children.

Domestically, medical education in the U.S. was radically transformed and improved through the publication of the Carnegie Foundation-financed Flexner Report; and the U.S. Supreme Court's landmark desegregation decision in "Brown vs. Board of Education" was profoundly influenced by Gunnar Myrdal's An *American Dilemma*, instigated and financed by the Carnegie Corporation.

Americans are not surprised to learn that of the world's 20 highest-ranked universities, 18 are in the U.S., with most carrying the names of their founders or major donors like Leland Stanford, James B. Duke, Johns Hopkins, Ezra Cornell,

Moses Brown and others. And if you return home without having been to the Frick Museum, the Morgan Library, Carnegie Hall or the Guggenheim Museum, you really haven't seen New York.

From Rockefeller and Carnegie, Vanderbilt and Rosenwald, Ford and Mellon to Bill Gates and Warren Buffett, America's mega-rich, largely "self-made," have long made a practice of "giving back." Andrew Carnegie's 1889 classic, *The Gospel of Wealth*, voiced a widely-held sentiment when he spoke of great wealth as a public trust. His challenge—to expend the same imagination and insight in disbursing a fortune as in creating it—has profoundly influenced American thinking.

338

This year Americans will donate over $325 billion to philanthropic causes. Over 80% comes from individuals, 12% from foundations, 5% from corporations. This is over 2% of our GDP, "off the scale" by international standards.

Private, non-profit schools and colleges educate one quarter of U.S. students and private, non-profit hospitals contain half of all U.S. hospital beds. Between one-third and one-half of Americans volunteer their time and effort to non-profit or community activities.

Alexis de Tocqueville noted this in 1835 in Democracy in America when he wrote, ". . .where in France you will find the government or in England some territorial magnate, in the United States you are sure to find an association."

The reasons for our traditions are clear. Envision a virgin continent settled by Europeans with no strong central government, no hereditary monarchy or aristocracy and no state religion. If the pioneers wanted a church or a school, they had to build it. Roads, hospitals, courthouses? They had to build them.

Respect and social prestige flowed to the leaders and financial supporters of those activities, Elihu Yale and John Harvard among them. To this day, American museum galleries, endowed college professorships, hospitals and libraries bear the names of their donors.

Will this continue? Will the American third sector in the future be what it has been in the past? Most likely, yes; because the American public wants it that way. Outside the U.S., many believe that Americans give because contributions are tax- exempt. The reverse is true: philanthropic contributions are tax-exempt because Americans give. Every major American private university and most major museums were created before 1913, when the federal income tax was introduced.

The huge increase in private wealth we see today will lead to vast sums going either into charitable foundations or direct grants to favored colleges, museums, hospitals, etc. Current attacks on charitable foundations by militants on the political Right and Left are unlikely to result in major changes, although we may see more public scrutiny and accountability, more admission of grant-making failures, more open discussion of measurable outcomes and what has worked and why (and, hopefully, less tax-exempt involvement in partisan politics).

The crucially important innovative and creative role of our third sector is often not recognized nor fully appreciated. It lies in the freedom and opportunity of third sector participants to "think outside the box"—to explore, experiment and innovate, to take risks which, if successful, help everyone but if unsuccessful are not at the public expense.

Our national 911 emergency response telephone system we owe to the imagination and persistence of the Robert Wood Johnson Foundation; the accident-preventing white lines (on our highways' right side) we owe to the Dorr Foundation-financed experiments on the Hutchinson and Merritt Parkways. The 2,509 public libraries Andrew Carnegie helped to build, the 4,977 rural schools for poor blacks that Julius Rosenwald financed in the Jim Crow U.S. South—showed the way and others have followed.

A new generation of donors places high value on innovations that can be life-changing. New York's Mike Bloomberg, for example, in his post-mayoral career, is devoting massive resources to helping cities worldwide solve urban problems.

Clearly, the world would be a better place if each of us contributed to the "common good"—at a time and in a manner best suited to our personal situation and to a cause or causes we feel important.

Life's material rewards will always be unequally distributed and private fortunes amassed. de Tocqueville faced this clearly when he wrote, "what is most important for democracy is not that great fortunes should not exist, but that great fortunes should not remain in the same hands." The hundred-plus American self-made billionaires who have signed the Bill Gates/Warren Buffett "Giving Pledge"—to give away over half of their net worth in their lifetime (for Gates and Buffett, it's 95%)—are on the same wave length. Heirs to great fortunes, on the other hand, like the Walton family, often march to the beat of a different drummer.

To which causes one should contribute is a subject open to discussion. The distinction between "charity" and "philanthropy" is expressed in the traditional observation that giving a starving man a fish (charity) feeds him for a day, while teaching him how to fish (philanthropy) feeds him permanently.

Whether your focus is on immediate, pragmatic help to those in distress—as many on the Left in America demand—or on research and experimentation in exploring "root causes" of long-term problems—which many foundations seek— Americans feel we should each do something!

The Duke of Wellington, who believed that the battle of Waterloo was won on the playing fields of Eton, might have attributed the magic of America's third sector to the quintessentially American celebration of Thanksgiving, at which all Americans acknowledge their good fortune by sharing.

All societies make some provision by which the rich help the poor, and draw a distinction between the mandatory and the voluntary (in Islam, between "zakat" and "sadaqa"). Endowments, too, appear elsewhere (in Islam, the "waqf"). But the American third sector is unique.

In an increasingly globalized "flat world," the case for "American exceptionalism" is weakening—our values of "fair play," "rule of law" and "equality of opportunity" are becoming universal. Let us hope that the American concept of the third sector will become universal as well, and that all of us will help to spread it.

International House
January 26, 2014

DEVELOPMENT CHALLENGES FOR AFRICA

To the development world, Africa is the future.

The necessary ingredients for healthy and sustainable growth are visible; now private sector entrepreneurial talent—working with and through government—must bring them to fruition. Small and medium-sized businesses created and led by imaginative and innovative risk-takers with their own funds invested will be the key to that growth.

Although government does not create wealth, along with providing for public safety and social stability it creates the pre- conditions and conducive atmosphere that permit the entrepreneurial sector to 'do its thing' for the benefit of all.

Necessary public investment, growth-encouraging legislation and social institutions, transparent business regulation, supervision of effective capital markets, etc. are immediate goals. The importance of public education is a given. For producers and for consumers, for the growing middle class whose demographics predict it can become the workshop of the world, for imaginative investors and for the creative entrepreneurs who can put those investments to productive use, for a submerged public yearning for health, education, safety and employment—for all those, Africa's future is bright if it is approached prudently, energetically and competently.

The failures and the successes, the boots-on-the-ground experience and similar efforts elsewhere provide important lessons for Africa.

Vast sums international groups dissipated in Haiti with little to show for it and the current state of Palestinian refugee camps after receiving billions of dollars of foreign aid should make us reflect on the next steps in Africa's development.

Our economic gurus' failure to predict the widespread financial disasters of 2007-8, and their failure to resolve them since should encourage modesty in a field often characterized by hubris; yet our economic thinking remains largely unchanged.

Bureaucrats love formal economic models—the more like mathematical equations the better—even though in the real world they often lead us astray, especially when dealing with economic development. The late Albert O. Hirschman, a dear friend who was never awarded the Nobel Prize he richly deserved, understood this clearly. He was a maverick who knew that economics is part art, part science and that on occasion appropriate metaphors may be more instructive than formal models. While his colleagues were obsessed with 'economies of scale' and conditions of 'perfect competition,' Hirschman realized that well-intentioned actions could have unintended adverse consequences, that capital markets can be inadequate for the demands upon them, that there could be local cultural barriers to change, and that insufficient local information, skills and entrepreneurial practice must be faced. While others focused on the "Big Push" from outside, Hirschman believed in local forward and backward linkages that were self-reinforcing. Others thought of development from the top down; Hirschman thought of it from the bottom up.

If he were here today, I believe he would endorse government and international focus on improving major infrastructure (with appropriate private involvement) but he would also emphasize the need for private investment (and access to loans) by and through local entrepreneurs with hands-on experience in coping with local obstacles.

This is true of all fields but particularly so of real estate, where he would have espoused smart growth, with a focus on long term sustainability as well as short term benefits; on prudent relationships between new development and existing utilities, infrastructure and public services; on transparency and public discussion, on community and stakeholder involvement in planning; and on the importance of cost effectiveness so often missing from development thinking.

Economic growth and urbanization go hand in hand, reinforcing each other as growing employment in services and manufacturing create an urban consumer class involved in finance, health care, higher education and distribution of retail and wholesale consumer goods. An increase in discretionary spending will be reflected in the purchase of durable consumer goods and a range of services marking a modern economy that is more than just a producer of commodities. The development of a thriving resource sector will stimulate the building of roads, rail and airports near natural resources, as well as investment in power and telecommunications.

Water and sanitation investments are crucial, not only for economic reasons, but for disease prevention and health, primary and secondary education and the freedom it gives women to participate more fully in national life. Production of clean water for those who lack it must be a high priority.

In Africa today, sound and stable governance and prudent macroeconomic policies are creating an environment in which favorable demographics, infrastructure development, rapid urbanization, consumer growth and new mineral discovery reinforce each other to signal a glowing future, as does the return of a talented, well-trained African diaspora.

If the future is to reduce Africa's heartbreaking social and economic inequality and remove the grinding poverty of the poorest, several steps must be taken. Most important of all is a fairer sharing of the benefits of national mineral wealth.

The chief threat Africa faces is the so-called 'resource curse' of massive new oil and gas discoveries where improperly-handled new revenues lead to corruption, with favored groups becoming rich and the rest of the economy suffering. To date, no African country has been able to apply its oil and gas revenue fairly for the public benefit.

U.N. officials believe Guinea and DR Congo are Africa's worst and Ghana the best, but even in Ghana the Auditor General reports that Ghana's share in some oil and gas companies is not on record, has not been disclosed to the Public Account Committee and has paid no revenue to Ghana.

African public opinion must demand more mineral rights transparency and accountability, an end to trade mispricing, country-by-country reporting of sales, profits and taxes, clear reporting of 'beneficial ownership', automatic international tax information exchanges on income gains and property of non- resident entities, and an end to money laundering.

The Washington-based Center for Global Development makes a convincing case for distributing the new mineral revenue directly to the public as taxable income, as some countries do successfully. Ghana could be a leader in this movement.

Other constructive goals would include an increase in productivity of subsistence farmers by the use of fertilizers, better seed, judicious use of water and the pooling of small land holdings and equipment so farmers can compete effectively with foreign food producers. The half of Africa's available piped water now unaccounted for because of leaking pipes and illegal connections by private tanker operators must be recaptured, and all water users should pay their bills. The tens of billions of dollars leaving Africa illegally each year could be stopped by greater transparency in the financial sector and the use of criminal penalties where indicated. Widespread tax-evasion must be remedied. Clarification and simplification of land tenure rights, (of ownership and use) and the simplification of visitors' visas for tourists and business travelers are long overdue. African central bank reserves, pension funds and sovereign wealth funds should be invested in cost-effective infrastructure improvements that offer investors a competitive return while helping society. Africa's mineral, physical, financial and human capital should be coordinated and applied for the public good.

Finally, the issue of corruption must be faced frankly and discussed openly. True transparency and accountability in the financial and legal systems and in government operations at all levels will have a positive impact on the continent's development. Trust and confidence in the ground rules are important factors in sustainable development. Africa's potential can be achieved if Africans will it.

The Yale Club of Ghana Conference
Accra, Ghana
July 19, 2013

AS AMERICA LOOKS AHEAD

Serious unknowns face America in the years ahead, but one thing is certain—those societies able to enhance the human capital and social capital of their citizens will outperform those that do not. Mineral, industrial and financial capital will recede in importance relative to the intangible strengths of an educated, motivated and future-minded public, one that is ably led, with a vision of "the good life" and an ethos of personal responsibility valuing both equality and excellence, one that encourages all to rise to the extent their talent and effort permit.

The undisputed American economic, military and geo-political primacy of 1945 to 2000 is now history. We still have the world's largest military, its reserve currency, most of its best universities and nearly one quarter of its economic activity; but forecasts are negative. The world's eight tallest buildings, seven longest bridges, six largest dams, most creative space exploration programs and cities with highest broadband connectivity and fastest Internet service are now overseas and the best stem cell research and work on renewable energy do not take place in America. Sadly, other nations are coming to value higher education more than we do. Traditional American optimism is giving way to widespread foreboding, and our tax-conscious public seems unwilling to pay for investments in education or infrastructure. Today, nations with larger populations, more effective leadership and more prudent allocation of resources present competitive challenges that must be acknowledged.

That challenge can be met by an American public that is better educated and vocationally trained, one that works smarter and harder, that has the necessary technological and social capital, whose goal is to increase productivity and to raise living standards for all. At the moment, our fiercely partisan leadership across the political spectrum focuses on immediate electoral issues at the expense of the longer term. Social issues, such as contraception, abortion or gay marriage, threaten to displace economic discussions dealing with our aging population, skyrocketing medical costs or the investments in education and infrastructure we must make to secure our future. No one has the courage to face the unsustainable unfunded pensions of our government employees.

The biblical Joseph's dream of 'seven fat years' followed by 'seven lean years' may be upon us, and in the period of austerity we are entering, harnessing our national brain power is more important than ever. Yet today public colleges in Florida and Texas are eliminating departments of engineering and computer science, and 41 states have made large cuts in their education budgets.

In 2008, 56% of the world's engineering degrees were awarded in Asia vs. 4% in the U.S. In 2009, 64% of U.S. doctoral degrees in engineering went to foreigners, chiefly from Asia, who were then forced by our immigration laws to return home. U.S.-based companies like 3M, Caterpillar and General Electric, now global, have spent billions of dollars expanding their overseas research labs. "Given the moribund interest in science in the U.S., this is strategically very important," says 3M's Chief Executive George Buckley.

A nation proud of Thomas Edison, Alexander Graham Bell, Eli Whitney and George Washington Carver (names unknown to most high school students today) must look to its laurels. Today, that requires 'mind workers' who process information.

For America to regain its forward momentum, we must understand why our national median wages have been stagnant for decades, why our students rank poorly in international academic ratings and why 75% of our young adults do not qualify to serve in the military, why our national transportation infrastructure is outclassed by international standards, why many of our 'best and brightest' college students choose careers on Wall Street rather than become engaged in the productive world. (46% of Princeton's class of 2006 entered finance.)

Fresh thinking is required and outdated conventional wisdom discarded. We must think of under-educated or vocationally untrained young people as potential national assets whose flowering will benefit the country at large, not only themselves, as they become taxpayers rather than tax eaters. We must recognize the relevance of Schumpeter's theory of 'creative destruction,' in which old jobs must yield to new jobs with more demanding requirements. Our dysfunctional, gridlocked Congress must face the pressing need for a national industrial policy and a national trade policy that will allow us to retain high-paying jobs supplying the needs of the growing middle class of the BRICs (Brazil, Russia, India, China). The leaders of our industrial trade unions must understand the constructive role they can play in restructuring labor policies (stultifying work rules, onerous jurisdictional disputes, etc.) to keep American industries internationally competitive. College leaders must give us a bigger bang for our educational buck; financial leaders must channel our nation's savings into productive uses that keep the economy growing; political leaders must encourage the proceeds to be applied wisely and fairly. We must balance the tension between short term self-interest and long-term national interest, between the demands of the young and the needs of the old; and we must not forget Oliver Wendell Holmes' observation that "taxes are the price we pay for a civilized society." Transcending petty tribalisms of color, religion and ethnicity, we must aim for a meritocracy of accomplishment; and our young should be encouraged to aim high and to prepare for futures that are demanding and rewarding.

Most importantly, a skilled and productive middle class is the key to national well-being, and we must do all we can to reproduce, sustain and expand ours. Today our middle class is threatened by two factors: a) increasing automation, performing ever more complex human functions, and b) globalization, which encourages the work traditionally performed by the developed world's middle class to be undertaken more cheaply elsewhere.

For the first time, Americans are looking over our shoulders to see how other nations meet these challenges. In rethinking the training and apprenticeship policies of our industrial work force, we can learn from Germany. In rethinking our narcotics policies on addiction, incarceration and rehabilitation, we can learn from Sweden. In rethinking the selection, training and retention of our public school teachers, we can learn from Finland. In rethinking our early childhood practices, we can learn from French crèches and écoles maternelles. In rethinking our national pension practices, we can learn from Australia and Chile. In rethinking our approach to transportation infrastructure, we can learn from the developing nations of Asia. In turn, if we can ever create a health delivery system that is cost-effective, efficient and whose financing is actuarially sound, we can show the rest of the world how to do it.

Singapore in the East and the Nordic countries of the West, although demographically small and relatively homogeneous, are increasingly setting the standards by which the success or failure of a society is measured; knowledge and skills are the new global currency and Americans are taking heed. International competition will encourage critical examination of means, and America will profit from being forced to view with fresh eyes practices and policies previously taken for granted.

When Americans learn, for example, that 15 year olds in Finland have the world's highest standards in reading, math and science, they should also recognize that teaching in Finland (at all levels) is a prestige profession; it is as hard for Finns to win a place in a teacher training course as it is to get into law school or medical school. No Finn can teach high school math, chemistry or physics without having majored in those subjects. Starting teachers there receive pay roughly equal to that of starting doctors or lawyers, and their careers are respected and rewarding. (And 98% of Finnish children attend excellent—and free—pre-school programs.)

In New York City, by contrast, too many of our public school teachers come from the lowest quartile of their classes in the least prestigious municipal colleges; they are granted tenure with just three or four years in the classroom. Teachers' unions fight fiercely against reasonable teacher evaluations; the union demands arbitration and appeal procedures for poorly performing teachers that can keep even alcoholics, suspected felons, sexual predators and violent offenders in the classroom (or at the least on the payroll) for years. Few low-performing teachers are fired; the best are often not rewarded nor retained. Outstanding, dedicated teachers struggle under great handicaps. Correlation is not the same as causation; but does ineffective teaching relate to the 84% rate of New York City public high school graduates requiring remedial courses in math, reading and writing when they enter CUNY community colleges?

"American exceptionalism" has been real—reflected in John Winthrop's vision of a "city on a hill," in Tocqueville's portrayal of our unique communal spirit of mutual assistance, in our unparalleled philanthropic traditions, in our culture of risk-taking and innovation, in magnificent national gestures like the Marshall Plan, in our universities and research institutes that produce a continuing dominance of Nobel prizes; and it can continue if we will it. Until recently, we led the world in social mobility, in the quality of our free public education, in the optimism and self-confidence of our public and trust in our institutions; and these can be regained.

To do so, we must re-orient public discourse which, sadly influenced by ideologically-driven foundations and their think tanks, sees government as an impediment, taxes as an unjustified imposition, unlimited political contributions justifiable as free speech, unregulated free markets as the ideal economic vehicle and socio- economic disparity as the Darwinian side-effect of a dynamic society. In all these areas, reasoned discussion rather than acrimonious polemic should prevail and thoughtful political compromise should be seen as reflecting prudence, not cowardliness.

In reviewing America's standing compared to the rest of the developed world, three areas in particular cry out for fresh thinking:

a) personal development(schooling and vocational training, along with psychological preparation for a full life);
b) prison incarceration (who goes to jail and what transpires there);
c) immigration (who enters the country and with what ramifications).

These three are the "low hanging fruit" which, if dealt with effectively, will have profound effects on the future of American society.

PERSONAL DEVELOPMENT

Most Americans feel they have the opportunity to achieve their potential; those who do not, deserve more attention, for their benefit and for ours.

All the factors that make us who we are, are what we simplistically think of as "education," with the child widely seen as a passive recipient of what a teacher drops into an outstretched hand. Parental cultural influences from birth through age three are widely ignored. Our educational establishment's hypersensitivity to charges of "blaming the victim" (e.g. William Ryan vs. Daniel Patrick Moynihan) encourages us to ignore or minimize home influences, along with peer pressure, community values and role model examples of family members and neighbors.

One notable exception, Nobel Laureate James Heckman, writes, "If I am born to educated, supportive parents, my chances of doing well are totally different than if I were born to a single parent or abusive parents." Extend that differential to the child of a semi- literate, traumatized and emotionally withdrawn 14 year old single mother

354

vs. the child of two well-educated parents who from birth talk, sing and read to their child. Imagine both children entering the same school in the same class. If the children react differently to the school experience, it is common today to blame the school, although studies show one-third of the later achievement gap is present at the start of first grade. Studies show that children raised in a home with two biological parents do better in school and in life.

As children age, some parents express high expectations, praise achievement, devote parental time and resources to the child, speak to the child frequently in grammatically correct and expressive language, dine with the child in a congenial family setting, serve as positive role models themselves. Others either do not or cannot. Since these factors defy easy measurement, social scientists tend to downplay or discount them.

As a child continues to grow, community values come into play. For example, drug dealers with fancy clothes and expensive cars may be seen as those to emulate, or they are not. Teenage unmarried mothers and high school drop-outs are seen as embarrassments to their families, or they are not. Religious leaders and community figures praise sustained, self-disciplined effort toward long term goals, or they do not. And lo and behold! A child emerges from adolescence ready for a productive, fulfilling life, or does not.

What next, college? The Department of Education reports that more than 500,000 American students who want to go to college have no access to Algebra II classes; more than two million would- be college students have no access to Calculus classes. And as the cost of college rises, public support for it wanes.

Our education problems are serious. Many on the Left refuse to acknowledge that teaching should be a high-skill, high entry level profession; many on the Right, to save taxpayers' money, attack Pell Grants, scholarships and student loans, not realizing that in doing so we are 'eating our seed corn.' Yet advocates for the children are silent.

Do schools help? Of course, especially those with great teaching—but we forget that 'teaching' is what someone does at a chalkboard, while 'learning' is what takes place in the head of a child.

We are all creatures of habit, subject to the influence of those around us. Inculcating life-enhancing values and habits and exposing children to constructive role models are continuing challenges. *McGuffey's Readers*, *The Autobiography of Benjamin Franklin*, the mythic stories of George Washington and the cherry tree or Abe Lincoln learning to write with charcoal on a shovel helped form American values in the past. What are the equivalents today?

Every nation has a dysfunctional segment of its population out of the mainstream. British physician Theodore Dalrymple's important book *Life at the Bottom* portrays those in England whose economic poverty is relative, not absolute, but whose mental, cultural, and spiritual impoverishment is a charge against society. Their nihilism, self-destructive patterns of behavior and social pathologies reflect a mindset in which they see themselves as helpless victims of circumstance, with no feeling of personal responsibility. Living in an eternal present with no sense of the future, they not only deride schooling for themselves, but attack those who seek it. Babies, for some of Dalrymple's dysfunctional teenage girls, are like pets for amusement or vehicles for their sense of self-importance, or an economic 'meal ticket.' Many other teenage single mothers, Dalrymple recounts, want to be good parents, but don't know how; they don't understand the difference between taking care of a child and raising a child.

Dalrymple despairs of Britain's ability or will to solve these problems. In the 21st century, America must resolve to face our similar problems, to deal resolutely with them and to solve them. Appropriate education is a crucial first step— pragmatic experience shows that education is not a consumable that costs, but a matchless investment that pays, not a zero- sum game of taking from Peter to benefit Paul, but a positive-sum game in which everyone wins.

There will always be differentials of achievement because of varying levels of ability, imagination, energy, ambition and effort. In the society we seek, however, one in which everyone can read,write and count, and all are exposed to as much formal education and vocational training as they can absorb, productive and fulfilling careers should be available to all.

Nobel laureate Edmund Phelps' important book, *Rewarding Work*, discusses employment as a chief source of an individual's personal and intellectual development, a potential source of pride (Thorsten Veblen's instinct of workmanship) and of self-esteem (Ralph Waldo Emerson's self-reliance). Providing jobs (earning one's way) vs. providing benefits (a culture of dependency) is a major challenge, especially for the working poor who deserve encouragement and help. Producers have a different mindset from dependents. If we provide employment opportunities for those ready, able and willing to work, we can recall that our Founding Fathers felt responsible not for our 'happiness' but for our 'pursuit of happiness.'

PRISON INCARCERATION

America has 5% of the world's population and nearly one quarter of its prison inmates. Germany, by contrast, has 93 people in prison per 100,000 of population; America has eight times that rate, or 750 in jail per 100,000. Yet no one feels safer in Chicago or Boston than in Berlin or Frankfurt. Furthermore, over half those in New York State prisons are recidivists. The American criminal justice system needs rethinking about those we arrest and what happens to those imprisoned. *The Collapse of American Criminal Justice*, by Harvard Law School Professor William Stuntz, provides a good overview of the problem.

We must understand that the same well-intentioned mindset that dealt with alcoholism by instituting Prohibition (1920-1933)— with its criminal aftermath— conjured up our badly thought out and ineptly implemented War On Drugs—with its destructive consequences. In one of life's great ironies, certified liberals like Joe Biden, Rahm Emanuel and Eric Holder have endorsed incarceration practices that have devastated our inner cities: more than half of all black men without a high school diploma go to prison at some time in their lives.

The quintessentially American application of technology to crime prevention (primarily the inspired work of New York's Jack Maples' and Bill Bratton's CompStat, implementing James Q. Wilson's "broken windows" theory) has increased police efficiency significantly but with unforeseen social ramifications.

Arrests for marijuana possession in New York went from fewer than 5,000 in 1993 to over 50,000 in 1999; arrests for gambling and prostitution remained unchanged. Marijuana use, studies show, is significantly higher among whites than among blacks, and much higher for whites than Latinos. Blacks, who comprise 28% of New York's population, account for 52% of the city's misdemeanor marijuana arrests, with non-black Latinos accounting for 31% of arrests. Whites, with 35% of the population, had fewer than 10% of marijuana arrests in the years 2004 to 2008.

One obvious conclusion is to call for the legalization— but high taxation— of marijuana, a substance studies show to be no more harmful than tobacco or alcohol. Sixteen states have legalized marijuana for medical use, and a dozen more have such legislation pending. Nationally and internationally (Mexico being a prime example), the War On Drugs as presently conducted has been a failure, and must be reconsidered.

Since data does show that marijuana arrests relate well to catching violent criminals, then encourage constructive dialogue on 'stop and frisk' and similar controversial matters between the police and the inner city community, which is more afflicted by violent crime than other areas, with staggering "black on black" homicide rates. Insensitivity by some over-zealous (and sometimes racist) police and hypersensitivity by some in the inner city are an explosive combination.

Some paranoid intellectuals (e.g. Michelle Alexander in *The New Jim Crow*) see the criminal justice system merely as a vehicle to oppress blacks; they make little effort to understand the problems of the police or to seek constructive solutions, such as more effective community policing. Public safety, on the one hand, and proper respect for the public, on the other, are important "rights." That is why the ancient Greeks defined tragedy as the conflict between two rights. Those who decry the use of metal detectors in schools must reflect on the impact of lethal hand guns and switch blade knives in those schools.

Best practices in criminal justice internationally treat drug use as a public health problem, with free detoxification programs for addicts; drug sale is treated as a serious criminal problem. First offenders are segregated from hardened criminals and are taught to read, write and count before release. Vocational training (as auto mechanics, pastry chefs, refrigeration and air conditioning repair personnel, etc.) is provided. The success rate in Nordic countries in rebuilding lives and in turning dysfunctional addicts into productive citizens is impressive. The financial return to any society on investment in "human capital" for first offenders is immense—for the former prisoner (whose life is turned around), for the taxpayer (fewer expenditures, more receipts) and for the public (reduced crime).

Many excellent studies have made constructive recommendations for U.S. reforms. Decriminalizing marijuana possession heads most lists, followed by: converting drug possession crimes to misdemeanors or civil penalties (e.g. California in 2010, Kentucky in 2011); limiting pre-trial detention to those who pose high threats to public safety; eliminating mandatory minimum sentences; reclassifying low level felonies to misdemeanors; and rethinking of parole practices.

No society wants to encourage drug addiction, but no society wants the violent and corrupting drug cartels or drugs' devastating impact on the lives of the poorest. The presidents of Guatemala, El Salvador, Costa Rica and other Latin American countries have pleaded with the U.S. to rethink its drug laws, and they are right.

The U.S. rate of homicide and of gun ownership is another scandal. Gun lobbyists have made certain that the issue receives little objective public discussion. Guns are more easily available in the U.S. than anywhere else in the world, including hand guns and automatic weapons like those used in recent mass murders; our homicide rates, though recently declining, are still "off the scale." Ownership of hand guns and automatic weapons is largely a "non- issue" in American life. Our Constitution protects the right to bear arms just as it does free speech. Libel, slander and shouting fire falsely in a crowded theater are prohibited, however, and so should be brandishing a loaded submachine gun.

After the assassinations of John F. Kennedy, Martin Luther King, Jr. and Bobby Kennedy, and the shooting of Ronald Reagan and Gabrielle Giffords, it is hard to believe that some states (such as Alaska, Arizona, Vermont and Wyoming) require no permit at all to harbor a hidden weapon. Thanks, National Rifle Association.

IMMIGRATION

A country that calls itself a nation of immigrants is hard-pressed to address calmly and rationally a subject with such emotional baggage.

On the one hand, we forget the "No Irish Need Apply" signs, the restrictive covenants against Jews, the Chinese Exclusion Act, etc.— all aimed at people whose children and grandchildren became full-fledged, productive citizens. (The current governor of Maine, a Republican leading the battle against immigration, is a direct descendent of French Canadians whose entry into America was fiercely opposed by his predecessors.) On the other hand, today's immigrants are seen by some as competitors for jobs or as expensive public charges.

Emma Lazarus' verse inscribed on the base of the Statue of Liberty was written in 1883, when the tired, poor "huddled masses yearning to breathe free" were welcomed as cheap labor for an expanding economy. Frederick Jackson Turner's "frontier thesis" was put forth in 1893, when the West, still open to settlement, was the home of rugged individualism, personal initiative and personal responsibility. Today, the American taxpayer is increasingly reluctant to pay even for increased educational opportunities or social uplift for the deprived in the hollows of our rural South or in our Northern inner cities, let alone pay for services to immigrants. The time has come for us to ask, "Which of the seven billion people beyond our borders should we admit to U.S. citizenship— and for whose well-being should we accept responsibility"?

Sealing our now-porous borders seems a 'no-brainer'. Encouraging the entry of immigrants we want and facing the eleven million-plus

360

undocumented immigrants already here are other challenges.

For the undocumented, those who unlawfully entered the country, pragmatism, common sense and a realization of the profound social upheaval attendant on any other solution would seem to lead to granting some form of amnesty, mandatory registration of aliens, and a procedure by which undocumented persons living here productively for a certain number of years—avoiding serious crime, paying taxes and not becoming public charges—could become legal citizens, with educated, upwardly mobile children. "Bad eggs" could be deported.

Thereafter, immigration could be limited to individuals meeting appropriate standards of education and skills, or with vocational abilities of value to the U.S. Severe penalties should then be imposed on employers of future undocumented workers.

Undocumented immigrants reflect a large percentage of adults in America not possessing a high school education, with little command of English, major handicaps to their advancement. It is in the best interest of the American public, to help them become full- fledged, productive members of society.

The third best financial investment ever made by the United States government was the G.I. Bill, providing for the educational expenses of WWII veterans (the best investment was the Louisiana Purchase and the second best, the purchase of Alaska). Case studies of lifetime earnings and lifetime income tax payments of identical twins, one of whom went to school on the G.I. Bill and one who did not, show a large return to the government on the funds invested.

There may be a better formula for achieving national well-being than by enhancing the human and social capital of all citizens; but if so, it is a closely guarded secret.

CONCLUSION:

America of the future will be what we make it.

We can choose to go the route of failed societies—self- indulgent, ignoring future rewards for present benefits, demanding more from the economy than it can afford, treating tax evasion as a game (distinguishing public from private morality), focusing on narrow self-interest rather than on the common good, with the richest and most powerful 'gaming the system' for their own benefit.

Or, with renewed acceptance of our traditional social contract, we can revert to an appropriately modified version of America's historic ethos—one that values hard work and savings, character and competence; that willingly sacrifices luxuries today for a better life for our children tomorrow; that is proud of contributing to the common good and that has trust in the integrity of our institutions and our leaders. That ethos sees universal education as the vehicle for upward mobility, with "need-blind" admission a goal. "And, yes," Americans have traditionally thought, "I am my brother's keeper!"

Equality and excellence are not mutually exclusive, and a healthy society reflects both. Equal access to public goods—education and health, museums and libraries, parks and playgrounds—does not require neglect of the needs of individuals whose achievements are national treasures. How to identify, encourage and reward greatness, while providing opportunity for all, is a continuing challenge.

America today is at a major inflection point as it faces a changing world beyond our borders and complex factors at home. The more wisely we set our national goals; the more prudently we allocate our resources—human and material; the more effectively our political system adjusts to the emerging challenges, the brighter that future will be.

The difficult choices we must make require more thoughtful, considerations than we are devoting to them. Our transition from creditor to debtor nation and from budget surpluses to massive deficits will force prudence on us. For example, the public must demand from our legislators commonsense balance—between the unrealistic profligacy of a California and the stingy backwardness of a Mississippi.

In an increasingly complex world, less government is probably not feasible; but more transparent, more efficient and more responsive government certainly is, if not corrupted by the legal bribery of im-

362

proper political contributions.

Our hope lies with the Internet Generation, the young people who will one day pay the bills acquired when we cut taxes as we increased military spending, stopped investing in infrastructure and promised government workers pensions we could not afford. Opinion polls say the young understand better than we do that productive free markets must work with government, that political institutions must regain public confidence, that taxation must be rationally apportioned, that we are not only heirs of the past, but stewards of the future.

The young are our stewards of the future, and our hopes are with them.

Pierson College
Yale University
March 26, 2012

ABOUT THE AUTHOR

Daniel Rose was born on October 31, 1929, attended public school in Mount Vernon, NY, then the Horace Mann School and Yale University. He spent the Korean War years as a military intelligence analyst in the U.S. Air Force.

During a 60 year career at Rose Associates, of which he is Chairman, he developed such projects as the prize-winning Pentagon City complex in Arlington, VA, the One Financial Center office tower in Boston, MA, and, as a consultant, conceived of and implemented the concept of "housing for the performing arts" for New York's Manhattan Plaza.

Winner of a number of national Cicero speechwriting awards, he has received Honorary Doctorates in Humane Letters from Long Island University; in Engineering from NYU/Polytechnic; and in Science from Technion-Israel Institute of Technology. He is a Fellow of the American Academy of Arts and Sciences. He has served as an 'Expert Advisor' to the U.S. Secretary of Housing and Urban Development and as an 'Expert/Consultant' to the Commissioner of Education, U.S. Department of Health, Education and Welfare.

A founding member of the NY Institute for the Humanities, he was also founding Chair of the Forum for Urban Design, Chairman of the national Jewish Community Centers Association,

Vice Chairman of the East West Institute, Vice Chairman of the Baltic American Enterprise Fund and is Treasurer of the Police Athletic League. He founded and is Chairman Emeritus of the Harlem Educational Activities Fund (www.HEAF.org).

Other honors include the Ernst & Young 'Man of the Year in Real Estate', the NYC Mayor's Award of Honor for Art & Culture and the W.E.B. Du Bois Award from Harvard University.

He serves on multiple corporate and philanthropic boards, has been married for 58 years, has four children and eleven grandchildren.